ALLEGORY AND MEANING

*Reading African, African American,
and Caribbean Literature*

I0585025

Ikenna Dieke

University Press of America,® Inc.
Lanham · Boulder · New York · Toronto · Plymouth, UK

Copyright © 2010 by
University Press of America,® Inc.
4501 Forbes Boulevard
Suite 200
Lanham, Maryland 20706
UPA Acquisitions Department (301) 459-3366

Estover Road
Plymouth PL6 7PY
United Kingdom

Library of Congress Control Number: 2010924018
ISBN: 978-0-7618-5121-9 (paperback : alk. paper)
eISBN: 978-0-7618-5122-6

The author and publisher gratefully acknowledge permission
for use of the following material:

Excerpts from THE INTERPRETERS, copyright 1965 by Wole Soyinka, reprinted by
permission of the author and Heinemann.

Excerpts from SEASON OF ANOMY, copyright 1973 by Wole Soyinka, reprinted by
permission of the author and The Third Press.

Excerpts from PALACE OF THE PEACOCK, copyright 1960 by Wilson Harris,
reprinted by permission of the author and Faber and Faber, London.

Excerpts from THE SYSTEM OF DANTE'S HELL, copyright 1965 by Imamu Amiri
Baraka, reprinted by permission of the author and Sterling Lord Literistic, New York.

Contents

CARIBBEAN

Introduction

Allegory and the Literary Imagination

Responding to a question in the 1982 *Times Literary Supplement* interview, Chinua Achebe declares among other things:

Language is our tool, and language is the tool of the politicians. We are like two sides in a very hostile game. And I think that the attempt to deceive with words is countered by the efforts of the writer to go behind the words, to show the meaning.[1]

In Lewis Carroll's *Through the Looking-Glass*, Humpty Dumpty initiates a dialogue with Alice this way:

"When I use a word," Humpty Dumpty said, in rather a scornful tone, "it means just what I choose it to mean—neither more nor less."
"The question is," said Alice, "whether you can make words mean so many different things."
"The question is," said Humpty Dumpty, "which is to be master—that's all."

Achebe's quarrel with the politicians' use of language reminds us of the Orwellian "newspeak." In his essay "Politics and the English Language," perturbed by the corruption of the truth-value of individual words and phrases, Orwell laments and equates political chaos with what he himself describes as "the decay of language."[2] Achebe's determination to go behind the words, to show the meaning parallels Orwell's resolve to bring about some improvement by starting at the verbal end. Both Achebe, Orwell, and Carroll are all concerned about the problem of meaning in the heritage of language. As James E. Miller, Jr. has so eloquently stated

there will always be those [like Alice] who insist, in a literal-minded way, that words mean what the dictionary says they mean, nothing more and nothing less; and there will always be those who, like Humpty Dumpty in *Through the*

Looking-Glass [and Achebe's politicians], insist that words mean whatever they choose them to mean" (98),

sometimes in opposition to shared conventions as in the subterfuge of political rhetoric, or in the masterly distortion and invention within a context of recognizable conventions such as is used by James Joyce in the novel *Finnegans Wake*.

And then there is the domain of allegory, the instrument of literary expression which, according to William Harmon, "represents one thing in the guise of another—an abstraction in that of a concrete image" (12). Angus Fletcher, in his critically acclaimed book *Allegory: The Theory of a Symbolic Mode*, states that allegory is an inversion, that: "in the simplest terms, allegory says one thing and means another. It destroys the normal expectation we have about language, that our words "mean what they say"" (2).[3] Willian Empson in *The Structure of Complex Words*, theorizes that

part of the function of an allegory is to make you feel that two levels of being correspond to each other in detail and indeed that there is some underlying reality, something in the nature of things, which makes this happen. . . But the effect of allegory is to keep the two levels of being very distinct in your mind though they interpenetrate each other in so many details. (346—47)

But making language mean has been quite a struggle, and according to Miller, "this is simply one more example of a crazy, mixed-up world, full of the paradoxes that make life interesting" (98).

For the African, African American, and Caribbean writers discussed in this study, the domain of allegory is the site of paradoxes. According to Fletcher, the fundamental point of allegory is that in addition to a literal sense, it manifests a peculiar doubleness of intention made deeper and richer by engaged textual interpretation. The writers' use of the allegorical mode is a serious attempt to recover the subtext or hyponoia, the real meaning behind words. The verbal corruption they perceive all around them is a direct consequence of the loss of shared meaning. Stephen J. Greenblatt suggests that "allegory arises in periods of loss" (viii). Seconding him, Hugh Kenner in "The Possum in the Cave" writes that allegory has its provenance in what he describes as "topos of loss. . . a sense of devastation. . . a vanished civilization" (quoted Greenblatt, 128—44).

For the African writers, in particular, the use of the allegory is a matter of personal safety. Many of them, in the height of their literary career, wrote at a time and in an environment increasingly fraught with personal danger as Soyinka and Ngugi found out the hard way. Both men knew first hand what writing in direct language as opposed to indirect verbiage of allegory meant. They were each clamped into jail—for Soyinka by the Gowon military junta in Nigeria; for Ngugi by the Arap Moi benevolent dictatorship in Kenya borne under the guise of liberal democracy. They and others came to the same sad realization as Cicero. During the crisis of 59 B.C., before his flight from Italy and the destruction of his house on the Palatine, Cicero wrote to Atticus: "Of the political situation I shall say little. I am terrified by now for fear the very paper may betray us. So henceforward, if I have occasion to write to you at any length, I shall obscure my meanings with allegories" (252).[4]

For Ngugi and Soyinka, as for the rest of the writers in this study, the use of allegory provides that safety net, for as Gordon Teskey has reminded us, "an allegory means something other than what it says and says something other than what it means" (6). All the writers practice their craft under tremendous authoritarian condition just as the allegorical mode flourishes under authoritarian conditions. For the African writer, the situation is political repression, especially in the era of military dictatorship; for the African Americans, it is racial oppression in an era of Jim Crowism; and for the West Indian (Caribbean), it is the colonial suppression and the anguish brought on by exilic consciousness. Each of the texts studied operates in a social and political environment that is stressful. As such their use of allegory is a natural by-product of the hunger for freedom under the present circumstances. The stories they tell are often thinly veiled. The events, characters, space and time in these stories are presented first in their literal context, and then in the other context—the ideas they are intended to convey or the significance they bear. One is presented in such a way that the surface meaning is held markedly independent of the other.

Of all the African allegorists such as Chinua Achebe, Ngugi Wathion'go, Ayi Kwei Armah, Kofi Awoonor and others, Soyinka unquestionably is the most engaging. His novel *Season of Anomy*, a narrative political allegory, both conceals and reveals. Soyinka veils his political narrative in Orphism to protect himself by the element of disguise and at the same time enable his narrative to make satirical revelations through the implied comparison. As a political allegory, the novel should be viewed in the same way that George Orwell's 1945 novel *Animal Farm* is an allegory of the irony of the Bolshevik Revolution in Russia. The only difference is that where Soyinka wraps his tale in the transplanted variety of the myth of Orpheus and Eurydice,

Orwell laces his in a moral fable. The end result appears the same: both writers launch satirical attacks on the political establishment, cataloging and castigating its laundry list of abuses. Soyinka, in transplanting the myth of Orpheus, recognizes along with writers such as Christopher Okigbo, Kofi Awoonor, and Amiri Baraka that allegory and the mythmaking process have enjoyed a mutual life of transparent interdependency. The meaning which allegory projects is encoded in society's basic assumptions in its stories and narratives, indigenous or transplanted.

Soyinka's *Season of Anomy* contains a distinct echo of the Bible in the sense that the latter is used to make a concealed satirical comment on politics. The novel exists though as an autonomous narrative, but for those who are familiar with Soyinka's writing and its hidden system of meaning, it has a clear and specific political agenda. The Orpheus–Eurydice story can be seen as an allegorical treatment of redemption and salvation for a sick nation such as Nigeria of the 1960s and 70s. We gain a better understanding of the novel as an allegory by considering it as a satire, for as John MacQueen in his book *Allegory* reminds us, allegory and satire are in fact intimately connected. The names and characters of Pa Ahime and Aiyero, Ofeyi and Iriyise, members of the Cartel and the military junta, Suberu and the Cross river, the Dentist and Taiila are all allegories of aspects of the human condition. They are each equated with meanings that lie outside the narrative itself. My point is that the narrative allegory of the myth of Orpheus and Eurydice must be interpreted in terms of the political and social realities of Nigeria's historiography of military dictatorship. Ofeyi's grueling search through the Cross river city of Temoko represents the sacrifices necessary if the soul is to redeem the lower self which it loves and without which it cannot find salvation/redemption. And as the prime traveler, Ofeyi becomes the natural hero since the primary motif in allegory is the journey. The processes of sacrifice and renewal are given legitimacy by the subsequent rebirth and the restoration of fertility to an otherwise waste and barren land.

Okigbo's allegorist stock in trade is the astrological image or astral symbolism which tends toward a kratophany—or as Mircea Eliade would describe it, toward a "revelation of power." Astral symbolism is replete in Okigbo, the same way as it is abundant in Marlowe's *Tamburlaine* or Schiller's *Wallenstein*. Like Marlowe or Schiller, Okigbo draws attention to the influence of the stars in the lives of human beings, and how the latter are under the influence of distant planetary bodies. Okigbo parallels the remoteness of the stars/starry firmament with an almost Gnostic alienation of man (including himself) from Ultimate Cause. Okigbo is "the stranger" on this earth because the poet's home, his astral resting place, remains so totally removed and severed from him. As Angus Fletcher has appropriately pointed out, astral imagery displays the highest degree of symbolic isolation, "for not only are the stars all separated from each other, like gems in a diadem, but they are even more distantly separated from man, who must adore and admire from a vast, alienating distance" (95—96). Fletcher also points out an added virtue for the poet-allegorist: the stars belong in constellations, and thus move in a strictly ordered system of mutually dependent relations. For Okigbo his hope is that the goddess Idoto can grant him the same kind of ordered system of mutually dependent relations.

For Okigbo, as for John Hughes in *An Essay on Allegorical Poetry*, every allegory has therefore two senses, the literal and the mystical; the literal sense is like a dream or vision, of which the mystical sense is the true meaning or interpretation. For Okigbo the value of the whole material world lies not in itself but in the spiritual meaning which it hides and reveals. As MacQueen has pointed out, the whole universe is a mystic pageant in which the immortal stars are the dancers and the sun the priestly torch-bearer. In this context, goddess Idoto appears as the swift messenger of the divine avatars and as the planetary protector of the poet. The allegorical mode has been of major significance in representing the cosmos and the cosmic forces. Okigbo's Idoto is a village goddess, and for the poet a cosmic force. In his long poetic sequence *Labyrinths*, Okigbo speculates about the abode of Idoto, the nature of her power, especially her power to take the poet into her watery bosom and give him that sense of belonging which he so desperately seeks and yearns. In *Labyrinths*, Okigbo sports in the wide regions of creative possibility, leads us from one scene to another, displaying a remarkable transumptive style.

Baraka's *The System of Dante's Hell*, aside from signifying on Dante's *Inferno*, bears resemblance to classical allegorical works such as Prudentius' *Psychomachia*, both in which vices and virtues fight for the possession of a human soul. As an allegorical novel in the tropological (a kind of allegory concerned about the moral conduct of life) mode, *The System of Dante's Hell* employs allegory's primary natural theme— temptation. But Baraka's *System* is not about Christian asceticism—the freeing of the faith believer from the tyranny of the passions. Instead Baraka turns tropological allegory on its head, counterposing the battle between the sacred and the profane for the possession of a black man's soul—where the profane and the temptation become redeeming qualities as part of Baraka's *fin de siécle*. In traditional Christian allegory, the passions are represented symbolically by animals, monsters and the like, the battle between higher passions and lower base passions against which the soul must defend itself if it is to arrive at the state of redemptive grace. Admittedly, the passions are synonymous with the world of the deadly sins. In Baraka's allegory, the deadly sins and the unchanneled passions fight for the soul of the black man, Roi, unfocused on blackness. Resisting the base passions and the deadly sins begins by Roi turning away from those influences that detract from his path of blackness and fulfilment.

Both V.S. Reid's *New Day* and to some extent Cyprian Ekwensi's *Survive the Peace* belong to the typological, prophetic and situational variety of allegory, the apocalyptic genre which contains symbolism intended to provide hope for oppressed people and/or forlorn masses who need to know that the forces of good will eventually overcome the forces of evil. In *New Day*, Deacon Bogle's sermons behind the pulpit are designed to encourage his faithfuls to endure their worldly suffering, at least for a time, until the Final Judgment when God will overthrow the British colonialism and secure for Jamaicans a just and free and independent society. Both novelists employ to a greater or lesser extent the New Testament method of Biblical exegesis which treats events and figures of the Old Testament as combining historical personage and reality with prophetic meaning in terms of the Gospels and the Christian dispensation.

Bessie Head's *Maru* employs allegory in the form of what William Harmon describes as an extended metaphor in which objects, persons, and actions in a narrative are equated with meanings that lie outside the narrative itself. By a process of double signification, the order of words in the novel represents actions and characters, and the actions and characters in turn represent ideas.

Returning to Achebe's comment in *Times Literary Supplement*, Achebe suggests that the African writer is an interpreter of his culture, and as such, he owes it to himself and his society to be clear about what language means. In his relationship to language, the writer must use language in such a way that it embodies society's prevailing attitudes toward life. Thus in his fourth novel, *A Man of the People*, Achebe makes it his cultural duty to expose Chief Nanga's Orwellian newspeak. Achebe is not so distressed so much about controlled indirectness or double meaning, the chief characteristic of allegory, fables, parables and proverbs (which he uses lavishly), as he is about the use of language for self-serving purposes of deception and subterfuge, an act which in fact alienates one from the shared conventions of a common cultural and linguistic community. For Achebe, the difference between the politician and the writer, in the realm of language, is that whereas the politician employs language in order to deceive and bamboozle, the writer, on the other hand, employs language in a way that encourages readers to look for meanings hidden beneath the literal surface of the narrative or verse or drama. In one there is outright disenchantment, in another rhetorical and mental resourcefulness and challenge and excitement. In *A Man of the People*, Achebe imparts cultural values, a passion of his, and his use of the allegorical mode awakens and arouses the impulse of his readers to question appearances, especially in a political culture where appearances are played up as reality. Through his use of the allegorical mode, therefore, Achebe warns us, at the very least, to be wary.

Chapter 1 discusses Bessie Head's *Maru* as an intensely moral idealist novel in which characters assume symbolic roles in the drama of resistance against culturally/ethnically engendered stereotypism, which in turn is imbricated within the discourse of pathology and perceptual categories. In his book, *Difference and Pathology: Stereotypes of Sexuality, Race, and Madness*, Sander L. Gilman posits that the literary text is a rich source of enlightenment in the study of stereotypes. His central thesis is that every society has generated a seemingly endless series of texts as a means of fixing stereotypes within a world of constant forms, and that these texts provide a very good basis for analyzing the historical forces at work in the shaping of stereotypes. In similar vein, Eve Kosofsky Sedgwick in her book, *Epistemology of the Closet* argues that literary texts are, in a rudimentary sense, domains of contention, sites of definitional rupture within which to interrogate constructs and perceptual categories of identity, truth and knowledge. Using Gilman's and Sedgwick's contentions as a point of departure, this chapter posits that Bessie Head's *Maru* is a site of resistance and rupture in which Head seriously interrogates the pathology associated with the identity of the San people of Botswana, otherwise known by such debasing appellations as Masarwa/Basarwa/Bushmen. The heroine, Margaret Cadmore, a member of the outcast group (the out-group), is an enduring allegorical symbol employed by Head to launch this resistance.

Chapter 2 examines Soyinka's *Season of Anomy* as an example of transplantation of literary imagination. By 70 A.D., Rome's armies had conquered nearly all of the kingdom of Judaea. Only one small Jewish enclave continued to resist the thousand men, women, and children in the mountain fortress of Masada, who endured a two-year siege by 15,000 Roman troops. When defeat loomed, Masada's defenders committed suicide rather than surrender. Such is the form and content of the story of Masada passed on to us the present generation. It is a story of indefatigable courage, of resistance, some might even say bravado. Armed with the story of Masada, located in the parched Judaean desert, and armed with a specific tragic circumstance—the violent killing spree that took place in the northern part of Nigeria in the latter part of 1966 (the militant Moslems as natives of Temoko in the Cross River cast as perpertrators and villains, and the Igbos, largely southern Christians, cast as hapless Aiyeros—victims of the murderous rampage), Soyinka tells a dizzying tale wrapped in myth and symbol, in particular, the myth of Orpheus-Eurydice-Persephone. The central character of the novel—Ofeyi—is both an Orphic hero as well as a defender of Masada (Temoko—a parched desert in the midst of the Cross River). Just as Orpheus journeys into Hades in search of Persephone, so Ofeyi, in the garb of the Roman Jewish historian Flavius Josephus, the avid archaeologist and the mythological hero (Orpheus), journeys to the Cross River hell of Temoko in search of his love Iriyise (cast as Eurydice) as our sole witness to the tragedy that has befallen the people of Aiyero.

Chapter 3 explores the divergent visions in Soyinka's first novel, *The Interpreters* and his second, *Season of Anomy* in terms of the one being an allegorical tale of a narcissian hero, intensely absorbed in the self, and another, an Orphic hero willing to enter the maws of death for the sole purpose of preserving humanity.

Chapter 4 examines the symbolic functions of four female characters in Kofi Awoonor's novel, *This Earth, My Brother*, Christopher Okigbo's *Labyrinths*, and Soyinka's novels—*The Interpreters* and *Season of Anomy*. In Awoonor's *This Earth. . .*, mythology and allegory blend, providing a radical image of a deeply wounded and penitent pilgrim—Amamu, angler in the lake of light—involved in what Chinua Achebe describes as "a tortured return journey in search of a lost beginning." In Okigbo's *Labyrinths*, we have the exploration of the subliminal interior of being, where the poet searches for those eternal images with which to assuage his violently sundered emotions as he gropes his way through the darkened maze that is modern, post-independence Nigeria. The poet returns to his primordial Mother—Idoto, determined but contrite, praying for self-renewal and self-regeneration. Soyinka similarly evokes the spirit of anima in the evolution of his two main characters, Egbo from *The Interpreters* and Ofeyi from *Season of Anomy*. In *The Interpreters*, Simi is conceived allegorically in terms of an erotic goddess whose fascination drives, lures and induces her countless male admirers, especially the hero, Egbo, to all the adventures of the soul and spirit. In *Season*. . . the use of the Orphic myth and symbol enables Soyinka to effect a kind of imaginative transformation of the mythos of the female from the phantom-lady to the Eurydice—Persephone figure.

Chapter 5 discusses Baraka's rewriting of the Cartesian cogito within the discourse of Marquis de Sade. The novel forces the reader to reassess his relationship to his own sexuality, his relationship to his own primary status—as being-in-flesh. The novel is an allegorical tale of a man's journey back to his flesh and beyond. We contain within ourselves the "degradations" of the erotic anima, Peaches. But in the heart of our pollution lies, waiting for discovery, the essential purity of existence. Pretty much in the spirit of the fin de siecle writers such as Swinburne, Beardsley and Wilde, Baraka transposes and dislocates the conventional, "natural" relations of whore and virgin, preferring instead the former vis a vis the latter. This is the same sort of thing Harris does in *Palace of the Peacock* as discussed in Chapter 11.

Chapter 6 goes beyond the Sadean logic in Chapter 5 to a tragic faith which channels the Baraka—Sade's dialogism into profounder essence—the chthonic archetype of the Dionysian spirit. For Baraka, the meaning of the tragic spirit is the meaning Nietzsche assigns to the Dionysian artist which Baraka is, true to type. Here Baraka can be said to have abandoned the moralistic orthodoxy of Dante and the Platonic-Christian orthodoxy in favor of a more socialized view of hell. For Baraka the tragic spirit is not about roasting in hell, but instead it is about emancipated spirits free to roam, transforming their basic agonies into moments of personal triumph and communal celebration.

Chapter 7 explores the way Baraka in *The System of Dante's Hell* skillfully blends romance (quest narrative), comic myth and cultural freight (blackness) into the lyrical and allegorical structure of the novel, and how that invites comparison with the banal schematism of Gower's *Confessio Amantis* and the comic realism of Boccaccio's *Decameron*. The chapter argues that the greatest appeal of the novel lies in the special moral appeal, an appeal not merely that of the cultural intellect, but of the urbane faculty of responding to the reality of intense moral experience. The chapter concludes by suggesting that the motive of Baraka's journey through modern American hell is cultural repentance, a rise of new native spirit almost to vertiginous heights, which contradicts the protagonist's earlier moral and cultural aberrations, a rise which is conceived as movement of discovery toward a better understanding of what it feels like to be a black man in America.

Chapter 8 examines Gwendolyn Brooks's novel *Maud Martha* as a

veritable initiation narrative. It is an allegory of a young black girl who
grows toward an awareness of self in a world of moral choices, toward
an eventful awakening of sorts, and this awakening implies a just
balance between the comic and the tragic elements of life, and between
the inner life of imaginative release, on the one hand, and the life of
social restrictions, of arbitrary measurements based on race and gender,
on the other; or as Patricia Meyer Spacks contends, an agonistic tension
"between fact (embodying circumstance) and interpretation (through
which the writer triumphs over circumstance).

Chapter 9 reads Soyinka's *Season of Anomy*, Baraka's *The System of
Dante's Hell,* Cyprian Ekwensi's *Survive the Peace*, V.S. Reid's *New
Day*, George Lamming's *In the Castle of My Skin*, and Ousmane
Sembene's *God's Bits of Wood* as varying aspects of the redemptive
fantasy where the artistic mind imagines a new beginning, very much in
the spirit of millenarianism, an alternate new world order. The dynamic,
always is toward a sanctified moment, a path out of the crustacean fate of
pain, wretchedness, and destructive tendencies that the black man has
found himself, some of it self-inflicted, some imposed by external forces.

Chapter 10 discusses Wilson Harris's *Palace of the Peacock* in terms
of the protagonist's quest for symbolic cosmic order within the complex
dialectic of thanatos (death instinct) and eros (life-affirming principle).
Along that quest Donne, the novel's monomaniacal prota-gonist,
awakens to a new sense of self, beyond the illusions of a false ego, a
fundamental transformation of being through the emergence of the
wedding of the mundane and the divine, the sacred and the profane. This
wedding imparts in Donne a critical lesson, that at the end, one no longer
sees oneself as an isolated point on the periphery of existence, but as part
of the Eternal One in the cosmic center. Donne and crew at long last
realize one unalterable truth, that 'Being' is discovered not in the faustian
will to power or territorial possessions, but instead in the will to
transcendent meaning, at the center of which is divine eros.

Chapter 11 examines the primordial female in terms of how she
provides fodder for the poet's artistic imagination. In his long, narrative,
autobiographical poem, *Another Life*, Anna is central to the poet's
reclaiming of his unique destiny as the privileged and eminent son of the
island nation of St. Lucia. Divided into four chapters or movements or
books, the poem charts the tortuous course of the homecomer-artist
humbled by guilt against the backdrop of a quintessential mother, Anna,
and a brooding symbolic landscape. In Harris's *Palace of the Peacock*,
the woman assumes a protean incarnation in a complex journey involv-

ing two dialectical forces: thanatos and eros.

The use of language, in particular, the use of allegory, symbol and mythological figures by the African, African American, and Caribbean writers engaged in this study parallels Ralph Waldo Ellison's ingenious use of symbolism in his fiction to advance the oblique process which he believes is indispensable for fiction and without which the latter becomes mere propaganda.[5]

1

Bessie Head's *Maru*: Existential Allegory, Pathology of Difference, and the Quest for Conscience

Critical responses to Bessie Head have generally tended to focus, even to a point of needless surfeit, on her autobiographical third novel, *A Question of Power*, published in 1973, many of them construing it as the most significant work in her oeuvre. Craig MacKenzie (1990) is convinced that the novel, cathartic in its measured formulation, is "pivotal to any examination of her life and work . . ." (p. xi). Lloyd W. Brown (1981) suggests that *A Question of Power* represents a touché in Head's literary achievement (175). Huma Ibrahim (1996) regards the novel as the most important work in the novelist's attempt to navigate the troubled waters of transnational identities and her exilic consciousness which she calls "Head's point of engagement" (p. 125). These critical opinions are quite tempting in their candor, and yet one is inclined, given all that we know about Bessie Head, to proffer a different conclusion, a conclusion very much in step with Head's own uniqueness as a writer which "marks her writing off from that of her contemporaries" (MacKenzie, 1990, p. xv). Just as Bessie Head from the start "set herself on a path that was uniquely her own" (MacKenzie, 1990, p. xv), so would I argue that Head's *Maru*, more than *A Question of Power*, distils the very essence of her creative enterprise laced with an overriding concern for what MacKenzie describes as an investigation into the enigma of human prejudice.

Although *A Question of Power* can be said to be an important site for "unravelling the strands of her anguished life story. . . [with] instances of immense suffering and privation. . . [and] crippling alienation . . ." (MacKenzie, 1990, p. ix), *Maru*, on the other hand, provides the fertile site for mounting a literary resistance to the mistaken ideology which often gives rise to that anguished life story. For without this insane ideology there would not be crippling alienation. Without this ideology, there would not be suffering and privation. Both the ideology and its accoutrements represent the two sides of the same morbid state. But while *A Question of Power* can be related in terms characteristic of a symptom, *Maru*, on the other hand, can be interpreted as the cause or aetiological source. This inverse relationship leads to my thesis: that in *Maru*, Bessie Head constructs a site not only for unravelling the very enigma of human prejudice, but also for mounting a stiff resistance to its ideological undergird. There is a second, more poignant reason why *Maru* may be viewed as the pivot of Head's "point of engagement." This has to do with what MacKenzie has appropriately identified as the one recurrent dynamo that fuels and drives her artistic consciousness. He writes: "As a South African-born 'Coloured', Bessie Head was subjected to all the brutalities meted out to those citizens not born white, and she, as a 'first generation' child of bi-racial origin, bore the full brunt of South Africa's discriminatory legislation" (p. x).

Botswana, a country two years shy of independence from Britain, is supposed to offer solace to the now displaced Bessie Head on a self-imposed exile from her native South Africa. The solace is supposed to provide a new beginning for the budding writer. However, Head's departure in March of 1964 for what would later become her adoptive country was, sadly enough, an ambiguous adventure at best. On the one hand, it offers her the basis for renewed hope in humanity for which she is grateful to her adoptive country. But, on the other hand, it ironically brings her yet again face to face with the old, recalcitrant demons of prejudice, an encounter far more unsettling in its stark horridness of entrance because of who the players are—victims and perpetrators alike—the Batswana themselves among whom she has come to launch her literary career and to predicate that career on charting a new course toward a redemptive world. At least so she thinks. Head, in one of her brilliant essays, once confessed that Botswana represented to her the height of irremedial trauma because it brought her face to face with racial hatred from an unlikely source—black on black.[1]

The taxonomies and stock roles usually imbricated in the insider—outsider dyadic construct become trenchantly reversed and usurped. The Afrikaners are now replaced by the Batswana, especially their social elite, the Totems, while the aggregate of the Blacks and the Colored of South Africa now become the Khoisan/Basarwa/Masarwa/Bushmen of Botswana. Head, through the ingenious resources of ascetic allegory and associative reasoning, attempts to correlate the two dichotomous and binary systems—one White on Black; the other Black on Black. For the writer, it is like being forced into a second *descensus ad inferos* (descent into hell); a dire strait requiring intestinal fortitude on her part.

Head's *Maru* is an intensely moral idealist novel providing a production site for literary resistance to a culturally and ethnically engendered stereotypism, which in turn is imbricated within the discourse of pathology and perceptual categories. In his critically acclaimed book (1992), *Difference and Pathology: Stereotypes of Sexuality, Race, and Madness*, Sander L. Gilman posits that the literary text is a rich source of enlightenment in the study of stereotypes. His central thesis is that every society has generated a seemingly endless series of texts as a means of fixing stereotypes within a world of constant forms; and these texts, Gilman suggests, provide a very good basis for analyzing the historical forces at work in the shaping of stereotypes. Gilman concludes by saying that the passion to create stereotypes has given rise to a fantastic variety of images of the Other, some of them quite remote from observable fact, but all of them at one time or another solemnly accepted as veritable truth. Reinforcing Gilman's thesis, Professor Eve Kosofsky Sedgwick in her book (1990), *Epistemology of the Closet*, argues that literary texts are, in a rudimentary sense, domains of contention, sites of definitional rupture within which to interrogate constructs and perceptual categories of identity, truth and knowledge.

Thus the thrust of this chapter is to interpret *Maru* as an allegorical tale of rupture in which Bessie Head seriously interrogates the pathological construction of ethnic identity and subjectivity as it affects the San people of Botswana, otherwise known by such ethnic slurs as "Masarwa/ Basarwa/ Bushmen." The novel's internal logic or *hyponoia* suggests that the ubiquity of the San people stereotyping is an unfortunate yet significant part of the larger culture's own perverse sense of collective self and nativity dovetailed into what Gilman has described as the primitive "illusionary image of the world divided into two camps, 'us' and 'them'"

In *Maru* Head, even with her politically charged rhetoric, is careful not to bore us with over-sentimental sociological statistics, but instead uses the opportunity afforded by the arrival of the new teacher—Margaret Cadmore—herself a Masarwa and intensely proud of it, in the village of Dilepe, a remote Batswana stronghold—to investigate the complex, volatile nature of human self-construction in general, the source of so much of the prejudice that gives rise to such pathological inscriptions of identity and subjectivity. A careful reading of Part One of the novel (pp. 10–11) will provide a critical point of departure for our discussion. On these pages, Head is not merely interested in cataloguing social instances of verbal abuse toward the Masarwa, nor is she simply content in suggesting the universality of racial/ethnic prejudice, but instead she hypothesizes as to the primal source of human prejudice in general. She suggests that in prejudice difference is constructed as an identity. Identity based on difference, quite often in many cultures and societies, is seen or represented and codified as pathology and degeneration. And this pathology and degeneration provides the pretext and justification for the oppression and exclusion of the members of various systems of difference—racial, ethnic, and sexual minorities, women, etc. One salient question seems to arise from these two passages, and that question is this—why is identity based on difference seen or represented or codified as pathological and degenerate? The answer lies beyond the bounds of the Masarwa world, and judging from the universal tone of the novel's ribald rhetoric, also beyond the bounds of any one nation or racial community. Instead the answer seems to lie in understanding the fundamental nature of human material consciousness, particularly the material consciousness of self in relationship to Other.

For answers to what Head describes in the passages as "the white man's mental outlook," we turn to Hegel (1977), the intellectual godfather of eugenicist occidentalism. Hegel sees human consciousness as operating in a divided arena. On the one hand, you have the transcendent or observing ego; on the other is the fixed self or the observed ego. French existentialist novelist, Jean-Paul Sartre (1966) renames this divided consciousness as *pour-soi* and *en-soi*. Hegel and Sartre contend that the two sides are in a perpetual dialectic, asserting that the transcendent ego (the *pour-soi*) attempts to move beyond the fixed, reified status of the fixed/observed ego (the *en-soi*), but at the same time needs the *en-soi* as an object against which to measure or define itself. Hegel insists that self-consciousness forever needs or desires other people to prove or validate its existence, if only by the negative proof that it is not the other consciousness. Hence this affirmation—denial takes the form of master— slave relationship, the master seeing the existence of the slave as the veritable truth of his certainty of himself.[1]

Weighing in on the issue, Martin Heidegger (1962) posits two kinds of existence between which the self (*Dasein*) is in perpetual tension.

The one existence he identifies as the object-level existence—that is existence as an object, living in an alienated, reified mode of existence. The other is existence as projective, creative and transcending subject—existence as subject. He adds that to live on the object-level of existence, "the they-self," is to live in an inauthentic mode. It is to conform to the dictatorship of the "they," a conformity which annihilates its own sense of self, authentic individuality in the public sphere. On the other hand, argues Heidegger, to live on the subject-level of existence is to live in an authentic mode with a supreme, sometimes narcissistic sense of one's self. It is a self which has individualized itself vis à vis the general crowd, which has achieved self-actualization through the paraphernalia of the authentic mode. It is a self which, for all intents and purposes, has achieved conscience. According to John MacQuarrie (1968) in *Martin Heidegger*, "conscience," for Heidegger, "is precisely the disclosure to someone of what he ought to be, of his authentic self" (p. 32).

For Jean-Paul Sartre, the self exists in a dyad—the *pour-soi* (for-itself) and the *en-soi* (in-itself). The one is the imperial ego, eternally self-projective, self-creative and self-evolving, refusing to be fixed or stereotyped; the other is the static, stock persona, the reified, contingent, immanent object-self, a false construction of the one. In order to constitute itself as a subject, pour-soi must cast the Other as object. "It is by the very fact of being that I exclude the Other. The Other is the one who excludes me by being himself, the one whom I exclude by being myself" (p. 212). Sartre views the dyad also in a perpetual agon. The only way, argues Sartre, that the en-soi can attain significance is that it too must get out of the reified status into the process of becoming. It is this participation in the agonistic process which constitutes human freedom, human liberation (Donovan, 1985).

Using the Hegel—Heidegger—Sartre trichotomy as a point of departure, I will argue that Head's *Maru*, on one level, is the story of one woman's quest for conscience, conscience here understood as the deliberate process of discovering her true authentic self. But on another level, it is the story of the Masarwa who must rise from immanence and the inauthentic pit-holes of *das Man* and find themselves once again reopened to the possibility of collective self-authentication. It is the story of Margaret Cadmore, a graduate of a teachers' training college who is appointed to her first post as a teacher in a remote, inland village of Dilepe, the heartland of the Totems, the village nobility. As members of nobility, the Totems are the lords of the socially stratified Dilepe as a microcosm of the larger Botswana society. Most of them keep the San people (the so called Masarwas) as slaves in their household. Social stratification in Dilepe has a discernible tripartite structure. At the top are the Totems themselves, those transcendent egos, eternally self-projective pour-soi, who have taken it upon themselves to cast everyone else as Other. At the bottom of the social stratification is the tribe of the Masarwa or Bushmen who bear the full brunt of Botwana society's exclusionary politics. The Totems and members of the dominant cultural group have constituted themselves into an exclusive, sole point of reference with apriori presumption of a normal human subject from which everyone else is a variation at best or an aberration at worst.. The Masarwa in Dilepe, as in the wider Botswana society, share this discourse of pathology with the mixed-breeds of Botswana (the third segment of the population), and thus are perceived as a threat to the arbitrary boundaries set within the stratification parameters.

From the time she was a child up until her adulthood, Margaret has been tortured with persistent reminders that she is an en-soi, a bushman, a mixed breed, or perhaps, a half breed, a low breed or a bastard. And yet she knows full well that she has inherited a savior role, one that would lead her people from the status of the reified en-soi to the transcendent position of the pour-soi. The principal of her training college had said to her: "One day, you will help your people" (*Maru*, p. 17). Once uttered, it has created a purpose in her young mind. But Ms. Cadmore, in order to fulfil that salvational role for herself and her people, must attain significance, and to do that, she must get out of the reified status into a process of becoming. Being trained as a teacher, and being deployed to a teaching post is the first toddler step toward that process of becoming.

To aid Margaret in that journey is Maru. Maru is a different kind of chieftain. Although he is one of the village nobility, he alone has the distinct honor of being a paramount chief elect, the heir apparent, of Dilepe. Thus his maverick decision to break with tradition—the long tradition of putting down the "Masarwa"—and in its place a new, more humane, gentler cultural and moral sensibility, is both groundbreaking and subversive. So when Margaret, a "Masarwa/Bushman" arrives in Dilepe, there is instant internal disquiet, a commotion of sorts. Although everybody recognizes the fact that she has an impeccable record as a budding intellectual, yet her quiet entry into Dilepe causes a stir, all due to the fact of her identity, her ethnicity. Ms. Cadmore is representative of those marginal individuals and/or communities whom Michel Foucault

(1988) seems to have forgotten when he opines in *The History of Sexuality* that the secret of identity is the secret of sex (p. 118). True enough, but Head reminds us in *Maru* that the secret of identity is not only that of sex but also the secret of ethnicity and race.

The reason for the internal disquiet that follows in the wake of Margaret's arrival in Dilepe is that her entry into the stronghold of the Totems is about to dislodge the age-long infamous binary tradition of "us" versus "them." The political stakes involved in the maintenance of this ethnic manicheanism are bound to get even higher with terrible consequences in the eyes of those who benefit from the status quo. Afterall the Masarwa are held as an anomaly in the taxonomy of Batswana culture not only because they do not conform to the hyper-Batswana image of a typical African of the Bantu extraction, but also because they are decentered in the hegemonic discourse of the class elitism, the elitism of the Totems. Because the Masarwa are alien or racial Other within the Batswana society, their difference is perceived in other forms of alterities. They are derogatively compared to wild animals—Zebra, Lions, and Buffalo who apparently do not feel any pain, no matter how much hurt you inflict on (*Maru*, p. 11).

Comparing the San people (the so-called Masarwa) to animals is part of the dominant culture's calculated attempt to deny them their basic humanity. And Margaret's entry into Dilepe is Bessie Head's own way of helping the San people reclaim their humanity and subjectivity, and for Margaret, fulfill part of her salvational role. The reference to the scientists of the old (*Maru*, p. 11)—is a reference to the 19th century human sciences whose authors engaged in discourses of racial science whose aim, according to Marylynne Diggs (1993), is "to constitute and differentiate the healthy and the sick, the normal and the abnormal" (p. 5) within the trichotomous context of identity, difference, and pathology. In treatise after treatise, these 19th-century pseudo-scientists adduced what they said was scientific evidence of the categorical differences in the human species with whites assumed to constitute the privileged norm, and every other race as a variation of the Caucasian, Anglo-Saxon stock. Bessie Head sees the same pseudo-scientific rubbish at work in the Batswana perception and treatment of the San people. In Botswana, the Totems and their kind are presumed to be the normal human subject, while the Masarwa, because of their association with beasts, are seen as biological curiosities. In fact, Head goes one step further and suggests that these perceived differences are invested with hierarchical meanings, with the Totems and their kind occupying the imperial position of master and transcendent egos, and the Masarwa, that of slave and immanent object-selves. Head further demonstrates not only the folly and inanity of such theorization, but also that it exacts a heavy political cost on the Masarwa as it justifies a social order that ensures that the Totems and their kind as insiders are kept in and the Masarwa as outsiders are perpetually locked out.

Thus when one of their privileged own, Maru—heir to the traditional throne of Dilepe—jumps ship, Head appears to have created Ms. Cadmore with the sole purpose of interrogating the Botswana society's binary racial paradigm, the Batswana racialism as the authorized discourse of knowledge and the parallel concepts of Bantu purity, health and pathology as the dominant paradigms of this kind of demented knowledge. The result is that as Maru sets his seductive eyes on the young, beautiful Margaret we begin to see the first crack in that amorphous, nefarious paradigm. We begin to see the first flicker of hope that, maybe, the exclusionary politics of Dilepe, as a microcosm of the larger Botswana society, is beginning to falter. By allowing Maru to fall in love with Margaret, Head appears to reject the iniquitous propensity of the Totems to normalize at will certain identities (their own) and categorize others (the Masarwa/Bushmen) as signs of pathology and degeneracy. Maru's renunciation of his high privileged position to marry Margaret, an act that stuns the villagers, represents an outgrowth/ingrowth of his encounter with the noumenal world, the realm of the gods. As a beyonder, the gods are constantly speaking to his heart and reminding him that he need not be like his fellow Batswana trapped behind the prison gate of prejudice. Maru knows full well that some fundamental wrong had to occur to precipitate in him an empathetic reorientation to the plight of those wronged. (*Maru*, p. 8). The gods constantly admonish him to think outside the box (*Maru*, p. 109).

Although many critics have called *Maru* a love story on some level, I would argue, however, that the love story is only a subplot that subserves the larger allegorical purpose in the novel—undermining an evil order in order to usher in a more humane, sympathetic order. Bessie Head shows insistently and consistently that Margaret retains moral superiority over her detractors, tormentors and persecutors. From the get go Margaret is cast as an outsider, in keeping with the exclusionary politics of Dilepe vis à vis the status of the en-soi which she and her people are forced to live and endure on a daily basis not only in Dilepe but also in the whole of Botswana society. Early on readers have had a bitter taste of the typical tragic life of a Masarwa—the inherited wretched life of degradation and debasement—in the heart-wrenching story of Margaret's biological mother at the hospital. The occasion is the death of her San mother at the outskirts of a remote village following the birth of Margaret. Apparently a passer-by had discovered her corpse.

Note that as in the case of her daughter, Margaret, years later when she is assigned as a teacher to a remote, inland village, her mother also bore her on the outskirts of a remote village. The symbolism cannot be overlooked and is never lost even on the casual readers. Emphasis always is on distance, on margins. Not just distance and margins in a physical sense, but more importantly in a social and political sense, in keeping with the fate of the Masarwa in this society, her mother's corpse is virtually ignored after it is brought into the hospital ward. Apparently no one wants to have anything to do with it, once they learn that she is a Masarwa. Subsequently, the missionaries are called in to handle her corpse, the corpse of one of the untouchables of Botswana. The person upon whose shoulders the responsibility of planning the funeral rests is none other than Margaret Cadmore Sr, the abundantly virtuous, atimes cantankerous English woman, wife of the English missionary George Cadmore. By naming Margaret after herself and by putting her through school, Mrs. Cadmore reclaims her humanity and significant selfhood.

Thomas Szasz (1970) in his important book, *The Manufacture of Madness*, applies the theory of the collective Other as scapegoat or repository for the undesired aspects of the dominant group in society developed by Sartre (1963) in *Saint Genet: Actor and Martyr* and in an essay "Portrait of an Anti-Semite." Szasz describes the treatment meted out by the so called "good, normal folks" on to those marginal folks as "existential cannibalism," and ends by asking a very poignant and weighty question: "Can we create meaning for our lives without demeaning the lives of others?" (p. 287). In similar vein, Cadmore, Sr. sees very clearly the existential cannibalism of the hospital supervisor, and especially the nurses, their coldness and soullessness in shoving the unwashed dead woman's body in the small back room where the slop pails are kept. In an angry, thunderous voice and fit of conscience, she orders the nurses to wash the dead woman's body immediately. And later in a reflective, somewhat plaintive monologue with her husband, she wonders where the Marsawa are buried, since in her fiercely blunt but honest opinion they are not perceived as belonging to the society (*Maru*, p. 13). Additionally Head tells us: "She took in also the hatred of the fortunate, and that if they so hated even a dead body how much more did they hate those of the woman's tribe who were still alive" (*Maru*, p. 15).

The truth, Head reminds us, is that what operates in Dilepe and the larger society is oppression, pure and simple. A visitor can see it; a sojourner can discern it. In her book (2002), *Becoming an Ally: Breaking the Cycle of Oppression in People*, lesbian feminist Anne Bishop discusses the basic common denominator among different forms of oppression, in other words, their essential common features. For our purposes here, I will summarize three of these: power and hierarchy, stereotyping, and ideological power. With respect to power and hierarchy, Bishop says that what we are really talking about is class or what she calls "power-over." The "power-over," she contends, can emanate from physical strength, weapons, greater wealth, resources, or information, or greater control of the decision-making and communication mechanisms of the society. These means, she argues, allow the oppressor group to control the oppressed group. The oppressed group can also effectively spread the idea that the less powerful group is inferior. Both the oppressor and the oppressed groups, however, internalize this hierarchical thinking and begin to act it out almost reflexively. Bishop concludes by saying that power-over and hierarchy are fundamental components of all oppression. They constitute the basic class structure in which all other forms of oppression operate.

In *Maru* the Totems and their kind constitute the real matrix of power. They own the Masarwa as servants and slaves. They oversee the economy and determine the forces in it. They alone are the big wigs, the administrators of hospitals, the superintendents and principals of schools with the sole power to decide which teacher goes where. The office of the education supervisor belongs to them and them alone, and the Dilepe Tribal Administration swarms like bees with them. In short, they are the gatekeepers of the Batswana exclusive club. In the novel, the most egregious example of this power-over is Pete, the principal of the Dilepe school where Margaret has been assigned. He is the one most perturbed by Margaret's presence. Almost to the point of having a nervous breakdown, Pete frets about, unable to conceal his intense discomfort that a Masarwa has been assigned to his school. He requests an urgent meeting with Seth, the education supervisor, convinced that there is some cruel artifice or connivance associated with the posting of a Marsawa to his school (*Maru*, p. 41).

Pete is a perfect example of what Sander Gilman calls the "pathological personality." In his book cited earlier (1985), *Difference and Pathology: Stereotypes of Sexuality, Race, and Madness*, Gilman identifies two polar opposite personalities in the politics of difference:

the one he identifies as non-pathological personality, the other he calls
the pathological personality. The non-pathological personality he defines
as one who recognizes that there are social stereotypes, that stereotypes
can and often do exist, but he is willing to create sophisticated rational
categories that transcend the crude line of difference in the stereotype.
On the other hand, the pathological personality does not develop this
ability and sees the entire world in terms of the rigid manichaean line of
difference. Gilman concludes: "The pathological personality's mental
representation of the world supports the need for the line of difference,
whereas for the non pathological individual the stereotype is a
momentary coping mechanism, one that can be used and then discarded
once anxiety is overcome" (p. 18). In the novel, the nonpathological
group includes Maru, Moleka and Dikeledi, and the pathological gang
comprises Pete—principal of LeSeding School, Seth, the school
superintendent (education supervisor), and Morafi, a dis-reputable Totem
and the cattle thief.

The second and third components of oppression identified by Anne
Bishop are stereotyping and ideological power. Stereotyping is part of
the concept of separation, dividing people rigidly into "us" and "them."
Bishop explains that in stereotyping, a dominant group sees itself
essentially as a collection of different individuals and a marginalized
group as a single collective entity. Bishop then concludes that most often
stereotypes are used in a damaging way against marginalized groups.
Many have suffered and died because negative images of their people
were established in the institutions with the power to imprison, kill,
forcibly hospitalize, take jobs and homes away, and separate people who
love one another. On ideological power, Bishop defines it as the power
of belief, of ideas, that allows an individual or group to influence others'
concepts of reality and their idea of what is possible and valuable. The
best example in the novel of both stereotyping and ideological power is
the obnoxious behavior of Margaret's students in the classroom. Word
had spread quickly around that a Masarwa teacher has been assigned to
the LeSeding school. So the pupils, who obviously have learned the
stereotypes of the San people from their parents, have come to class
ready to insult Margaret with their virulence and obnoxious demeanor.
No sooner had Margaret walked into the classroom than the assault
began. The principal Pete had engineered and stage-managed the whole
damn freak show ((*Maru*, pp. 45–46). The rudeness and assault
continues unabated until Dikeledi, her mentor, comes flying into
Margaret's classroom, and in a rage that sounds like the clap of thunder,

she curses at the pupils (*Maru*, p. 46).

This classroom scene illustrates the fact that, as with the Batswana society in which the shaping of stereotypes is more than a mere casual preoccupation, Dilepe in particular and Botswana society in general have manufactured a set vocabulary of images and beliefs about the San people, the externalized Other. The novel suggests that these images of the Masarwa are rooted in the tribal history of Botswana, and in a binary culture that perpetuates them. Calling the Masarwa whatever names they may enables the dominant Batswanas to construct a model that best reflects their common presuppositions about their externalized Other, the Masarwas. These presuppositions underscore the Batswana people's need to structure the world in familiar stock terms exclusively advantageous to them. The derogatory names suggest the use of what Gilman calls "root metaphors" (p. 22) in the construction of binary categories in the culture, which in turn subserve the morbid intentionality of classifying the Other. As Gilman asserts, "these categories reflect the cultural categories of seeing objects as a reflection or distortion of the self" (p. 23). Furthermore, the derogation erects false categories of difference and somehow suggest that the Masarwa are the puns in the sickening game of structuring perceptions in terms of binary difference. For as Gilman also notes, the concept of difference is needed to distinguish the healthy and the sick, or as Head says in the novel, to erect "false barriers people usually erect toward each other" (p. 38).

Maru's love for Margaret, a Masarwa and subsequent marriage to her is an attempt to weave what I call the Bessie Head's monomyth. In Head's monomyth, there is a sense of promise, of renewal, and of rebirth. In this monomyth, there is a sense of the Masarwa emergence from oppression and marginality and a sense of their gradual participation in the fruits of Botswana promise and Botswana dream. I, therefore, take exception to the conclusion of Cecil A. Abrahams (1990) that "the marriage does not change the prejudice and narrowness of the Botswana, they simply close their doors on their chief and withdraw their allegiance" (p. 7). Instead, I would argue that there is in that marriage both a certain exuberance, a will to change things for the better, one totem at a time, one individual at a time. Beneath the surface of fairy tale magic, lies supreme human confidence in the possibility of moral order, a moral order in which true equality and opportunity can manifest its genuine effulgence.

Thus *Maru* ends on a sanguine note of rebirth, the possibility of leaving one kind of life behind and passing on to an entirely new existence. For

Maru, the sensation of being reborn in the image of his gods, of beginning a gentler, more humane life is fundamental to his sensibility as a beyonder who understands the language and world of the gods where there are no dualities. He knows full well that the transformation which Botswana must undergo is not one merely restricted at the physical and material level of consciousness, but more importantly also involves the element of inwardness, inner spiritual renaissance, what we might call ontological rebirth—rebirth into another being. This other being is that larger and greater personality maturing within us—far greater and far above the elemental, base ego from which all the prejudice spews forth. Once transformed into that other being, one begins to see that there is more to life and oneself than the base, twisted intelligence from which prejudice spews forth. One's horizons expand beyond the limited loyalty to class and tribal culture. For Maru his old attitudes and assumptions about the Masarwa suddenly seem insufficient, and so he must leave them behind, cast them off like the slough of a snake, the old skin which can no longer contain his growing body and consciousness.

Head distills this process of Maru's maturation in the form of an initiation rite—the rite of marriage, albeit untraditional. The purpose of the marriage rite between Maru and Margaret is to transform the former into a new man. Allegorically, the process represents the death of his old self. Elopement functions symbolically as that sense of removal which is necessary for rebirth to occur. Elopement is an allegorical passage of sorts. Every passage most often is unnerving. But those individuals courageous enough to accomplish this passage without regard to social convention, in Maru's case, regal comfort, often discover at the end of their passage a way of life far more satisfying, far superior than the one they leave behind. Similarly, by getting married and then eloping, both Maru and Margaret serve the allegorical function of leaving one life behind to seek a new existence, a place where a second chance is possible, where they can start life anew and be, in a sense, reborn. As Oladele Taiwo (1985) argues, "Maru's marriage to Margaret is presented not only as a personal act of enlightened self-interest. It is also a major political achievement. By it the novelist makes an important statement of hope and redemption for all oppressed people in Africa and elsewhere" (p. 192).

Finally, Head intimates that change in Botswana will come by way of fundamental dismantling of the apparatuses of prejudice and exclusivism, a dismantling of a mind-set inimical to a segment of the Botswana population. It will manifest a three stage process—birth, death, and rebirth. The birth is that of the prejudice lodged in the hearts of men, women and children. The death implies that for a new life, a new society to emerge, this prejudicial culture has to die. Confronting ethnic prejudice in Botswana is like descending into darkness and danger, and this descent represents what amounts to death, casting off established social attitudes toward the Masarwa. The beginning and the ending of the novel inform this death-rebirth dialectic. The first paragraph of the novel reads like a dark foreboding with the rains coming so late that year, like prisoners trapped in tumultuous clouds. (p. 5). This picture suggests a man's later awakening to a new life preceded by a symbolic death. Watching the darkening sky, readers are given this picture of descent into a dark realm, a dismal underworld of prejudice and hatred that has imprisoned everyone, victim and villain alike. At the end we witness an emergence from darkness into daylight, the brooding sky clears up a bit, and life resumes its tempo with a new vigor. The novel shares in the new-fangled optimism (p. 127).

Bessie Head's *Maru* is thus an important post-modernist work which rewrites the Masarwa into significant existence. Teresa Ebert (1991) says that rewriting, as a strategy of resistance post-modernism, "articulates the unsaid, the suppressed, not only of texts and signifying practices, but also of theories and frames of the intelligibilites shaping them" (p. 888). Similarly, in *Maru*, Head articulates and voices the suppressed and the silenced and the oppressed in Botswana society—the Masarwas, and in so doing, displaces the hegemonic logos of the Batswana, thus unleashing an alternative potential in the life and work of Margaret Cad-Cadmore. The fact that Margaret is a teacher, a profession that demands the exercise of instructional intelligence disrupts the dominant culture's stranglehold on knowledge. Inscribing or rewriting ethnic difference means that the concealed Other—the Masarwa—must be revealed. Thus Margaret must come to Dilepe to cast off the slough of the old snake, a symbolic analogue that must accompany the displacement and destabilization of the dominant cultural logic or illogic. The novel recycles the heritage of common humanity by foregrounding change as an agathological instrument for establishing a new social and ideological frame of reference, for charting a truly egalitarian future for Dilepe (Botswana) and the rest of mankind.

2

Masada as Symbol in *Season of Anomy*

Current interpretations of Soyinka's *Season of Anomy,* including this writer's, have tended to focus almost exclusively on its mythic significance. Dan Izevbaye's article "Soyinka's Black Orpheus"[1] (Lindfors) is perhaps the most illuminating to date. The basic narrative structure of the novel may indeed be Orphic; and in fact, it is undeniably so. But unless we are prepared to admit that Soyinka is working on a number of intellectual levels, we are far likely to fall in the way of those critics who think that by posing as pious curators in the live museums of Yoruba mythology, the ultimate truth of Soyinka's artistic vision becomes readily available. But the plain truth is that *Season of Anomy* is basically a human tale about the wanton destruction of human lives. However, to appreciate the full hideous impact of the killing of the Aiyero people in the Cross-river region of Ilosa (Soyinka's imaginary dystopia of present-day northern part of Nigeria), Soyinka demands that we go back to the history of the Jews, particularly the history of their tragic and heroic struggle against the murderous tyranny of the Romans.

The poet-hero of the novel, Ofeyi, is not merely a mythic hero in quest of his abducted love; he is also an archaeologist prodding through the rubble of extermination to find what possible clues, if any, exist on the nature of the genocide and the way the innocent victims of it managed to hold out to the last painful throbs of their breath. The place of his search is Masada which, curiously enough, finds its geographical transplantation within Soyinka's imagination in the desert hills of Temoko, particularly in the grotto of the Tabernacle of Hope Church.

Season of Anomy is a perfect example of the transplantation and adaptation of creative imagination. By 70 A.D., Rome's armies had conquered nearly all of the kingdom of Judaea. Only one small Jewish enclave continued to resist: the thousand men, women, and children in the mountain fortress of Masada, who endured a two-year siege by 15,000 Roman troops. When defeat loomed, Masada's defenders committed suicide rather than surrender. Such is the form and content of the tragic narrative of Masada passed on to us, the present generation. It is a story of indefatigable courage, of resistance; some might even say bravado. Armed with the story of Masada, located in the parched Judaean desert, and armed with a specific local circumstance—the violent and gruesome killing spree that took place in the northern part of Nigeria in the latter part of 1966 (the militant Moslems as natives of Temoko in the Cross-river cast as perpertrators and villains, and the Igbos, largely southern Christians, cast as hapless Aiyeros-victims of the murderous rampage), Soyinka tells a dizzying tale of genocidal murder and colossal betrayal, wrapped in myth and symbolism, in particular, the myth of Orpheus-Eurydice-Persephone. The central character of the novel— Ofeyi—is both an Orphic hero as well as a defender of Masada, cast in the novel as Temoko—a parched desert outpost in the midst of the Cross-river, beyond the Niger-Benue confluence line (northern Nigeria). Just as Orpheus journeys into Hades in search of Persephone, so Ofeyi, in the garb of the Roman Jewish historian Flavius Josephus, the avid archaeologist, and the mythological hero (Orpheus) journeys to the Cross-river hell of Temoko in search of his love Iriyise (cast as Eurydice) as our sole witness to the tragedy that has befallen the people of Aiyero.

But in recasting story and myth, Soyinka insistently and consistently plays on a very painful irony. For the poet-hero, just as the Masada cave was destined to be the last stronghold held by the Jewish people against the Romans, so the Tabernacle of Hope grotto serves as the last hiding place for the citizens of Aiyero in preparation for their forced return to their native land. But painfully enough, it is here that most of them—men, women and children—met their untimely death just as it was in the Masada crypt that some Jews asserted their own response to the immutable law of the inner conscience. Besides, the irony works in another equally significant way. For instance, most of the archaeologists involved in the Masada Expedition, notably Professor Yigael Yadin, formerly of the Hebrew University of Jerusalem, perform their task with a kind of avid relish. But for the poet-hero of *Season of Anomy,* the search, by its very nature, raises fresh disturbing questions about the ultimate necessity of the whole archaeological venture, since what it does is simply exacerbate his skewed emotional disquiet over the entire tragic scenario. Ofeyi muses: "Why do they bother, these antiquarian hands forever disturbing the ghosts of history. . . These futile reconstructions, of what use ultimately are they since they neither stop nor caution against the reenactment" (272).

Clearly enough, the poet-hero is here expressing his apparent doubt over his search. There is a temptation to view this self-doubt as the hero's grave cynicism about the ultimate value of archaeological researches in general. But if we can distance ourselves from the problem of teleologism and view his self-doubt within the broad schema of sensitive humaneness, we might see that the hero's questionings clearly in some curious way underscore basic universal human frustration and outrage against the killing of other human beings. What seems to support this latter viewpoint is that immediately after, he begins to be fascinated by a more positive aspect of his apparent archaeological excarvation—one that would unearth for us evidence of a more vital linkage: "Strange history. . . must look into what evidence there is of a Nilotic link" (273). The "Nilotic link," of course, refers to the Nilotic group of Sudanese languages spoken in the Nile Valley above Khartoum and southeastward into Kenya and Tanganyika, divided into western containing Acholi, Alur, Dinka, Lango, Luo, Nuer, and Shilluk and eastern containing Bari, Karamofong, Masai, Nandi, and Teso, and variously considered as a family or as a branch of the Chari-Nile family. The mention of these language groups is crucial in understanding the full dimensions of the huge irony being played out here. There is a strong suggestion that the attendant sense of national and gentilitial unity which it evokes appears to have been shattered. We recall Soyinka's passionate belief in the transcendent power of a common medium of communication, notably Kiswahili, in forging a new sense of cohesion in mother Africa. If that is what is adumbrated here in fictional terms, then the painful irony seems to be that the basis of that anticipated unity appears now to have been demolished in the massive ruins and rubble of castrated bodies.

So that an archaeologist, armed with certain vital tools, is likely to grow in confident belief that at the end some sort of a creative essence could begin to form. But Soyinka's archaeologist isn't quite sure whether the whole search, as an act of recurrent ritual pattern of sacrifice, will not prove futile, like the futile sacrifice of the nameless traveller in Soyinka's poem "Death in the Dawn"[2] Thus the basic difference between the real life Masada Expeditionists and the poet-hero expeditionist in *Season of Anomy*, at least for now, is that unlike the latter the former seek to discover in the Masada debris a basis upon which to forge what Roland Sanders has described as "the memory of Jewish heroism, of refusal to accept any alternative to living and dying in the Jewish homeland that this spot invokes" (8). The point is stated even more poignantly by Yadin:

We, the sons of new Israel—as we stood in the ruins of the Roman camp above the cave on which we pitched tents of the Israeli Army who helped us to retrieve the precious documents of our past—could not help feeling at that moment the strength of our deep-rooted belief that the Eternity of Israel shall not fail. (41)

It is the absence of a deep-rooted belief in anything that our poet-hero appears to regret. We shall return to Yadin's statement later and examine it in terms of its crucial impact on the correlated allegoric meaning of Masada in *Season of Anomy*.

A number of parallels exist on a number of divergent levels between the Jewish Masada of the Bar-Kokhba cave and the grotto-cave of the Tabernacle of Hope Church in Soyinka's Cross-river. There is first what I would call the generic-ethnological level. Then there is the similarity in geography, in architecture and stratigraphy. Finally, there is the symbolic—what the whole Masada episode means and why it is of such intense fascination to Soyinka. First, some general background statement. The subject of Masada in *Season of Anomy* is not a product of mere abstract thinking, or perhaps of a perception based on mere subjective relations of one thing to another, relations which one perceives exclusively in symbolic terms. The symbolic is unmistakably there and inheres in the dynamic action and events in the novel, and in the novel's intricate web of images. But I think that Soyinka also means to paint a little physical picture of the Masada crypt as a way of leading us closer to its ultimate symbolization within the broad allegorical framework of the novel. On page 271 of the novel, Soyinka calls a spade a spade, moving the poet-hero to ask: ". . . Messala. . . Mesalla?. . . Was it Masada? Was this how it always began, these treasures that brought scholarly salivation to the lips of burrowing fanatics? Dead Sea Scrolls and dead men's bones that are never permitted rest" (271).

These questions posed here relate advertently to the tragedy of Masada. The "brave self-immolation that slept for a thousand years" refers to the brave death of the one thousand Jewish people at their own hands in the caves of Masada under the leadership of Eleazar ben Yair. Thus the answer to the poet-hero's question whether this was truly Masada is that like the Jewish death, the death of these innocent Aiyero men, women and children is the death of glory preferable to a life of captivity and infamy and loss of freedom and liberty. With this notion, his heart appears to steel against this delicate moment of truth that afterall these people, like the 960 Jewish men, women and children, had performed a telling act of valor by ostensibly taking their own lives. If that is the final picture presented here in this mass rubble of human waste, then the best moral and intellectual suasion appears to have been innocuously framed for dealing with the cruel necessity, the hideousness of the whole act. This means also that the first spark of optimism appears to have been kindled to replace the initial doubt and pessimism.

Soyinka's "carbon-dating scrolls that disintegrated and writings that turned invisible at the first touch of sunlight," recalls the biblical scrolls and the scrolls of the Dead Sea Sect, discovered by archaeologists in the cave of Masada at the dawn of the Masada Expedition, which, according to Yadin, "can be absolutely dated from before 73 C.E. . . , the first time that ancient scrolls can be specifically and absolutely dated." (24) Viewed in this light, the task of the poet-hero in *Season of Anomy* is of immense value to humanity, at least for two reasons. The first is that it recreates for us the patterns of life in the grotto of the Tabernacle. But even more crucial is the fact that by discovering these scrolls, he has succeeded in preserving not only for historians but also for posterity, in fact for all concerned humanity, the most significant leads and artifacts necessary for the understanding of the lineament of that gory and tragic event. The discovery of these ancient scrolls, therefore, suggests not only Soyinka's deliberate universalization of the Temoko carnage, but also the high esteem to which he devoutly holds its innocent victims whose death is then primordially linked to the lost and buried biblical relics, which discovered, have served mankind up till this day. Once again, as in all Soyinka's works, the negative and the positive (the Heraclitean law of enantiodromia), the creative and the destructive, coexist so ingeniously that the resultant sense of triumphant humanism becomes a new shrine upon which the estimation of human nobility even unto death could be securely forged.

I have said that there are levels of correspondences between Soyinka's grotto in Temoko and the cave in Masada. The first, as has been pointed out, is the generic-ethnological. This provides what is clearly an extraneous level of realism admirably refined into art and stylistic dynamism. Although some critics might with some legitimacy object to raising issues outside the universe of a work of art, we cannot, as we wade through the heart-wrenching pages of *Season of Anomy,* but suspect that Soyinka has fictionalized one of the most tragic chapters of Nigeria's national political history—the cold massacre of the Igbos in the north of the country in 1966. It is a brutal event which even the most pious plea for artistic dissociation could not easily conceal. This is not surprising at all given Soyinka's very controversial stand on the event. One of his best poems (in fact, one of the best poems coming out of Africa), titled, "Massacre October, 1966," is dedicated to that tragic event.

Aside from his poem, Soyinka had spoken out quite vehemently against the killings. He even made a trip to Eastern Nigeria in which he sought to accomplish two things: first, to express his sympathy for the victims of the Igbo pogrom, and second, to persuade the Igbos against secession. Therefore, while it may be extraneous in the sense that it is not rendered as a prosaic historical chronicle, I think that as in Chaucer's *Canterbury Tales* a more appropriate appreciation of Soyinka's vision in *Season of Anomy* must be based on the historical context within which it is securely conceived. In the absence of any proof of the inviolate reliability of art as an aesthetic-stylistic construct of dynamism, and without trying to trivialize the artistic richness of *Season of Anomy*, I think it is fair to say that what Soyinka is attempting to accomplish is to employ the power of his consummate art in order to create valid aesthetic remove between himself as social critic and his raw material, the historical reality, at least for the preservation of the unique integrity of art.

Besides, the mention of Auguste Rodin's bronze masterpiece, *Burghers of Calais* on page 272 reinforces the historical dimension. The *Burghers of Calais* as an art work that trnnsmutes powerful emotion into physical stature is perhaps one of Rodin's most memorable sculptural works next to *The Thinker*. It is not so much that the *Burghers of Calais* is a master bronze work. That much has been vouched by critics. What is even more important to Soyinka is the story behind the bronze work; perhaps, not just the story, but the very meaning which it conveys. The story, put quite simply, is that it is a monument erected by the city of Calais in memory of its heroes of 1349 who volunteered to surrender themselves to Edward III, King of England in exchange for the liberation of their besieged city, which lay strategically on the northern coast of France. The story was recounted in the chronicles of Jean Froissart written around 1360–65.[3] Why, you may ask, is this art work whose story is about an event that took place in Europe more than six hundred years ago relevant to the situation in Soyinka's Cross-river. The truth of the matter is that both events celebrate the idea of sacrifice for the greater good, and the idea of salvation and the individual will. Eldred Durosimi Jones explains the whole concept this way:

Soyinka sees society as being in continual need of salvation from itself. This act of salvation is not a mass act; it comes about through the vision and dedication of individuals who doggedly pursue their vision in spite of the opposition of the very society they seek to save. . . The salvation of the society then depends on the exercise of the individual will. (11)

In a somewhat similar vein, Obi Maduakor writes:

Associational linkage of events recurs at the Tabernacle of Hope where the condition of the entombed congregation reminds Ofeyi of previous religious persecutions, especially the Spanish Inquisition. In one instant the underground church is transformed into an archaeological catacomb in which archaeologosts are digging out the remains of religious martyrs of history. (147)

The underlying point of all these historical-ethnological details is that we are dealing with the near extinction of a race; from the standpoint of Masada—the Jewish people, and from the standpoint of *Season of Anomy*—the Aiyero race. In each case, the near extinction is suffered in a crypt or desert cave—in Masada, it is the Bar-Kokhba cave; in *Season of Anomy*, it is the grotto of the Tabernacle of Hope in Temoko. Just as the Jewish followers of Bar-Kokhba and Eleazar, himself a priest, sought refuge from the Roman terror in the cave of Masada, so the Aiyero people (refugees in their own country) seek temporary refuge in the grotto of the Tabernacle in the desert wilderness ofTemoko under Father Elihu.

Aside from the ethnographical, the nature of the topography, part of which we have touched upon, reveals even more curious similarities. The first is that Temoko is in the wilderness of the Cross-river (the northern part of the imaginary country, llosa) just as Masada is in the wilderness of Judaea. Aside from the desert quality, each town is on a boulder or boulder-infested terrain. Masada is helmed by desert cliffs, and according to Yadin, "with a sheer drop of more than 1300 feet to the western shore of the Dead Sea" (19). Temoko is in the midst of desert hills yawning their way down to the river around which the Mining Trust Company carries out its prospecting operations. Again, Masada is an outpost for the fleeing Jews, just as the Temoko grotto is the final outpost for the fleeing Aiyeros

But nowhere is the similarity between Soyinka's grotto and the Bar-Kokhba cave more striking than in the nature of the archaeological finds. It is startling the way in which the tangible items and artifacts discovered (or imagined) by Ofeyi in the grotto correspond fairly closely to the finds in the cave of Masada, architecturally and stratigraphically speaking, that is. A list of the Masada finds is culled from the final report by Yadin who, as Director of the Masada Expedition worked tirelessly in the huge excavations of the ancient relics of Masada.

In Yadin's Masada Expedition and Soyinka's *Season of Anomy*, there is mentioned a small Christian chapel, named in the latter the "Tabernacle of Hope." There is the mention in both of a rectangular structure. Then there is the accumulation of ash underneath a gruesome discovery of dead, pulverized bodies. There is a grissly picture of an anguished male survivor. Mention is also made of deliberately set fire, perpetrated by a bloodthirsty marauding horde and heartless vandals.

Then there are references to the Dead Sea Scrolls. And finally, there are enamel chips and small potsherds broken and scattered all over the place, evidence of breached rooms. Both Dead Sea Scrolls mentioned in Yadin's archeological finds and Soyinka's *Season* are associated with sacrifices. But while the real life Judaic scrolls are sacrifices for renewal of life those of the Tabernacle of Hope are for death, mass death, that is. It is one of the painful ironies which Ofeyi, our poet-hero, finds particularly hard to swallow. But the poet-hero's final prayer and consolation is that ". . . grass grow upon it all and let fresh, rich millet (one of the grains grown in the North of Nigeria) feed the children of survivors"[272]. This is the only way in which Ofeyi could possibly conceive bringing in line his own discovered or imagined Tabernacle scrolls with the ultimate, higher purpose of the Judaic Scrolls.

The intent in providing these preceding comparative data is to reinforce the point that definite parallels do in fact exist between the real-life Masada of the Judaean desert and its fictionalized version of the Temoko desert in *Season of Anomy*. Having seen all these more or less physical details of the Masada cave:, the question that arises is this: What is Masada?[4] What, really is it about Masada that has fascinated Soyinka, so much so that he decided to even weave it into the inner logic of *Season of Anomy?* Yes, to critics Masada seems to have paradoxical possibilities for the Jews: survival and accommodation and heroism and annihilation. But to this writer, the answer to this question is not to be sought in what Masada means to Soyinka per se. Rather, the answer lies in what Masada as a prototypical human tragedy meant and still means to some of the Jews. Of all the writers who have had to write on Masada, particularly on its moral implications, no one has done it better than Louis Finkelstein—Chancellor of The Jewish Theological Seminary of America.[5] So I think it is fair to take his lead in understanding the ultimate message of Masada. In "Masada and Its Heroes," Finkelstein makes the following eminently crucial claim: "Masada stands today as a monument to freedom, and to the courage and heroism of those who laid down their lives for it It is a reminder sadly needed in a world which all too often forgets that man is made in the image of God" (8).

These immortal words of Finkelstein state the point succinctly and eloquently. For Soyinka, the Aiyero people, murdered in cold blood, are people who love freedom. They have fled to the Tabernacle of Hope church because as its name suggests, albeit ironically, it is the last fortress of hope and freedom from death and destruction. Although they do not choose to die by their own hands, as did their heroic antitypes—Bar-Kokhba and Eleazar followers—their fate is essentially the same. It is as Finkelstein has put it, "the right of man to live according to his own conscience; and under certain circumstances, even to make the supreme sacrifice for conscience" (15). That Soyinka espouses this ideal is hardly arguable. His own chequered life is filled with moments of rigorous defence of freedom and justice. In an interview with the magazine *Spear*, he says pointedly:

I believe there is no reason why human beings should not enjoy maximum freedom. In living together in society, we agree to lose some of our freedom. To detract from the maximum freedom socially possible, to me, is treacherous. I do not believe in dictatorship benevolent or malevolent. (20)

Soyinka himself knew what freedom or denial of it really tasted like when he was unjustly arrested and subsequently clamped into solitary confinement by the military junta headed by General Yakubu Gowon between 1967-1969. This tragic experience has led him to re-rhetoricize in his prison memoirs—*The Man Died*—what has now become one of the grandest, memorable clichés of our time, reminding us of Timerman, Socrates, Norman Thomas, Edmund Burke, the Russian dissidents, and, of course, the Jews: "the man dies in all who keep silent in the face of tyranny" (13). That is why the poet-hero, like the Child Roland of Robert Browning has to thrust out into the African wasteland of Temoko, risking life and limb, to secure the release of his loved one—Iriyise. In this way we are assured of the basic freedom critically needed for any real meaningful operation of human life. Soyinka's poetic sequence, *Ogun Abibiman*, is an expression of his condemnation of the geo-political tragedy of denied freedom, as the South African case, prior to the release of Nelson Mandela, reveals quite clearly.

In conclusion, let us return to Yigael Yadin's earlier statement at this point because of what I have indicated to be its unique significance. When Yadin speaks of "our deep-seated belief that the Eternity of Israel shall not fail," we are reminded of Soyinka's almost prophetic candor with respect to the history of modem civilization. Soyinka is an optimist, or better still a meliorist, and his use of the Masada event as a symbol of the human spirit, appears to be a reinforcement of that optimism. For Soyinka, Masada's true testimony is that it underlines for him the search for a final system of stable equilibrium in a world of constant flux and topsy-turvydom. It serves ironically as a penultimate human statement about the reconstruction and renewal of human society which finds its appropriate form in the Aiyero utopian scheme. So that aside from the ideal of freedom, the Masada episode reflects Soyinka's fundamental preoccupation—the search for the true shape of things to come. In a period of exceptionally bloody chaos in a country like Nigeria, "Africa's Giant," so much depends on the ability to foresee the direction in which

African societies are moving. That is why the poet-voyager in *Idanre,* a lone ranger, had to trudge up the hills, the untrodden path, to ascertain the secrets of the gods. In *Season of Anomy,* he goes beyond the hills down into the cave of Masada-Temoko, prodding through the rubble, a task which has become a life and death response to this demand for reliable information about coming thing—the Aiyero alternative ideal. In this regard, Soyinka becomes the horizon-watcher of our time.

The ideal of freedom, that is what it is. Soyinka's grotto like the Masada Bar-Kokhba cave may contain ashes and rubble, yet out of them must arise a new era of congenial human relations, a secure ideal of freedom, a new epoch far more human, and even humane than the present set of Junta-and-Cartel crotchets, an Aiyero ideal—the finest alternative to the masochistic reign of terror, hate and extermination that was Africa's recent past. And if Soyinka had taken the pains to poke through the ashes of the Masada-Temoko cave, it is because he believes passionately that human beings must be free to live their lives far beyond the welter and above the clangor of motiveless malignity. Upon this canopied niche, sane human beings can pitch their tabernacles, once more hope to enshrine their most sacred destiny, and begin to pursue their legitimate fortunes, free from the menaces of a home-grown leviathan. This is the message of the Masada grotto of the Tabernacle of Hope. This is the fundamental message of *Season of Anomy.*

3

Soyinka: From the Failed Narcissus to Heroic Orphism

Wole Soyinka's two novels, *The Interpreters* (Heinemann, 1965) and *Season of Anomy* (Third Press, 1973), reveal significant distinctions, in spite of Juliet Okonkwo's ingenious effort to underscore certain affinities between them. To move from the world of *The Interpreters* to that of *Season of Anomy* is to cross a liminal threshold, away from the Narcissian self-indulgence of the former to the heroic artistry of Orphism of the latter. It is like moving from man as a self-seeking voyager to man as exemplifier of what Jung calls the transcendent function, the Orphic man cutting through death and destruction, driven by the ineffable power and the unconquerable will to endure and to prevail. Richard Hughes, taking a cue from Joseph Campbell's *The Hero with a Thousand Faces*, reveals that the basic difference between the Narcissian hero and the Orphic is that the former lacks the daring spirit of the latter, the spirit to confront obstacles and not be overwhelmed by them. Incidentally, it is this heroic obstinacy that distinguishes Ofeyi from Egbo; it is a distinction that reveals a significant point of departure in Soyinka's artistic, social, moral, and ideological vision. For instance, where Egbo in *The Interpreters* is overwhelmed by his journey, dispirited by the death-like impediments—canoe hulks and the like—that litter his path, Ofeyi in *Season of Anomy*, on the other hand, dares into the maws of death.

Furthermore, Egbo is no Orpheus like Ofeyi. His dream of reintegrating with his past vanishes at the shadowline, in the depths of the creeks. He returns with no clear image, no icon, no treasure. He travels a crooked path that seemingly has no depth or discovery or supreme sense of salvational rescue. Perhaps the only thing he returns with is the self-annihilating choice of drifting with the surging tide. The ironic image of the quester-hero as perpetual drifter is somewhat checked in Ofeyi, who as a person who seeks security from the present dangerous moment must uproot himself from it and so comes pretty close to becoming a perpetual drifter himself. Soyinka, however, avoids the drifter image by conferring upon Ofeyi's journey a clear archetypal, prefigurative paradigm of Orphism and by making the present state irritatingly unsurvivable. Besides, Ofeyi, on the other hand, is Orpheus, and as Orpheus, he fuses two roles in one: he is both an artist (poet-musician) and a seeker. Herbert Marcuse, in *Eros and Civilization*, considers Orpheus the prime symbol of the poet as liberator and creator, the pacification of man and nature through art rather than force (154-55). In fact, Ofeyi, as poet, composer, and song-writer, must not only descend into the underworld of the Cross-river, but must also return with Iriyise and with the whole arcadian image of Aiyero, which incidentally incarnates his quest and his anticipated return. A closer examination of the quests in these two novels would ascertain the patterns of heroic failure versus heroic success, even triumph, and subsequently reveal the distinction afore-mentioned

The Interpreters begins with Egbo's journey to his maternal hometown, Osa. The occasion for the heroic quest is not so much external as it is more of an atavistic urge born out of some internal disquiet, a feeling within Egbo for his personal past. It leads down into the darkness of his sundered personality, into the depths of his unexplored interior, and it is here, in this alien world within, that he must confront and learn to accept the concealed and unpleasant parts of himself. For Egbo, the confrontation must lead back to the primal swamp, the dark river of energy and dissolution out of which he has come. In fact, Soyinka's marsh is marked by something like Freud's death-wish to return to a prior inorganic state of matter. The problem, however, is that Egbo, in spite of his journey, is not yet disposed, and probably will never be, to deathly things or mortuary images. In response to Kola's disdainful remark about the depressive mangrove, Egbo confesses that he loathes deathly things.

In fact, all through the journey, the thought of death is clearly the chief threat his Narcissian vision has to overcome. It is solely for this reason, this failure to confront death, that makes Egbo's voyage of discovery a failed mission. By balking at the spectre of deathness, Egbo betrays unwarranted despair and fails Jung's transpersonal archetypal test. Jung rejects the ultimate despair that yearns for liberation from suffering. Death is described in Jungian iconography as a counterpart to birth, indicative of renewal, a symbol for the exuberance of all life-processes regardless as to whether they constitute a beginning or an end. However, the journey provides Egbo with the opportunity to encounter the supreme life of the god, Ogun, a life, that is, in its own nature, contradicts death. At such auspicious moments, like the one provided by this journey, or the one afforded by watching a woman in a baptismal seance in Prophet Lazarus's beach congregational church, Egbo opts for a quest, a quest for a qualitative immortality representing man's longing for a unified personality outlasting the vicissitudes of time. It is a longing for an instinctive release of soul that carries no particular deontological prerequisite except that Egbo be quite capable of achieving it. Quintessentially it will bring him the assurance of an ever-present life beside which death is simply unreal and unimaginable. Considered as an intrinsic element in the formation of the Egbo self, the quest becomes a longing for the mystique of ascension which Erich Neumann suggests is intimately connected with the mystery of wholeness and integration (25). Against this backdrop, Egbo, in the company of his friends, begins a homebound journey that he hopes would change his life in subtle significant ways (see 8-10).

Egbo's musing also reveals an interiorization of time through hallowed memory which for him represents a deeply troubling encounter with his own past. But apart from being an archetypal search for a personal past, the journey is a longing by Egbo to return to the center of existence (see 70-77). At the end of it all, however, Egbo returns from his journey, a failed Narcissus, convinced that Osa after all is no more than "a place of death" (12), an impassable homestead that "built a faded photo of the past" (8), with a pungent smell of "its archaic menace and violent undertoss" (12).

In *Season of Anomy*, on the other hand, Ofeyi, unlike Egbo, must confront death, massive death. The quest narrative in the novel is defined in terms highly suggestive of death-rebirth symbology, a symbology which reminds one of Eliot's use of the Grail Legend in *The Waste Land*, and which gives to the novel's leitmotifs and metaphors the exciting range of correspondences which *The Interpreters* could not achieve completely. As Orpheus, Ofeyi must go in search of his beautiful damsel, Iriyise, abducted by the military junta, aided and abetted by the Cocoa Cartel, in the desert town of Temoko, where she is subsequently held in a mental ward. Ofeyi journeys through a wasteland to an underworld, a territory ruled with relentless terror and brutality by Anubis, described by Soyinka as infinitely flagitious and as the jackal-headed one who "had fallen asleep thinking, this is the fifth face of the Apocalypse, the eight plague that the Judaic sorcerer had omitted to include—the plague of rabid dogs." Undaunted by this, Ofeyi moves with his guide through the land of death while their "living bodies felt clammy hands about them sucking their vitality into a universal deathness" (22). Ofeyi's perseverence and determination to look death straight in the eye and to subsequently defy it is justified by the final pay-off; he finally rescues

Iriyise and together they head back to Aiyero, land of order and ritual harmony.

The parallels in *Season of Anomy* with the Eleusinian Demeter-and-Persephone myths are infinitely clear, hardly fortuitous. Among the ideas earliest impressed on the mind of primordial man was the yearly stealing away of the treasures of the earth or dawn-mother by the greedy and pitiless winter into the regions of darkness. These regions became a prison or store-house, containing the germs of all future harvest. The lord of this cheerless abode, according to Hellenic belief, was Hades or Aides, the third of the three Kronid brothers and children of Rhea. Similarly the abduction of Iriyise is like the stealing of the dawn-mother in the Eleusinian myth, because after Ofeyi finds her, life resumes its normal rhythm (see p. 320).

The landscape through which Ofeyi journeys is tellingly wintry and grotesque (see particularly 175). Soyinka does not merely depict the perceptible attributes of the landscape; instead he demonstrates that its center is the stark horridness of entrance, the slow penetration of the landscape by an awakening, disconsolate voyager. We follow the thrust of the allegoric imagination downward, through obstacles and impediments, to a new abrasive assessment of the physical environment. The progression in the novel is literally downward. Ofeyi moves from clouds across a distant view of scorched fields to the stunted plant life right before him. The panoramic view, with its patches of dry land, offers nothing with which Ofeyi's imagination might joyously connect itself. It is starkly, unabatedly dreadful.

Soyinka's description of the Cross-river—Temoko—Funtua tri-setting stands between Eliot's *The Waste Land* on the one hand, and Saul Bellow's and Browning's on the other. Eliot's "stony rubbish," dead trees, and dried up pools, for instance, parallel Soyinka's drought, dwindling trees, and stunted branches. Like the setting, however, in Henderson *The Rain King* and "Childe Roland to the Dark Tower Came," Soyinka's infernal topography is also peopled by strange monsters, weird creatures, and rabid beasts like tongue-steaming dogs. These are creatures which are drawn heavily through the force of nightmarish imagination upon the uncanny forces of the Apocalypse, the beasts of Revelation. Childe Roland's black bird parallels Ofeyi's rapacious kites and vultures circling the sky. Soyinka's dog is more like the dog in Baraka's *The System of Dante's Hell* and the one in Awoonor's *This Earth, My Brother*, the whelping bitch, the howler by the nightly road. As Ofeyi continues his quest, the landscape becomes increasingly ominous and shrill (see 212).

The desolate eeriness of the landscape is carried into the making of Soyinka's characters. Suberu, for instance, the club-footed guard at the Temoko prison-gate where Iriyise is held, is a brilliant pun upon the Eleusinian Kerberos (Cerberus) who guards the gates of Hades. To enter the Cross-river underworld, Ofeyi must cross the river beneath the Labbe Bridge because Labbe Bridge apparently marks the boundary between hell and earth.

The Labbe river parallels the Eleusinian river, Acheron, the boundary which separates the world of the dead from the world of the living. Just as in the Eleusinian myth, those who are accepted as righteous by the three judges of Hades pass to the happy abode of Elysion, far away in the west where the sun goes down beyond the bounds of the earth, and where no grief and sorrow, nor sickness and pain can ever touch them, so Ofeyi, Iriyise, Zaccheus, Pa Ahime, Demakin, and the whole contingent of Aiyero refugees, absolved of the blood of their own kind, return to the arcadian clime of Aiyero (presumably in the western region of Ilosa). They return to a people who, instead of gloating over strife, blood and animal vengeance, participate in the nobility and grandeur of arcane rituals that forge the resplendent affirmation of life principles and innermost sympathetic and affectionate bonds. They return with an image, which is an image of the vicarious anguish crucial for man's chastising pilgrimage to the "center of the world."

Soyinka's Season of Anomy is a classic example of what is termed: *descensus ad inferos*. That the novel chronicles a man's descent into hell is clear even to a casual reader. The very terrain and the characters that people the novel are drawn somewhat from Hades or Hades-like environment. Mircea Eliade, one of the first to introduce the concept into general literature, links it with the experience of initiation, cast as agonistic drama involving battles with monsters and demons, real or imagined. As has been pointed out in chapter 2, the Cross-river region of Ilosa is Soyinka's version of Hades, a part of the world which is an abnormal variant of Aiyero, and which, for all intents and purposes, is a remote, dark, menacing underworld of unimaginable terrors, monsters and demons, a subterranean domain of death and destruction. Soyinka describes one tiny segment this way:

Knowledge of death filtered through the crypt, a chilly current through air that had only begun to warm up. The shadowy inmates underwent changes of infinite subtleties, drawing together even more, purging individual fears in the font of shared loss. Prayers rose in hushed voices from one corner to the other, a mother embraced her children in a sudden spasm of love, hugged them until they hurt. Her tears fell in mourning for the unknown one, death spread its cold tentacles through the festering gloom but it bred no fear in the breasts of any. They had seen too much. (270)

This is a dark picture of almost unparalleled horror and unrelieved afIliction. Soyinka comes close to what Eliade believes is the very end of afIliction in the descensus ad inferos mode. When Soyinka writes that "death spreads its cold tentacles through the festering gloom but it bred no fear," it is not because he is not convinced that their plight is real, but rather because as symbolic death and suffering, the whole situation at this stage has a clear ritual value—the spiritual transmutation of the victims. The church setting and the endless prayers lend weight to such transmutation.

The task of Soyinka's quester-protagonist is infinite and complex. But it is a role that must be assumed and subsequently fulfilled if the world is to be salvaged from the miasma of carnage and recurrent existential negation. Oftentimes, it is a selfless and sacrificial role fraught and enacted in the transpersonal mode of liminal encounter. It is an encounter that involves not just the path but the depths, and perhaps, not just the depths but the ability to penetrate them, perceive meaningful patterns, and finally emerge with a new sense of reality, perhaps one much profounder. Egbo, like Verne's Professor Lidenbrock, ventures into the liminal path, but somehow falls short of craving the gloomy twilight. Fernando Savater says that "to descend is indeed a task for the tenacious man, not for the merely resourceful" (49). Evidently, Soyinka realizes that mankind does not have much hope of redemption without this penetration, this unbending tenacity. Egbo, though unquestionably resourceful, weaves nothing more than a fragile thread of the spirit, but hardly consummating it in fundamental essence. Ofeyi, on the other hand, crystallizes the spirit into an incarnate image. The Orphic-man, Ofeyi, like Baraka's Peaches- man or Verne's Axel-man, fords the direst depths for the image, the liberating image of Iriyise and Aiyero, that alone is capable of mending our battered lives.

4

Awoonor, Okigbo, and Soyinka: Nostos Symbolism, and Prima Donnas

Creative imagination, particularly literary fantasy, is replete with a rich variety of symbolic representations of the woman, which representations are efforts not only at re-visioning the role of women in our lives, but have for all intents and purposes marked a movement one step beyond the sexual politics of cultural feminism. Upon us are the days when prominent figures of the *fin de siècle* such as Swinburne, Beardsley and Oscar Wilde constructed an altar-site where it is now fashionable to venerate and exalt the 'heathenized' woman. In western tradition, prior to the age of the *fin de siècle*, particularly during the great tradition of the emergence of the novel, this worship of the heathenized woman was frowned upon as satanic. Instead what we had was a dualized image of the woman, dualized into opposing values—the whore and the virtuous woman—with the latter being the positive instrument of heroic redemption, and the former being the one that distracts the hero from his enlightenment[1] or shiny path. Such was the familiar dichotomy that, as Mark McWatt has written, "became an established feature of the literary language of the time.." (33). The African *fin de siècle* group—Kofi Awoonor, Christopher Okigbo, and Wole Soyinka—uses the same figure as the European *fin de siècle* in privileging the 'paganized' woman as the intercessionary symbol of their hero's redemption and/or enlightenment. For these three writers, A.S. Altekar's observation on the position of women in Hindu civilization is right on the mark. Altekar has said that "one of the best ways to understand the spirit of a civilization and to appreciate its excellences and realize its limitation is to study the history of the position and status of women in it" (xiii).

In Kofi Awoonor's novel, *This Earth, My Brother*, mythology and allegory blend, providing a radical image of a deeply wounded and penitent pilgrim involved in what Chinua Achebe describes as "a tortured return journey in search of a lost beginning" (x). This return journey, despite its obvious limitations at the level of concrete experience, does provide an aboriginal via media of fantasy for a homecoming "wombwards to a rendezvous. . . [with joyful tidings of] golden-age innocence" (Achebe xi). In *This Earth, My Brother*, Awoonor plays out this fantasy in the drama of the spirit of Amamu, the activist-lawyer who lives in Kaneshie-Deme (modern Ghana). The author associates him largely with his mermaid, the maternal lake of light, and to a lesser extent, with maternal darkness and cosmic dissolution from which his sense of worth, all sense of worth, emanates:

The protagonist, Amamu, is presented as an avid angler in the lake of light, thirsty for a badly needed mystical image. The mermaid's bodacious rise from this lake momentarily blinds him, providing Amamu just that crucial image. It is an image of the world that, though sensuous, does endow the life of an angler/seeker with a dignity that a corrupt society of modern Ghana in which the hero exists and supposedly lives summarily denies. Though partially mentally ill, suffering from marginal psychosis, Amamu does recognize that this maternal sea is fundamentally one of light, evoking in the language of its mystical aliveness a sense of what Bronislaw Malinowski terms "phatic communion" (315), a principal source of pristine vitality and containment. Awoonor invites us early enough in the tidal effulgence of the sea into this phatic communion with a voice reminiscent of biblical eschatology and Dantesque spiritualism. The call is to return to the magic hour of our birth.

Home for Amamu is the imaginal unconscious wherein lies the immanent presence of the maternal crown of light. He must descend when driven by the excessive demands of Demean (Ghanaian) lycurgus—the blind tyranny of the political establishment. The images of the blind tyrants, the political buffoons, seen in people like Mr. Attipoe—the fat drunken road overseer, Mr. Kodzo—the derelict and inebriate towncrier, and the elders—those stupid-looking old men—are particularly frightening to Amamu. Then there are the more horrifying images of maggots and decay, of death and self-annihilation, of "the yellow lights of streets paved with human excrement from flying trucks," (108) of the sexual torture and perversion, of madness and hysteria, of possession by devils and despicable people, of uncontainable rage, and of unmoving lives of speechlessness containing the scatological visions of lunacy. Amamu's response to these destructive, chthonic images is to resist their deadly allurement for a gullible returning pilgrim, and to try instead to develop a mystical rapport with kindlier, life-affirming images, images that constellate in the maternal unconscious of a mermaid, whose anagogic power would lead him out of his present rut onto peaks of a more meanigful life comprising all the loftier aspirations such as ethics and sound morality. We are simultaneously told that "he sat down at its feet gazing out to sea. A sudden calmness descended upon him. . . (178), and that at last this is his moment of salvation.

Amamu's visit (and there are several such visits in the novel) to his mermaid of the sea, like Okigbo's penitential call before his watery deity—Idoto—is less a private dream and more of a public one. To the extent that it evokes rather concretely the more ordinary elements of his present experience, Amamu's visit is a private affair. But it is also a much more serious public dream, because in a way Amamu dreams for us, for the entire Deme (Ghana), thus becoming a primordial metaphor of collective initiation and carrying a portent for the community. Perhaps his visit is symbolic of the mystical unconscious and the Malinowskian sense of community, which sense appears to have been lost in the post independence Ghana. This maternal image is so consuming and pervasive for Amamu and the Deme community that it summarily symbolizes for Amamu a return to the certainties of the old primeval order and ritual bond, away from the amorphous transgressions and odious indulgences of the anarchic, degenerate modern Ghana.

Jung calls this kind of dream, "big dream." It is the kind of big dream that had moved Gilgamesh to seek in the depths of the sea for the herb of immortality—the secret of rebirth. It is the kind of big dream that had moved Zarathustra to attempt to lift the veil of illusion and behold the "womb of being."" And it is the kind of big dream that had facilitated Faust's entrance into the "realm of mothers," to see what binds the world together in its innermost essence. It is like descending to the aboriginal matrix of creation to reenact the archetypal quest of the prototype hero, in Amamu's case, to answer the heart-felt call to "deliver my soul from the sword/My darling from the power of the dog." (3) The power of the dog here is the power of the mythical dog that guards the gates of Hades; Deme, as contemporary Ghana, is the modern equivalent of Greek mythological Hell. Amamu, very much like Theseus, must confront the minotaur or the leviathan that has ravaged his native land, not in the pose of a faustian conquistador, but in the patronage of a greater power—the feminine principle. Thus encountering the maternal image is like descending to the depths of the undiscovered self, experienced not as mere faceless surrender or withdrawal, but as downwardness which is a measure of man's heroic spirit. And when Amamu does just that, he is no longer out of his elements.

Besides, Amamu's mermaid is drawn upon the inherited pattern of behavior celebrated in the Mother-of-the-Sea tradition. But unlike the latter, the convention which Awoonor draws on is somewhat unique, a uniqueness which allows full sway of private vision. The traditional Mother of the sea figure is not a particularly attractive personality, according to Stephen Larsen in his book, *The Sharman's Doorway*. Larsen offers this interesting explanation: "The Mother of the Sea creature is a rather unappetizing creature herself, smelling of fish, of course, and with her hair matted and tangled—in a Greenland version, full of vermin and lice" (85). Awoonor's mother of the sea, on the other hand, still retains a peculiar quality of sensuous beauty despite the ravages of time. Her long hair still shines "like flames of jet streaming down," (4) and still drops "millions of golden stars behind her" (5). Like the virgin figure in Derek Walcott's *Another Life*, her breasts, we are told, "are balls of flames," are shiny and erect upon the water (4). But like all mothers of the sea, Awoonor's mermaid is the anthropos image in the depths of the unconscious, cut off from a life of instinct, from the unconscious. Visiting the sea of his mermaid is like visiting the forgotten or the hitherto unplumbed depths of the psyche wherein lies the therapeutic image of wholeness.

In sum Amamu's mermaid is Awoonor's affirmation, or shall we say, reaffirmation of water as the symbol of the unconscious which lies underneath consciousness. His watermaid is a Jungian equivalent of the water spirit, psychologically, the unseen denizen of the unconscious. The significance of this symbolism for Amamu, who is suffering from the the neurosis of alienation, is that down by the sea he could experience the working of the living spirit in the process of individual healing. Awoonor's creation of his mermaid is part of what Jung perceives as the inexorable urge to rediscover the redemptive gods within each one of us, that is, the gods as psychic factors, as archetypes of the unconscious, an urge which Jung categorically attributes to an unparalleled impoverishment of symbolism (de Laszlo 308).

Awoonor, however, is not interested in the mermaid as a mere symbol of the unconscious "that contains nothing but the silent, undisturbed sway of nature" (de Laszlo 308). Jung writes:

Our unconscious, on the other hand, hides living water spirit that has become nature, and that is why it is disturbed. Heaven has become for us the cosmic space of the physicists, and the divine empyrean a fair memory of things that once were. But 'the heart glows,' and a secret unrest gnaws at the roots of our being" (de Laszlo 308).

Amamu's visit to the lake to confer with his anima, his *soror mystica*, therefore, shows a peculiar kind of sympathetic concern for the unconscious which is mirrored in his very inner being. He knows that the treasure of emancipation from the sickening ills of modern day Ghana lies in the depths of the water. By the power of this knowledge, he becomes a veritable Jungian fisherman who must catch with hook and nets that which swims in the depths of the unconscious. He recognizes the infinitely timeless meaning of his visit; and when he peers into the sea, he sees his own image behind which are living and chthonic metaphors of the unconscious. That is the symbolic meaning of the symbolic female in *This Earth, My Brother.*

Just as Awoonor seeks the image of the buried, unknown self in the maritime surroundings of his mermaid, Christopher Okigbo lets that image be the center of his obsession with inner peace and cultural palingenesis. In his only volume of poetry, *Labyrinths*, Okigbo explores the subliminal interior of his being, searching for those eternal unconscious images with which to assuage his violently sundered feelings as he gropes his way through the darkened labyrinth of modern Nigeria caught in the suffocating cobweb of cultural dialectic. The poet, like Robert Graves before him, knows that he has wronged his goddess of creation, rebirth and fertility by pandering to foreign gods who had distracted him from the world of his revered goddess and its life-enhancing ritual. From this distraction, follow all the tribulations and indignities that the poet has had to endure. Okigbo knows full well that the apparent cause of his tribulation is the poet's estrangement from the goddess, his true muse, and his loss of the original and essential language, the aboriginal voice of his poetry, namely, gynocentric mythos which is based on a close knowledge of the divine realm, the seasonal cycle, and vegetative life.[3] Thus at the center of the poet's feelings and thoughts is the image of his primordial mother constellated in four symbolic patterns—the vegetal, the labyrinthine, the canaline, and the astrological. Incidentally, each one of these symbolic patterns represents a crucial stage in Okigbo's quest for self-renewal and self-regeneration

The vegetal symbolism represents one of the most traditional and recurrent forms for representing the archetypal feminine figure, and Okigbo employs it artfully to his end. In "The Passage," the very first poem in *Heavensgate* (part 1 of the sequence), the poet prostrates and prays before his goddess—Idoto.[4] In *The Golden Bough*, James G. Frazer stresses the vegetal aspect of other goddesses like Idoto, their anthropomorphic embodiment of that form of fertility on which pristine peoples depend for their sustenance. Frazer traces in considerable detail the precise plants, trees, and flowers held sacred to the individual goddesses.

Okigbo's incorporation of the elements of myth and ritual shows a subtle reliance on *The Golden Bough*. Partly in thematics and detail, and partly in constructive genius, *Labyrinths* invokes Frazer's *The Golden Bough*, although the influence appears more Lawerentian and Eliotian than Gravesian. Okigbo's identification of Idoto with her familiar totem tree—oilbean—parallels Robert Graves's linking of the Summerian Belili with the willow, and Frazer's ascribing of corn to Isis. The poet's leaning on Idoto's totem tree suggests his hunger for physical and emotional security under Idoto's infinitely caring arms. Sunday O. Anozie is absolutely right when he suggests that goddessess among other things play a dominant role in Okigbo's poetry, and that the goddess Idoto mentioned in the first movement—*Heavensgate*—is the original source of the poet's being to whom he must return in humility and penitence. In this respect, Idoto resembles other figures like the Babylonian Ishtar and the Greek Demeter. As mother of vegetation, Idoto is for the poet the fruit-bearing oilbean tree which nourishes, shelters, and thus transforms. And if in "Lustra," the poet has seen Idoto in her full glory that is because he realises that his goddess, like Graves's white goddess, has become the tree of life which nourishes his famished soul, a benevolent divinity of telluric abundance and vegetal fecundity. Thus the myth of Idoto subserves the larger mythology about the genesis of the edible plants which Mircea Eliade suggests is associated with the primordial Mother (183).

It is not only in the vegetal realm that Okigbo conceives of his goddess. His vision of her also draws from the age-long labyrinthine tradition; in fact, it is not surprising that the sequence is titled *Labyrinths*. Of all the studies done on the labyrinthine iconography, none is more fundamental than John H. Layard's. In *Stone Men of Malekula: Vao*, Layard reveals a number of primordial characteristics of the labyrinth. The most salient, for our purposes, is that it is almost always connected with a cave or more rarely a constructed dwelling, and that the presiding personage, either mythical or actual, is always a woman.

In section six of the fourth movement, *Distances*, the poet is invited into the maternal cavern; he responds with as much religious fervor as that seen in the paleolithic aeon. For the poet, it is at once an unconscious abode of initiation into the inner mysteries of the mother principle. To penetrate into the body of the goddess, now seen as the labyrinth or cavern, is for the poet the equivalent of a mystical return to the mother, an end pursued in a determined rite of passage. The resultant passion is a dream, a sense of divine accommodation that compels a time-hallowed invitation. The poet, stepping on mythical stones, is invited inside, deep into the cavern. It is an invitation that grounds Okigbo's vision in the paleolithic tradition, with all the suggestions of the geological dimensions of the mother-figure. In mythical tradition, stones serve as an organic and animated creation of the mother archetype. The poet must step onto these stones because as the mythological analogues to the bones of the earth-mother, he realizes that these stones stand for the source of life, the very source of his own life.

The poet thus comes to a place where apparently he is no longer out of his element, where he is with a redeeming, lively image, the maternal image. He is no longer the estranged African chasing after dead foreign values, but a true native changed radically in the imaginal cavern of a beckoning sympathetic, forgiving primordial mother. Going into the cavern then becomes for the poet not a mere matter of preserving himself in a strange, unfamiliar terraine, but rather of returning home after a period of cultural bastardization. It is experienced not as inward defeat but rather as downwardness, the downwardness of a self molded back in what Adi Shmueli says is "the dialectic of 'inward transformation' which is a process of becoming (5). It is from these very mythical stones that the poet will derive the strength with which to mold his past fugitive and wayward ego into a new stable self imbued with a sense of resurgent cultural pride. There is a clear echo here of the paleolithic myth of Deucalion, who by scattering stones, is really sowing the seeds of the new humanity; in the poet's mind, a new, more level-headed native son, living in right relationship with the cherished deity of his native land.

As we follow the poet in *Distances IV* through the marbled pavement, which is like and in *Distances V*, through the molten rocks, the metallurgical process suggested here is very much akin to the agricultural season associated with goddesses like Mother Idoto. Both the metallurgical and the agricultural processes suggest the fertility of Mother Idoto, and have therefore tended to create in the poet a feeling of supreme confidence and pride.

The labyrinthine symbolism is further enlarged upon by the canaline (vessel-like) symbolism. Here Okigbo begins to perceive his goddess as the symbol of quintessential containment. The main canaline symbols employed by Okigbo are basically traditional and typical, and include water and the abyss. We have already seen that Okigbo's main goddess, Idoto, is a village stream worshipped in his own hometown, Ojoto in Anambra State of Nigeria. The very first stanza of "The Passage" referred earlier establishes Idoto's power as a water goddess. Into this watery sanctuary the poet, driven by the demand for mystical wholeness, must descend for refuge and purgatorial cleansing. Mother Idoto is a goddess of moisture, and the poet's descent is for symbolic moistening. In other words, we have a penitential prodigal-son sadly yielding to the psychic gravitation of the maternal instinct now seen as a water vessel. He stands there pleading that he be allowed to drink from the maternal vessel which contains the water for which he has been thirsting for a long time. To drink from it is for the poet to be initiated into the primordial womb of life. It is the symbolic water of the depths of his soul. This water will also nourish and transform the poet, since all living things build up and preserve their existence with the water of milk of the earth. That is why the poet's prayer in "Elegy of the Wind" (*Path of Thunder*), is to be warmly received as a forlorn sojourner, and this suggests that the earth water has now become the milk of the maternal body, and the poet's goddess, like those in the lyrics and songs of the Kagaba Indians, has become the mother of the Milky Way. In primordial iconology, water is the life-milk of the world body, and the cosmic space is a sea of milk. And when we hear the poet's joyful lyric, we get a sense of the primordial man for whom the archetypal female still owns everything in the plenitude of her vessel. For mother Idoto, and her cohort, the watermaid, "bright with the armpit dazzle of a lioness," their goal is not to devour but instead to procure and shower riches generously.

The second canaline symbol—the abyss—is the symbol of the feminine earth-womb. It has two aspects—the positive, in which case the goddess is the Good Mother of creation and birth; and the negative, where she is the mistress of death, the engulfing entrance to the dark underworld. Okigbo's poem that best exemplifies this dual symbolism is *Distances V*. Here the word, "abyss" is mentioned three times. In each case, the abyss is the numinous place, the maternal sanctuary where the famished soul of the poet can experience both effervescent joy, the warmth of a maternal kiss, as well as the pacification of the mythical darkness of the mother, the coldness of her funerary rose. The canaline motif here has profound intimations of the Osiris myth and the Gnostic tradition. It is a primary feminine symbol, a maternal womb in which the home-bound poet, seeking psychic and higher consciousness, is transformed and reborn into a new positive self.

Okigbo's primordial vision of the symbolic female in *Labyrinths* finds its most trenchant expression in the zodiac. Here Okigbo employs the three principal luminaries: sun, moon, and stars, correlating the starry firmament with his primordial mother figure. We have already seen how, in *Path of Thunder*, the poet associates his mother-figure with the Milky Way. But while recognizing that these luminaries are somewhat governed by the immutable laws of fluidity, Okigbo, however, infuses his own maternal zodiac with permanence and stability. It is absolutely essential that he, like Parmenides, cultivate this stability, for the poet drifting through the labyrinth of meaningless and senseless modernity must, as a matter of personal survival, hold on to some kind of symbolic intangible around which he may find some consolation.

In the first poem of *Watermaid III*, the poet-prodigal looks rather solemnly and reflectively at the heavenly bodies and the majesty of the starry constellation. In the second poem of the same movement, the poet savors the incandescent vision of her mystical queen who emerges with the effulgence of a mooncrested lioness. And he the poet must ride the angry firmament, fording angelically toward the solar system, with Eunice at the gateway. To ride with the angry stars toward the great sunshine is, for the poet, to embrace the maternal sunshine that would hopefully brighten up his weary days on earth. The passageway of the returning pilgrim is manifestly oneiric, clustered around certain symbols which represent life as passage, both ontologically and epistemologically. In fact, the ethos of Okigbo's poetry strongly suggests that Being has taken on a character of tension in the charged gradient of radical becoming. The poet knows that the ontological mutation which he seeks in the Mother-archetype can actualize only by deliberate rite of passage. That rite of passage is, for the poet, a matter of flight, of elevation and ascension, of mounting the astrological stairway. The astrological passageway, therefore, serves as a symbol of a passage from one mode of being to another, securing a just liberty of movement, a freedom to alter the poet's present moral and psychological ordeal, to annul the poet's conditioned unnative propensities.

In fact, Okigbo makes it perfectly clear that an understanding of the astrological determinism of his delicate encounter with his anima is absolutely essential to a comparable understanding of the very meaning of the feminine primordial mystery and its seemingly strange hold on him. But in the movement, *Lament of the Silent Sisters III*, the poet fears that the possibility of reaching this understanding may be stalled by "Unseen shadows like long-fingered winds/Pluck from our strings/This shriek, the music of the firmament." Nonetheless, the poet is determined to swish through the phantoms of darkness, to partake of the celestial promise of self-regeneration sounding off in the beautiful euphony of the heavenly music.

Thus through the delicate kinship of Okigbo's goddess with the moon, sun and stars, the poet's celestial goddess assumes her rightful place in the monistic world of the primordial female. His goddess is now the very personification of the eternal feminine principle of life, identical with the primeval water in the tunnel and the genetrix of the sun whose rays, in conjunction with the lunar consciousness, manifest life, beginning and ending, and within it, the questing poet must seek light, his eternal soul's passageway embodied in the goddess.

Finally, *Labyrinths* is an ingenious attempt to give a distinct poetic form to serious mythopoeic and philosophical doctrine. It offers Okigbo the very possibility of satisfying his profound desire to configure a millennial reality forged out of his personal moments of pain and suffering. The poem dramatizes the state of moral agitation of a penitent soul in which a profound concern for the spirit of a Madonna-figure predominates, and in which there is a burning desire to live in right relation to her. In other words, *Labyrinths* distills an anagogic meaning which subserves a deep reverence for an all-encompassing, infinite, benevolent gynocentric divinity. Through the four symbolic patterns, Okigbo transforms the deontological objective of his homecoming into a deeply felt penance and self-mortification, a paean and a beatitude for a beloved Mother-figure.

In Soyinka's *The Interpreters*, the symbolic prima donna is constellated in Simi, the whorish diva of unbridled passion. She is conceived in terms of an eroticized goddess, the instinctual embodiment of the anima, the prime exotic mover whose fascination drives, lures, and induces her countless male admirers, especially the fugitive Egbo of the Foreign Office, to all adventures of the soul and spirit, of creation and recreation in the inner and outer worlds. She is "the goddess of serenity, Simi, Queen Bee, with the skin of light pastel earth, Kano soil from the air" (51). Assuming the Queen Bee image links Simi to the natural potency of earth mother-figures. Johan Jacob Bachofen sums up the symbolic significance of the bee this way:

This makes the beehive a perfect prototype of the first human society, based on the gynocracy of motherhood, as we find it among the peoples named. Aristotle goes so far as to place the bees higher than the man of that period, because in them the great law of nature is expressed far more perfectly and firmly than among men. The bee was rightly looked upon as a symbol of the feminine potency of nature.It was associated above all with Demeter, Artemis, and Persephone. Here it symbolized the earth, its motherliness, its never-resting, artfully formative busy-ness, and reflected the Demetrian earth soul in its supreme purity. (114)

Simi's Demetrian earth soul is aptly reflected by the light pastel earth of Kano. When she sits "motionless, calm, unacknowledging, and indifferent to a host of admiring men," (51) she insists upon her "virginal" pride, her uncompromising independence of the men after her. Her indifference is an unconscious function of her Demetrian character, the relative "purity" of Demeter, whom Bachofen respectfully regards as the "pure mother bee" (584). However, being a bee may also carry some negative connotations—the terrible aspect of Simi's protean personality. Afterall, what else is she but the femme fatale inhabiting the bee-hive, from where men

> . . . had gone, bluster emptied, pocket drained, manhood disgraced—for Simi matched them glass for glass and kept her mystery while the men were hollowed out and led out flabby or raucous, sadder but never wiser—then would Simi make her choice, her frozen eyelids betraying nothing. (51)

As a symbol of creative female power, Muse-like, Simi has the uncanny capacity to inspire both practicing and prospective poets into spontaneous songs of homage. We are told that

> There were songs, of course, the various episodes of Simi's loves, praise-songs and many which spun abuse, not on Simi, not ever on Simi, but on the women who dared profane the goddess of serenity. . . Simi never paid to have her praises sung; the men did. But mostly it was an act of spontaneous homage; the poet saw, and burst forth in song. (51)

Thus Simi is cast in the image of a mantic woman, a muse who is the center of magical songs and of lyric poetry, the source of the songs that stream upward from the unconscious depths. Indeed she is like Robert Graves's goddess, the inspiring anima of the poets. But as the universal goddess, she also challenges men, leading them into the darkest reaches of their souls, the result of which, however, is ironic since the men are not led to muster any will to overcome, or to assimilate and transmute their less exemplary traits, or even to achieve any semblance of self-mastery. The statement: "in company Simi would sit motionless, calm, unacknowledging, indifferent to a host of admiring men" strongly suggests that Simi's apparent mystery is her dualism, the enantiodromic dualism of the feminine archetype of the cosmic Queen Bee. Thus in her positive aspect, and in the archetype's most concrete crystallization, she represents procreative energy, like Joyce's Molly Bloom. But in her less charitable, men impelled by what Colin MacCabe calls "neurotic negation of desire" (35), are in danger of being engulfed, blinded, emasculated, even humiliated by her. Joseph Campbell has said that "the universal goddess makes her appearance to men under a multitude of guises; for the effects of creation are multitudinous, complex, and of mutually contradictory kind when experienced from the viewpoint of the created world" (302).

What Soyinka is attempting to do with Simi, whose role as an awe-inspiring courtesan, reminds us of the archetypal heroine in "The Respectable Harlot and Tin of Lemon-Drops," one of the many ingenious tales in Anderson-Rosendal's *The Moon of Beauty*, is to defract the hour-glass through which woman is perceived, in effect, as mere footstool or puny object of men's degenerate sexual fantasies. Soyinka reinforces this point again and again in a series of other striking passages (see p. 54). There was a continuing saga in other passages (see p. 56).

In these passages, several notions are established regarding Simi's symbolic ascendancy. The first is that enunciated by John Vickery. Vickery asserts that "the notion of the beautiful woman who is whimsical, capricious, cruel, and tyrannical, and nonetheless passionately desire and sought after has a long literary tradition, of which the medieval court of love portion is perhaps the best known" (35). In this context, Soyinka shares in the early Keatsian vision of the La Belle Dame Sans Merci prototype "whose sexuality ruined many a 'knight at arms'" (McWatt 33) as well as in the Frazerian iconography of the great orgiastic fertility goddesses, taking into account the awesome honor and responsibility of cohabiting with the "divine" woman. The second notion is the "phantom-lady" image. According to Barbara Warren, the phantom lady is a spiritual being who causes the hero (or any other man for that matter) endless suffering and remorse and who leaves him "alone and palely loitering" on some "cold hill side." Warren maintains that "whether she is viewed as seductress, "femme fatale," succubus, or divine muse, she is essentially the man's vital spirit, his soul, without which he is inwardly dead, merely existing, wandering, lost in a gray world. She is his fate-living hell or divine madness; and he is not fully alive without her" (8).

Thus the picture we have of men after Simi is demonstrably that of hunters, of venatic dreamers and disconsolate seekers, seeking a phantom-woman, at once so passive and withdrawn, so complete in her own self-indulgent fulfillment and power. Simi appears to these men as mysterious as the elusive image of the primordial woman manifests to the primal man; in fact, as an infinitely uncanny female personality superstitiously akin to the magic of nature. The men swing between something in the form of pious simulacrum and a kind of inscrutable morbid fear, underlying, on one hand, their tamed protestations of self-presumptuousness, and on the other, the turgidity with which Simi has struck in them the first note of their infantile imagination. Warren suggests that the man who pursues such a phantom lady can only waste away in a fantasy world if he seeks her as a real woman, for he will never find her in the flesh; she is an imaginary creature of his own making who will always elude him in the outside world because she is part of his own psyche. This, concludes Warren,

is the nature of ideal images, dream-lovers, and inner spirits when they are projected onto people in the outside world. Eventually, they vanish from external reality because they are part of that world; flesh-and-blood reality is contrary to their essence. . . that is why she is an airy substance like all things that are purely intellectual in nature and spiritual in source. (8)

Apart from her capacity to inspire songs and awe, Simi can also inspire passionate love. The most intense is the love affair between her and the rootless Egbo of the Foreign Office. The author is far from idealizing that affair the way Derek Walcott in *Another Life* idealizes the love between the questing poet and Andreuille ("Anna"). But Soyinka does utilize the love to build up Simi into a towering Aphroditic figure.[6] She is a love symbol, proclaimed by Soyinka as having universal human essence. As we will see shortly, the author refuses to reduce her to a level of frivolous girlishness, this in spite of the fact that she is an unabashed courtesan. In fact, as men that have come in contact with her realize, Simi is more than a mere suggestion of the obscene, the perverse, or the erotic as is, for example, Cyprian Ekwensi's Jagua Nana. Rather, Soyinka invests her with a quasi-religious stature, a figure who symbolizes profound values and profound ambivalences, meriting the epithets: "Goddess of serenity. . . Simi, Queen Bee." Her relationship with Egbo exposes the love of a superior being for a human, a love based upon spiritual and emotional contentment as well as upon sheer physical animal sexual gratification. It is a love that expresses Egbo's desire for an understanding between the erotic emotions of human creatures and the quasi-spiritual love of the godhead.[7]

The worst we can say about the love affair between Simi and Egbo is that it remains at bottom a fragile affair precariously balanced between seduction and symbolic suicide. But otherwise, ultimately, it is a life-long affirming love emanating from a love goddess, for there is little doubt that the relationship benefits both, but especially Egbo, rather immensely. Egbo himself has never been in any shadow of doubt about the arcane significance of their love. In fact, insistently and consistently, he has grown to see it as the freeing outlet of his own intensely eroticized soul; and he knows that ultimate freedom, in terms of the accessibility of the divine, lies squarely in the creative capacity of his own emotion expressible through his very carefully orchestrated physical rapture.

The thought of taking Simi as his wife shows that the conscious part of Egbo's personality now yearns for some kind of indefinable harmony. Were his life to amount to anything remotely meaningful, were he to discover the hidden self within, then his life would have to be channeled, and supposedly Simi's love is there to meet that need. That is why "he felt in danger now, so that to retrieve himself from a wound he feared he asked, 'Do you never love any man?'" (59). Egbo's desire for the love of the feminine principle is heightened in that moment of ecstasy when Simi is uncannily proclaimed "the filled bag in a stiff breeze, high grass on the air field" (60). This is where male desire is transformed by the feminine vision of love, a vision which transforms naked eroticism into something vastly different, into a symbolic function of the anima's nurturing of the life of the animus. Simi retains her spiritual integrity even in the consuming venality of erotic magnanimity. She is no longer just Simi of Lagos; she has become in effect larger than life, an icon resembling the epitome and dynamic channel of affective life, or shall we say, affective femininity. Thus in yielding her body to the sexually starved Egbo, Simi symbolizes for him the matrix of unconscious self-fertilization, the via media of creative dynamism, in short, a stimulus to his inner craving.

When Simi prompts seductively for love—"You are not undressed. No leave it. I'll do it for you" (59), she invites him into the mystery of her inner world. It is here that Simi's power as essential transformative erotica is foreshadowed. Because there is a quasi mystical side to their love affair—"for he [mused] about Simi, and her near mystical desertions" (57)—Simi becomes the keeper of the mystic center of this love. She has become for Egbo, for all intents and purposes, his highest known potential and so can be said to rule him through the physical onto the psychical plane; in psychological terms, from the conscious onto the unconscious. This awareness nourishes Egbo's fragile faith and thus figuratively fulfills his inner desire for ritual participation in cosmic vitalization. Note the following description: ". . . When it lay flooded, when it lay flooded. There were tassels for the man, sweet roots for the child, and above cloud curds waited for the chosen one of God. . . (60).

The rhythm and imagery in this short ejaculation by Egbo is a hypostatizing analogue to the religious and ritualistic rhythm by which Egbo witnesses his blood tie to the cosmos. The half-submerged, dotted metaphor of the coupling of earth and sky, of the man of tassels and the elect of God, suggests the meeting of the human and the divine in which Simi takes on some of the power and status of a creative, vitalizing goddess. When we hear Egbo blubber: ". . . through hidden floods a sheath canoe parts tall reeds, not dies, God, not dies a rotting hulk. . ." (60), and Simi half-responding, "My dear, tell me, what is the matter?," the picture we have is that of an inchoate, epiphenomenal man, though now intensely consumed in orgasmic-voyeuristic frenzy within the maternal womb of an epiphanic love goddess, still probing the dimen sions of the woman in him, his anima. Egbo is now in perfect, close psychical oneness with his whole inner ambience, alive and throb-bing in orgasmic, dark communion, overwhelmed by his own chastened flesh, with Simi as the intercessionary channel.

The hidden floods through which a sheath canoe parts tall reeds suggest much more than the sexual act itself. Archetypally, they are the final proof of Egbo's assurance and serenity at this time, a serenity very much anchored in his responsiveness toward the tremendous living flood which carries and sustains him in his vital relation to the encompassing female. Because Simi is the channel for his responsiveness, Egbo discerns in her, graciousness, delight, freedom, and even protection traditionally associated with the Good Mother figure. To lie or to want to lie in darkness alone with Simi is to consummate a primoridial union with Simi, his love goddess. To lie so close to her body also means to repeat the mystery of his own conception. Egbo's submission to the Simi archetype, the identity between the act of conception and the unconscious, is brought out again and again: "Egbo forgot himself then when he looked at her , ...sensing such sadness that he feared for her and wondered if this was love. But the moment passed, for she had become playful, always in grave aspect even when she teased. . ." (59)

Soyinka's apt portrayal of Egbo-Simi relationship, there-fore, is visualized in a form resembling a chiasma, which in Jungian psychology, is nothing but a male and a female coexisting in the same body. Jung states that such a chiasma is usually "projected in the form of the divine *syzygy*, the divine pair, or in the idea of the hermaphroditic nature of the creator" (Laszlo 494), and the idea of the androgynous inner man. For Egbo, the sexual act is neither an act of venality or sinness against the divine order as might be deontologically interpreted by Prophet Lazarus nor a mere act of unbridled youthful sport as seen by Dr. Lumoye, nor even an act of moral turpitude as might be viewed by the austere Professor Oguazor. Rather, the darkness that enevelopes Egbo and his goddess, Simi, is the darkness of the unconscious, symbolical of the womb into which they two must withdraw and where, as in the case between Egbo and the unnamed University girl, conception takes place. The literal and the metaphorical, conscious and unconscious, levels of meaning meet when those that seek the darkness of the maternal womb anticipate a return to a kind of prenatal bliss that daylight reality, pulsating with the stink of corruption, witholds from them. It is a return to primeval simplicity and erotic innocence where primal values are duly indulged and arcane rituals performed in the abyssmal depths of man's unconscious, not prepackaged nor abjured in the incisive homiletics of self-righteous evangelism.

The subject of sex and religion is especially significant in our perception of Simi as an archetypal feminine. Through her character, Soyinka attempts to deal with the living connection between sex and religion, especially the phallic cult or sex-worship of polytheism. As we have seen, Simi is a goddess, a Queen Bee, imbued with mystical qualities. We have seen that Egbo has a hard time checking his rising delirium as he prepares to 'worship' at Simi's 'temple,' suggesting that Soyinka is trying to resurrect the continuity of phallic worship in which the world is perceived as an emanation of sexual desire. Besides, the fact that the sexual act itself takes place in a dark room underscores Egbo's symbolic, unconscious return to the womb which, in many myths, represents the earth womb, a maternal place safe from the turbulent world of masculine restlessness suggested in the opening pages of the novel. Ivan Bloch has said that "in a certain sense, the history of religion can be regarded as a peculiar mode of manifestation of the inner human sexual instinct" (97). E.D. Starbuck suggests that "the religious life is an irradiation of the reproductive instinct" (quoted in Cohen 90). And yet another critic has opined that "the language of devotion and of amatory passion is often identical" (Cohen 90).

Clearly, if Egbo espouses any particular faith at this point, it is one securely wedged between naked amorality and an acute but muted "erotic divinity." Simi, because she is the direct object in that uneasy equation, becomes its receptacle. The point is that whether or not we are prepared to interpret Egbo's "devotedness" to his love goddess as part of the modern renewal of ancient signs and portents of female dominance, the inference that there is such a manifestation, that Simi occupies at the moment of her entry anything but servile position seems plausibly admissible. And when ". . . she touched him about and Egbo felt himself lifted, there was no earth beneath his feet" (59), Egbo desires to come to terms with his anima, the feminine container of his emotional security, but requires a strength he apparently does not have. The "rising delirium" in Egbo is a neat pun upon ecstasy, the mystical attempt to seek divine harmony in which woman, Simi, plays a commanding role. We may be dealing here with Soyinka's allusion to the ancient mysteries that derive from this frenzy to reach to the freedom of the godhead. This somewhat explains why Egbo's religious affirmations are fundamentally divested of the ascetic moralizations like Lazarus's. For Egbo, the most flagrant contradiction of Simi's quintessence comes when Lazarus enjoins chastity and freedom from sin as the price for overcoming death and for entering the kingdom of God. In assuming that erotic abnegation is generally possible for and desirable to the faithful, Lazarus contradicts

Egbo's increasingly pragmatic belief that the sexual act may be the ultimate unconscious channel to the godhead, suspecting ultimate deception.

Egbo's confrontation with Lazarus symbolically reenacts the primordial clash between priest of the sacred king and defender of the fertility goddess, male and female religious principles. Their struggle to assert the superiority of their respective deities culminates in a momentary victory for Lazarus when he leads Barabas, the Oyingbo thief, through the dedication rites culminating in the latter's baptism as Noah. Apparently savoring this moment, Lazarus taunts Egbo: "'You are mistaken. That youth has received the holy spirit of God'" (177). Egbo shrugs it off with a lackadaisical remark: "'I don't like apostasy'" (177).

Egbo's rebuff lies in the full faith that Simi's capacity to provide him bio-physical satisfaction and security, a role that places her on the same mystical footing with the Madonna, much compensates, more than adequately, for this apparent loss of the gift of the Holy Spirit before the baptismal font. In fact, it can be argued that part of Soyinka's dialectical vision in *The Interpreters* lies in setting up the sacred heart Christ and the profane courtesan Simi on opposite poles, with the latter's affirmation of the truly grand pre-eminence of the female deity matched against Lazarus's Christian redemptive hero-Christ. The tension resulting from the clash of these two contrary impulses, Christian and Simian, provides an intrinsic segment of the anima-animus encounter. The substitution motif provides an analogue to the ransom paid by Christ for fallen man. For the love of mankind, Christ descended from the state of pure spirit, much to the horror of the neoPlatonists, to that of the flesh, and assumed the suffering of that flesh to redeem mankind. Simi, by and large, does the same for Egbo, descending from the level of illusory, airy, phantom-ladishness to that of a worldly courtesan to provide some saving grace for psychologically inadequate and culturally fallen man. To Prophet Lazarus, that is heresy. To Egbo that is salvation and amazing grace.

The same image of the primordial-mythological feminine principle is continued in Soyinka's second novel, *Season of Anomy*, albeit on a much more complex level. The complexity of the feminine image in *Season of Anomy* derives from the fact that in it the unconscious contrasexual images of animus-anima encounter are almost literally withdrawn. This allows the unconscious to reveal a superior mother archetype, which in men like the novel's hero means the aid of a wise old man, and in women like the heroine/shero of the novel, the redemption of a great mother, a mistress or of goddess who is both Kore and Demeter.[8] Jung calls this aspect of the unconscious, the *Self*.

In the novel, the use of the Orphic myth enables Soyinka to effect a kind of imaginative transformation of the mythos of the female from the phantom-lady to the Eurydice Persephone figure. We can find the mythological parallels to her situation in the story of Persephone abducted by Pluto and taken to the underworld. But her story also shows very close resemblance to the Orpheus- Eurydice mythology; Orpheus, heart-broken at the loss of his wife, journeys to Hades to try to bring her back (Zimmerman). In the novel, Soyinka renames Eurydice Iriyise—which name literally means "dew on the feet" (Izevbaye 153), marking her out as what Erich Neumann would call "the great nourisher." Dan Izevbaye has rightly suggested that Iriyise's story is Soyinka's rendition of the Orphic myth, adding that "Iriyise, like the dying goddessess before her, and especially like Persephone, is the Spirit of spring whose departure marks the descent of winter on the landscape" (153).[9] The result, according to him, is that "Iriyise is made to represent the claims of life. She is the silent arbiter in the struggle for Ofeyi's allegiance carried on by his two 'angels,' the Dentist, an extractor and agent of brute violence, and Taiila, an exotic character with other-worldly ideals. . ." (155).

Besides, Iriyise is also the nautical star that shines through the thick darkness caused by the "blood-lit evocation of biblical horrors." Spyhole, the iconoclast-investigative journalist, given to tantrums of 'lyric journalese wailing,' even in his characteristic mysogyny, cannot help but acknowledge Iriyise's extraordinary power. "I despise women," Spyhole scowls, ". . . but I finally met a woman that wasn't a woman" (62).[10] And this frank, uncharacteristic admission of sorts forces him to lionize Iriyise with an appelation of infinite grandeur—'Celestial Certainty' (60)— appropriate to her preeminent primordial stature. Seen against this epithet, Iriyise becomes the celestial mother associated with the stars and the cosmic entity. She is Soyinka's version of Mayauel, Mexican goddess of the Agave, whom Lewis Spence tells us, is regarded as the cute Queen of Heaven (116). There is also the suggestion of the dependency of all the luminous bodies on the Great Mother. She holds the tables of fate, the all-determining constellations of heaven. The fact that Iriyise's abduction causes such radical change in the seasonal pattern, as Izevbaye rightly points out, marks her out as the goddess of fate, to whom are subordinated very clearly discernible natural seasonal changes.

But Spyhole's unusual eulogy quite ironically lands him in momentary embarrassment. Although he means well and has spoken the truth, most people just could not concede to him any benefit of doubt, even in this

his rare encomiastic mood, to hone Iriyise's 'holy' name. Once he had been caught snooping around a pub, and three irate students had accosted him. Iriyise—the celestial queen—the students swear, is so special, so endearing to most people's hearts, that she could not and must never be the subject of such tattle-tale profession as tabloid pseudo-journalism. But granted that Spyhole is morally inadequate in the sense for which the three students reprimand him, in one particular instance, on this particular occasion, at least, he seems to have gotten it right, and they are prepared for one time only to forgive his previous egregious transgressions. Iriyise is no ordinary woman, her abduction by the military junta bears this judgement out. The whole grim affair becomes a matter for universal grief and lamentation (see pp. 61-62). Spyhole, in sinc with tabloids' tattle-tale hypes, raises this universal lament to a somewhat mock-heroic prosaic level: "Where is that Iridiscent face that lit us through the abyss of universal ugliness?" (61).

Clearly, Iriyise's power to provoke this kind of profuse out-pouring of emotion is similar to that aptly evinced by the charisma of ascendent-transcendent primordial females. She is undoubtedly the Mother of mothers, the Lady of ladies, or as Wallis Budge designates such figures, the "creatrix of the world" (440). Even the authorities themselves, here represented by the multinational corporation, the Cocoa Cartel, and the Brigade, a brutish arm of the ruling military junta, recognize her power and eminence, even though, envious as they are, they would prefer to couch that power in anarchic, less charitable terms. We are told that

Once in a while she unleashed the caged tigress in her at some trivial or imagined provocation, . . . engaging the riot squad and fire brigade in a nightlong siege which ended only when, on the stairway or on the lavatory bowl or even in bed she fell suddenly, immortally asleep. . . It was the Brigade who named her Firebrand. . . And the name was taken up and absorbed into the lyric repertoire of her legend. (62)

Iriyise's capacity to generate "fire" may be interpreted psychologically in two, but not mutually exclusive ways. In her destructive temper, Iriyise may be said to be the Earth Mother that springs from social chaos. But in her creative role, the fire within her acquires a fresh psychoanalytic and spiritual dimension. Her inner fire may be responsible for awakening the people to the consciousness of evil in their midst and of the new moral choices they potentially have in combating that evil. Even when the biological factor of illness momentarily intrudes, the drama of Iriyise's spirit still retains enough psychoanalytic fire capable of exuding warmth in the hearts of those engaged in passionate love. This possibility leaves Ofeyi wondering: "Is this the same Fire-brand for which flying sparks ignite dead flesh?" (63). Of course, the answer is emphatically and unequivocally yes. The only thing that can dispel the chill that hangs over the people's lives is Iriyise's symbolic fire. It is this that associates her with the other fire goddesses in mythology.

But the thing which best establishes Iriyise as the feminine principle is the Earth-Mother image which combines the elementary and transformative qualities of her personality. Hence she is associated with the earth of Aiyero, and therefore with its fruits, its water, but above all, its staple cash crop, cocoa. This inexorably links her to Demeter and Persephone, to the preeminent role of women in agricultural rituals, most specifically, to the metamorphic and sacrificial character of Aiyero's Custodian of the Grain. What sustains the people of Aiyero is their land. Even in their work songs and ballads, we hear familiar rituals of mystical identification with the Aiyero earth. At the center of these auto-chthonous rituals, "The forest was cleared, sown. The founding ballads of Aiyero were unearthed, a new body of work-songs grew from the grain of the vanguard idea. . . Aiyero held her deeper than any bed of eiderdown" (20).

Iriyise's deepening love for Aiyero is also vividly expressed on the eve of her departure from Aiyero back to the neoned city, after a temporary stay. She has felt a certain reluctance, "her face fell with disappointment but he [Ofeyi] promised: 'We are coming back. Right now we have work to do'" (18). Ofeyi is struck by the way in which she is passionately drawn into the inner space of Aiyero landscape. Iriyise accepts the rhythm of nature, and by celebrating its fructification and flowering (cocoa growing), she learns her subjection to the value, beauty, and eternal joy of the seasonal rhythm of natural fecundity. Thus she is an anima suitably associated with the gestation and full blossoming of the fruits of Aiyero's pristine forests. She is presented as earth, as sympathetic relatedness to the personal and human aspects of pastoral life which it crystallizes, and to the problems of empathy, feeling and love which it evokes. The following passage represents the most lucid example of Iriyise's symbolic power as both earth goddess and mother figure: "In wrapper and sash with the other women of Aiyero, . . . her bared limbs and shoulders among young shoots, . . . Iriyise weaving fronds for the protection of the young nursery, bringing wine to the sweating men in their struggle against the virgin forests" (20).

Underlying Iriyise's earth-mother disposition, therefore, is the African representation of natural reality with its emphasis on the qualitative primacy of consciousness, on integrativeness and sympathetic related-ness. The ritual of Iriyise's pastoral initiation, described early in the first chapter of the novel, contains homologous expressions of love and reverence for the Aiyero earth. That is why people keep coming back to it time and time again, because in their thoughts of their homeland, they do not regard the land as mere possession which they own to exploit, but regard themselves as possessed by it in an infinite drama of participation mystique. It is an inscrutable truth which the hitherto inchoate mind of Ofeyi could not possibly apprehend until the moment of his epiphany. Thus Iriyise, in her archetypal position, symbolizes creativity, fertility, and eternal love of life. By presenting a continuum of agricultural seasonal cycles, coupled with the transformation of her persona, Soyinka endows her with the image of fertility as well as the inner justification to crystallize that image into a unified emblem of symbolic feminine power.

5

Baraka, Marquis de Sade, and the Individual Will

For Amiri Baraka (LeRoi Jones), the vehement repudiation of Cartesianism has meant an unrelenting Hegelian celebration of the quintessential African aesthetic principle "I feel, therefore I am." ("The dichotomy of what is seen and taught and desired as opposed to what is felt," Baraka writes in *The System of Dante's Hell* 153).[1] But beyond this negritudinal responsum lies, I think, a more serious primal embrace of the Sadean poetics of libertinism. Baraka's persistent use of the word "fuck" parallels the Marquis de Sade's rewriting of the Cartesian cogito, "I fuck, therefore I am," which Angela Carter designates an axiom that not only constructs a diabolical lyricism of fuckery but also makes of sexuality itself a permanent negation (26). Going beyond mere existential negation and self-annihilation (although these are clearly recognizable in his novel), Baraka's poetics has two principal elements. The first is what I like to identify as the Sadean ritualization of sexual villainy, or what James Melvin Reinhardt calls "manifest psychosis. . . psycho-sexual degeneracy" (140). The second may be referred to as the symbolization of mythologized, sacral sexuality. Both illustrate the persistence of the ruling passion, which represents Baraka's sexualized view of the world, a view which blends social reality and moral dilemma but which, unlike Sade's view, does not verge on misanthropy.

Before I examine the use of these two principles in *The System of Dante's Hell*, some background information is necessary. The influence of the Marquis (Donatien Alphonse François) de Sade, the eighteenth—and the early—nineteenth—century French libertine—writer, extends beyond such authors as Swinburne and his PreRaphaelite coterie, Flaubert and the Goncourt Brotherhood; beyond Apollinaire, Guy de Maupassant, Baudelaire, André Breton, Gide, and Genet to Amiri Baraka. All these writers share with Sade a certain deviltry, iconoclasm, heresy, and unconventionality. They share the Baudelairean insistence that one must always return to Sade to observe mankind in its natural, passionate state and to understand the essential quality of evil.[2] Just as Flaubert's mind was unceasingly haunted by Sade, so Baraka's *System* is haunted by Sade's vision of hell, which is linked ultimately to the iconography of sodomy and sexuality and its manifest perverseness.

Although Baraka is not a self-confessed disciple of Sade in the way that Frederick Hankey, Baudelaire, and Apollinaire were, based on their own self-pronouncements (Donald Thomas 194), his novel *The System of Dante's Hell* though is in many noticeable ways a powerful revival of Sade's influence on the literary imagination. The book employs a nihilistic vocabulary of sexual psychology in literature designated as a form of pleasure-seeking cruelty that is primarily erotic.

Baraka's exploration of human sexuality, as I mentioned earlier, has two antipodal dimensions, and is ultimately designed to manifest the pathology of art. The first, sexual villainy, assumes the manifest forms of homosexuality and rape. Throughout the novel, homosexuality and rape illustrate Baraka's encounter with forms of sexuality which suggest an avoidance and negation of reality. In contrast, the book's second Sadean dimension, sexuality as a symbolic process, represents an involvement with, as well as an affirmation of, Black American reality. Baraka insists that both elements be viewed as in a complex dialectic.

In the novel, the exploration of sexual perversion takes the form of a psychodrama of erotic turbulence, as the hero, Roi, is gradually introduced to a dark, satanic street underworld. Armed with Swiftean irony and bitterness, Baraka begins to assert the power of this psychodrama over Roi's personality. Turbulent images begin to assail Roi in the form of a world deranged with "violence/ against others, against one's self, against/God, Nature and Art" (36).

This is a world of moral anarchy; and as Roi contemplates and savors the sinful world of sex, he hears a strange, accusatorial voice: "You have abandoned God" (113). All at once, he seems to have found a new "tone, to set some fire in dry wood. An inferno. Where flame is words, or lives, or the simple elegance of death" (111). The tone is that of not only a Dantean creature severed from a divinely ordered universe, but also of one who manifests his own solitude. Henceforth, Roi's solitude will become the perpetual, daily ritual of the Sadean prisoner on the loose in a godless universe whose final place of confinement is the self. Henceforth, Roi would be initiated into the ideology of the flesh, which will later become an elaborate metaphor for erotic abuse, merging finally with the devil's dung. Henceforth, Baraka will rivet the cool eye of an atheist and heretic, casting it nefariously on the world and finding Satan a more likeable ally as a ruling principle than is the Savior. Consequently, Satan leads Roi to survey the world under, and Roi reports back to him that "the figures I saw were fucking. 'Huge' shadows, sprawling open their cunts," whereupon Satan gives him the injunction to "create a new world. Of Sex and Cataclysm. The rest," he mocks gleefully, "let them languish on their Sundays. Let them use shadows to sleep" (50-51).

With this Mephistcphelean contract well in place, Roi is ready to plunge into the world of villainous sexuality. It will be a world of declining religious belief, a world in which mental images of Paradise appear to have faded or corrupted or both. It will be a menacing world of demonic lechers, brutal lovers, and sadistic perverts trapped within a kind of hideous prison. Within this prison, Roi turns in upon himself and discovers the universe of the libido, of the sexual instincts as an eternal part of the landscape of human existence and consciousness.

Roi soon becomes involved with a violent gang of sexual outlaws in Newark whose activities introduce us to the form of sexual villainy in the novel, rape. Having accepted damnation as his lot, Roi and five gang members (Calvin, Donald, Sanchez, Leon, and Joe) plan to delight in an erotic whipping that will awaken in them the memory of the social fiction of the female wound. This is precisely what happens when they meet their first victim: "A drunken girl, woman, slut, moved thru the trees. Weaving. I folded my arms and watched the trees, green almost under the porch lamp paste her in. They turned to me to see what noises I was making. Stupid things I'd thought I heard" (109).

The drunken girl asks for directions to Jones Street, and the males seem to oblige, whisking her away in a car with Donald "at the woman's left, I at her right. The others packed in the front" (112). Then, suddenly, they stop, pulling up by the side of the road against the engulfing darkness of the night, a threatening forest, and barking dogs. At this point the novel operates on the level of grotesque farce made brusquer by the secured ingredients of erotic cruelty. Roi is the first to act. The woman, dreading what is coming, lets out a protesting scream. Her life now resembles that of a woman martyred by the circumstances of her life as a woman. We recall the title character in Sade's *Justine or The Misfortunes of Virtue*, desecrated by Saint-Florent in a forest, raped, robbed, and left alone and half-naked. Roi's victim, like Justine, is a lamb led to the slaughter, a victim defenseless against male predation. She is not dead, but in a world in which the function of her own flesh is to reveal to her the gratuitous inevitability of erotic pain, her present plight has sufficiently demonstrated to her the shocking tragedy of femaleness, the fact that in a man's world her female flesh must be transformed to meat.

According to Norman Kiell, rape usually involves force, humiliation, and degradation (446), and G. Legman suggests that "there is in sex a normal component of sadism" (61). Roi and his pals are bent on exploiting their picaresque universe with all its picaresque fortunes. The woman's screams for help and protests notwithstanding, they are determined to see their victim in the most primitive terms of use. They are all too ready to take advantage of Sade's injunction: Exploit and meatify the weak. Man's primal condition cannot be modified in any other way: it is fuck or be fucked. To them sexuality in this estranged form has become a denial of a basis of mutuality, sexuality stripped of the slightest idea of consent, of free exchange. It admits of no entreaties, however importunate:

I wdn't have that easy copout [that she should be left alone because she has v.d.] Fuck that. . . goddamit, no pleas./I made Donald put his hands back. I scowled the way I can with one side of my mouth, the other pushing the woman back. 'Shit, I don't believe that bullshit! Prove it, baby, lemme see! I wanna see the sores. . . see what they look like'" (115).

The erotic cannibalism of the gang-raping of an unsuspecting, defenceless woman here is as shocking as that in a typical Jacobean blood-tragedy, the Gothic novel, or the Victorian melodrama. The eroticism, with its display of violence and pain, preserves something of the demonology of primitive man. The act of cruelty with the violence of the copulatory process is the assertion of the abyss between master and victim. To Roi, this assertion represents in his own twisted mind "new life now. Reinforced, the others laughed. I pushed again. 'O.K., mama, runout them sores. . . lemme suck 'em till they get well'" (115).

Roi would imagine himself like a mad butcher wielding an insensible knife. He upholds savagery, denouncing virtue and compassion. When Roi views sexual cruelty as an expression of new life, and when he admits of no plea from his victim, we see masochism in its goriest form, coming about as a kind of a cavalier escape from an unendurable sense of guilt. He possesses at this moment the omnipotence of the Sadean tyrant-villain savoring the abjectness of his victim-heroine. Ihab Hassan has said that "the Sadean self permits no encounter, no negotiation. It solves the problem of evil by converting all pain, whether inflicted or received, into a source of personal pleasure" (54).

Reinhardt opines that the mutilation of a rape victim shows the craving of the fiendish lust, the degeneration of the total personality (138). As in Sade's fiction, we encounter in Baraka's book an opaque world of base matter, a Mettriean universe in which the characters, especially rape victims, are reduced to the status of instruments that provoke the macabre ecstacy of destruction. The nadir of this destructive impulse is reached when, their lust turned to uncomfortable joviality, Roi and his pals brutally roll the woman out of the moving car: "'Throw this dumb bitch out.' Calvin grabbed her by the arm and Donald heaved against her ass. The woman tumbled over my knees and rolled, I thought, slow motion out of the car. She smashed against the pavement and wobbled on her stomach hard against the curb" (117). This is the consummation of the Sadean will,[3] the negation of all that is virtuous in man; it is the expression of man as a purely physical structure uncooked in the effusive cauldron of its own malodorous bestiality.

If rape signifies Baraka's encounter with the demonology of primitive man latent in all of us, homosexuality[4] or sodomy, or perhaps what Michel Foucault calls "interior androgyny" (and Walter Perrie "homo-eroticism,"[5] signifies Baraka's encounter with the baroque force which threatens the integrity of the self, a form of instinctual bondage which destroys discernment, but which later must be countered by some kind of ethical renunciation. The rationale which underpins the homo-sexuality==heresy equation set up in the novel is that each is unnatural because each unwillfully defies the laws not merely of man and self but also of God, who ordains the natural order. This is what makes Baraka less a passionate atheist than is Sade.

Unlike Whitman, who in *Leaves of Grass* views male—male friendship as virtually coextensive with democracy and the independent spirit, unlike the poets of the Oxford Movement who idealize it with romantic and religious fervor (Perrie 172), unlike Johan Huizinga's transfiguration of it into illusionary forms, and unlike the Aesthetes' commuting of its malodorousness toward a redemptive aestheticism and artistic integrity, Baraka's attitude is Freudian[6] and Dantean. Theodore Hudson reveals that, for Baraka, homosexuality is symbolic of the misuse of creative energies, of a deliberate turning from what is natural and good, as a degeneracy, as an avoidance of reality (114). As in his encounter with rape, Roi, confronted with homosexuality in Chicago, is saddled with a sense of guilt. "To be pushed under a quilt, and call it love, To shit water for days and say I've been loved" (138—39). Roi is here referring to his numerous unhappy early experiences with boys and girls in his Newark, New Jersey neighborhood, followed by overwhelming feelings of guilt. Finding himself afraid to accept normal heterosexual outlets and suffering a heavy sense of guilt, Roi escapes into himself with the powerful warping impulses that such an inverted escape would create. Like Oscar Wilde in *The Picture of Dorian Gray* and André Gide in *The Immoralist*, Baraka knows that homosexuality is inevitably accompanied by fear, guilt, and self-hatred. This is the nadir of what Stekel calls "a strangely aberrant self."[7]

The most effective and most sustained homosexual scene in the novel occurs in "The Eighth Ditch (Is Drama." Here two men, 46 and 64, are sitting on bunks within a tent. 46 is reading; 64 is staring at 46's book from across the room. Baraka uses 46, a smooth-faced black youth, especially in his homoerotic seduction by 64, to demonstrate what Kimberly Benston regards as a form of self-negation caged within a kind of moral estrangement (15-17). Baraka portrays the seduction as a supreme test of one's authenticity. Although 46 is a highly knowledgeable man, he does not know who he really is, whereas, when he asks 64 to disclose his identity, 64 replies: "The Street! Things around you. Even noises at night, or smells you are afraid of. I am a maelstrom of definitions. I can even fly" (80). "The Street," in addition to its scatological suggestiveness, embodies a dark meaning, a dark vitality which is beyond the immediate grasp of 46's Cartesian rationalism. The street is the spirit of place, the sharing in a hidden harmony, what Benston calls "dark certainty." 46, by dissociating himself from the street, has become culturally rootless.

This motif is emphasized by 46's namelessness. Baraka suggests through the dialogue between 64 and 46 that the art of naming is part of the expression of a man's identity and his belonging to a definable ethos. 64's real name is Herman, and even hipsters like Otis (62) have names. But throughout the drama, 46 remains unnamed—in Benston's words, "trading the body he ignores for the 'blues' of a foreign heritage" (16). The final drama of 46's inauthenticity and lack of personal identity is rendered in his surrender to 64's advances, an act of sodomy accompanied by all the trappings of a Gothic seduction. The portrayal of this scene recalls the homosexual seduction scene in T.G. Smollett's *Roderick Random* and Honore de Balzac's *Comédie Humaine*, and the painful self-scrutiny of Proust's and T.E. Lawrence's language. As 64 mounts 46, he taunts him: "What do you know? You. sit rjght now on the surface of your life. I have, at least, all the black arts. The smell of deepest loneliness. . . I know things that will split your face & send you wild-eyed to your own meek thoughts!" (83). 64 is culturally alive, born and nurtured in solitariness, the supreme crucible of the black American experience and one capable of articulating with vigor the rich creative artifactual imagination of black people. It.is a possession which woefully eludes 46, a man out of tune with his time and estranged from a dark certainty of which he is very much a part but to which, regrettably, he does not relate. In artistic terms, 46's inauthenticity typifies what Jeffrey

Meyers calls the divorce between the modern artist and the rest of society (9).

But Baraka's portrayal of sexuality is not all dark and grotesque. In portraying the problems posed by rape and homosexuality, Baraka journeys to the depths of the sexual underworld. But having journeyed and having allowed ourselves to be damned with him, we must once more ascend to make, as the Narrator tells us in "The Eighth Ditch," "some blank gesture towards light" (84). We cannot leave ourselves and humanity in the charnel pit of erotic anarchy. Unless we can emerge from it, there is no hope for us. Baraka, conscious of that, has Roi lured by an archetypal woman, a black Southern whore named Peaches, who uses the power of her sexuality to initiate the alienated Roi into the black lifestyle, to bring him into meaningful contact with those who truly want and need him. He is freed from the control of the white world's constrictive influence, apart from 46's sterile Cartesianism. Roi at first shuns Peaches world, for he cannot discriminate among kinds of flesh. For him, all flesh must be dubbed "crazy as anything in the world, and sad because of it" (128); he regards fleshly delights as lewd distractions from the contemplation of higher aims. But his perceptions soon change. initial rebuff yields to a moment of supreme realization and edification. Roi articulates it well: "She loved me, she said. . . We could live together and she would show me how to fuck. How to do it good" (146).[8]

Unlike homosexual sodomy, heterosexual intercourse between Roi and Peaches indicates the closest possible human interaction, which Roi needs to assuage his earlier alienation. Unlike his former sexual exploits, there is in this one a mutually beneficial, intimate giving and getting, a community feeling savored by a profoundly becoming self. Homosexuality and rape result in separateness and attendant guilt. Here, however, sexuality has become a striving toward the goal of a balanced and "sanctified" life. Philosophically, aesthetically, and socially, Roi's ideal is the self-containment, the retention of the creative impulse of sexuality, a kind of Indian *brachmachari* or *purusa*.[9] Roi, in a moment of purest sexual encounter, describes it as "a real thing in the world. See my shadow. My reflection. I'm here, alive. Touch me. Please. Please. touch me" (139). This is the notion of culture as sublimated sexuality. This is the emergence of Baraka's perverse imagination, which for Roi provides a moment of historical clarity, compelling inexorably a re-examination of the entire concept of repression brought about by rape and sodomy in which he has been trapped. Baraka suggests that the geography of the female body, here of Peaches,' may serve as a historical and cultural metaphor for such a critical re-examination.

Irving Buchen has said that the enormous stress put upon sexuality and perversion is meant to dramatize the castration of man's wholeness. Historically and psychologically, he maintains, man has been forced to be half a man and lead half a life. The perverse imagination, by contrast, demands that the range of the body's secret-desires be granted the same span of fulfillment and free play previously reserved for those of the soul (30). Buchen also links the perverse imagination to the concept of identity, the search for self-continuity. Abandoning its heroic isolation, the self must yield to the collective fluidity of the body, which, by virtue of its tactile totality, sets a new standard of multiplicity for the mind. The supreme enemy of the perverse imagination, contends Buchen, is separatism (31).

Baraka's portrayal of the sexual encounter between Roi and Peaches dramatizes the perverse imagination. Here Roi, after an intense period of isolation, bad company, guilt, and a feeling of horror at the prospect of castrating death, finally achieves a kind of Hegelian completeness grounded in self-knowledge. The penitent prodigal returns to the black ethos from which he has hitherto been severed. He now knows "how to be in this world. How to be here, not a shadow, but thick bone and meat. Real flesh under real sun. And real tears falling on black sweet earth" (140).

The essence of twisting, "spitting tears, and hitting my hips on hers, pounding flesh in her. . . (141), is to consummate an orgasmic return to the source of his being, leaving him to hear for the first time in his troubled life "daytime voices thru the window up and fat with optimism (147) and to relish the times that have "soft black harmonies and color (148). Having passed from airman to Peaches' man, he can now hold his head up, and walk right "into that sun. The day was bright and people walked by me smiling. And waved 'Hey' (a greeting). . ." (149).

The idea of being the "Peaches' man" is the closest Baraka comes in the exercise of his perverse imagination to the equation of spirituality with sexuality and its corollary, the neo-Christ figure drenched in erotic turbulence, animality, and romantic agony. Roi is no longer going to be subjected to "the torture of being the unseen object, and, the constantly observed subject," no longer will he be subjected to "the flame of social dichotomy. Split open down the center, which is the early legacy of the black man unfocused on blackness" (153). Peaches' man is a child of quasi sacral sexuality, a man remolded in the crucible of phallicism. Aware of that, Roi can heave a sigh of relief and say ". . . the world is clearer to me now, and many of its features, more easily definable" (154).

Baraka, through the mediation of the Sadean image and the perverse imagination, forces the reader to reassess his relationship to his own sexuality, his relationship to his own primary being.[10] His perverse imagination, insofar as the relative marginality of the artist is concerned, partakes of the pathology of sexuality and so the pathology of art. But the fact is that the pathology grounded in an aesthetic dimension inevitably transforms erotic cruelty into patterns of liberation. Baraka is caught between Sade the desecrator and Freud the consecrator and sublimator. He shares the Marquis de Sade's Manichaean catechism of libertinage and excrementalism but rejects his Dolmancé doctrine,[11] his disdain for the piety of a cultural tradition. He accepts Freud's psychoanalysis of the sublimated Eros but balks at his suggestion of its adversarial potential.

In a society that all too often denies racial dignity, Baraka, like Sade, insists that the greatest possible attention to the human situation is conveyed within flesh. The will to be which Roi epitomizes is the basic aspect of sexuality rooted in a despair that had become typical in the mid-1960s. The agony of black history is a perpetual variation upon the primal suffering rooted in the myth of the expulsion from Eden, white Eden. The intensity with which Baraka's characters sexually attack, cajole, and devour each other comes from the recognition of human cultural isolation and the desire to get back to Eden, the black Eden, to find that perfect and final security and relief from anxiety, which beyond Freudian analysis relates to the basic facts of human identity in terms of separation from and reintegration with the universe. Unlike Sade, however, Baraka's vision does not include a permanent disintegration of being in spite of the marked surrealist suggestiveness of the novel, nor does it amount to a complete Schopenhauerian self-surrender or renunciation of selfhood.

What Baraka seems to be suggesting is that imprisoned, and conscious both of the imprisonment and of the scope of freedom beyond our confinement, we all, in one form or another, crouch in the dungeon of a sexual inferno and contemplate the exploits that will eventually redeem us. We contain within ourselves, one way or another, the "degradations" of Peaches and the demonic urges of rapists and homosexual libertines; we are all contaminated beings. But in the heart of our pollution lies, waiting for discovery, the essential purity of existence. Roi emerges from the Dionysian orgies of *The System of Dante's Hell* as a consecrated carrier of a revivified black history just as Sade's double, Duc de Blangis, in Buñuel's film *L'Age d'Or*, emerges from the orgies of *The 120 Days of Sodom* dressed as Christ. Like Nietzsche, Baraka would vigorously contest with professional moralists to effect this kind of quantum leap, this kind of radical transformation.

6

Baraka and the Allegoric Meaning of the Tragic Spirit

In chapter 5, I discussed the feminine principle in Baraka's novel *The System of Dante's Hell* and the ways in which that principle related to the homecoming of the black prodigal, Roi, within the broad schema of Sadean poetics. I established that, toward the end of his mythopoeic quest, Roi had changed from Roi—Airman to Peachesman. However, the meaning of that symbolic transformation lies not merely in the carnal relationship between him and Peaches, the Cyprian archetype, but instead within the broader context of a tragic faith which channels that relationship into profounder essence. I am speaking, of course, about the more potent archetype in the novel—the chthonic archetype of the Dionysian spirit. An in-depth exploration of the configuration of this archetype brings into focus the prima facie convergence of Friedrich Nietzsche's metaphysical thought and Baraka's voluntaristic vision in *The System of Dante's Hell*.

Generally speaking, Nietzsche's influence on modern and contemporary art and literature has long been recognized by Western scholars. For example, the dramas of Pinter, Ionesco, Beckett, Brecht, and many others, "in their attempts to come to terms with the absurdity of human existence, and to preserve human dignity in the face of a reality that seems paradoxical and senseless" (Pfeffer 65),[1] contain radical manifestations of Nietzsche's tragic faith and metaphysical conceptualization of art, grounded in the categories of becoming and the senses. The symbolic quintessence of this tragic faith is Dionysus, who, according to Nietzsche, represents the passionate and tortured search for a meaningful life, beyond any objective ground of moral principles.

In *The Birth of Tragedy*, Nietzsche makes a distinction between what he calls the Apollonian and the Dionysian imaginations. The Apollonian artist, he explains, is much like the philosophical worker who creates values, who determines and formalizes some large reservoir of value judgments. The Apollonian artist overpowers, abbreviates, and makes visible an ordered past. On the other hand, "the Dionysian artist plunges into time, risks himself and his world in the flux, dark to all except his desire, to the elan of the dance to which he abandons himself" (Dooley 158). Douglas Jones, expounding on the thesis of Dionysian aesthetics, has said that, in a time of disintegrating culture, it is the Dionysian imagination which we need to cultivate, abandoning ourselves to Eros and the deepest springs of our desire. Cultivating the Dionysian imagination is in keeping with the Nietzschean aphorism that "the greatest epochs of our lives come when we gain the courage to rebaptize our evil as our best" (Dooley 158).

My position is that, in *The System of Dante's Hell*, Baraka assumes the role of the Dionysian artist, an artist opposed to Dante, whom Baraka sees very early in the novel (in the Epigraph) as being allowed no other function except that of watering down the moral ideas of Platonic—Christian orthodoxy. The meaning of this Dionysian role is played out within the context of four symbolic frames: the nihilistic, the tragic, the Dionysian, and, finally, the frame of the heroic individual, or what Nietzsche has called the "Overman" and Baraka the "Peachesman." The nihilistic frame is, for Nietzsche, the frame of despair and anxiety. Nicholas Berdyaev calls it "Nietzsche's torment" (82). Baraka's nihilism, like Nietzsche's, derives from what Jules Chaix Ruy refers to as "the decomposition of culture" (96). Its genesis is in the uncompromising viewpoint that all traditional values and beliefs are unfounded, and that all existence is consequently senseless and useless. Like Nietzsche, Baraka is haunted by nihilism, the devaluation of values. Again like Nietzsche, Baraka knows that no longer can we trust our old gods, our traditional, orthodox values and goals; no longer can we believe in the exclusive power of reason and science.

Religion and morality appear to have lapsed into a state of crisis, vitiated into what Martin Buber has characterized as "the eclipse of God" (see Pfeffer 68), Nietzsche as "God is dead," and Baraka as "jewchrist, that's hunkie bread, turned green." Baraka vents his nihilistic anger on almost every page of the first half of the novel. The nihilistic chord is first struck in the novel's epigraph, leaving a rather jarring, disturbing note:

I put The Heretics in the deepest part of hell, though Dante had them spared, on higher ground.

It is heresy, against one's own sources, running in terror, from one's deepest responses and insights. . . the denial of feeling. . . that I see as basest evil. (7)

This quick, unapologetic swipe at Dante has colossal Nietzschean implications. Like Nietzsche, Baraka insists that the feeling for life, not for some otherworldly existence, provides the only sane justification for man. Dante's quest for eternal meaning among the cloistered tombstones of Judeo-Christian morality is misguided, given the phenomenal fact that this morality summarily deprecates life; that is, this life here on Earth. The epigraph echoes Nietzsche's repudiation of the eternal, immutable values and axiological assumptions of Plato's realm of ideas and the transcendent, supersensible norms of Christianity. Both philosopher and novelist suggest that the transcendental metaphysics of Western civilization denies reality to the world we live in—the world of the objective senses, of feeling and emotion, of mutation and dialectic (change and opposition)—and ultimately degrades it into a secondary world of semblance, simulacrum, and pathetic illusion.

Baraka carries his nihilistic sentience even on to the very end of the novel. In the postscript, titled "Sound and Image," for example, Baraka attempts a personal transvaluation of Hell:

What is hell? Your definitions.

I am and was and will be a social animal. Hell is definable only in those terms. I can get no place else; it wdn't exist.

Hell in this book which moves from sound and image ("association complexes") into fast narrative is what vision I had of it around 1960-61 and that fix on my life, and my interpretation of my earlier life. (153)

In other words, Baraka like Nietzsche rejects the mythology of the traditional Christian interpretation that places hell in an other-worldly realm. Nietzsche himself claims that nihilism is deeply rooted in Christian morality. "For our adherence to Christian morality, Nietzsche says, "we must pay dearly: by this adherence we are losing our equilibrium and are on the verge of adopting opposite valuations—those consisting of nihilistic elements" (see Wright 278). Baraka's nihilism, Nietzschean and nonpathological, does, however, hold out the possibility of some redemptive alternate order. His alternative to a transcendentalized noumenal inferno is a distinctly socialized hell, for there is no world, reality, or realm which transcends that in which we live and move. So the hell of traditional, orthodox Christian theology and metaphysics appears, in the author's view, more contrived than real and substantive, more a state of mind, whereas the more phenomenal hell of Baraka, the Black nihilist, and Nietzsche, the white agnostic, represents the closest thing to the existential truth.

Baraka's nihilism, like Nietzsche's, also expresses a longing for a new, uncoerced relation with and definition of the divine:

Finally, God, is simply a white man, a white "idea," in this society, unless we have made some other image which is stronger, and can deliver us from the salvation of our enemies.

For instance, if we can bring back on ourselves, the absolute pain our people must have felt when they carne onto this shore, we are more ourselves again, and can begin to put history back in our menu, and forget the propaganda of devils that they are not devils.

Hell is actual, and people with hell in their heads. But the pastoral moments in a man's life will also mean a great deal as far as his emotional references. One thinks of home, or the other "homes" we have had. And we remember w/ love those things bathed in soft black light. The struggles away or towards this peace is Hell's function. (Wars of consciousness. Antithetical definitions of feeling(s). (153-54)

Though anti-Christian, and short of endorsing a blind impulse toward an anthropomorphic Black deity, Baraka cannot be charged with anti-religion. He may be one of Nietzsche's "great despisers," but he is also, by the same token, one of his "great reverers." Baraka's world, like Nietzsche's, consists mainly in the repudiation of the dualistic separation of God and Nature. It does not express a negation of all faiths, but rather reveals the tragic predicament of modern man who has lost his faith in a transcendent, anthropomorphic God. Baraka's God, like Nietzsche's or Goethe's or Spinoza's, faces an entrance into the qualitative primacy of consciousness, into the totality of being, without moral deduction, without axiological pontification, where good and evil, the ugly and the beautiful, the normal and the bizarre, the finite and the infinite, the sublime and the ridiculous, the limited and the limitless, dwell side by side in a kind of reciprocal Manicheanism, where, in Nietzschean terms, "even the ugly and the horrible are redeemed and made meaningful in the fatality of the whole" (Quoted in Pfeffer 260).

For Baraka, the relation of God and the oppressed/ down-trodden people should not be construed in purely abstract, theoretical terms, understandable by the discursive intellect alone, but must proceed instead from the totality of being, touching the very depths of the black soul, the unconscious black psyche. It must be a relation that is lived, experienced, and suffered. It must take place within the sphere of the daemonic and the Dionysian, within the checkered reality of struggle, dialectical tension, negation, and despair, and be understood essentially as a desire and drive to connect and relate and unify Black history, and thus express the fundamental essence of the Black world, the Afro-centric world view. The alternate image of God on which Baraka insists as a sine qua non for black selfhood has all the glorious resonances of Rastafarian philosophy. It is coterminous with the peculiar attainment of unassailable harmony with oneself and the whole, the whole represented by the enjoined, redefined image of God. Baraka like Nietzsche demands that redemption be found in this world and not in the world beyond, within tragedy and suffering and historical/dialectical materialism, not necessarily beyond it.

This sense of the tragedy of life and the devaluation of all values is not for Baraka a freak accident. In fact, insistently and consistently Baraka draws attention to this fact. In "Neutrals: The Vestibule," for instance, Baraka admonishes us to:

look at things in another light. Not always the smarting blue glare pressing through the glass. Another light, or darkness. Wherever we'd go to rest. By the simple rivers of our time. Dark cold water slapping long wooden logs jammed 10 yards down in the weird slime, 6 or 12 of them hold up a pier. Water, wherever we'd rest. And the first sun we see each other in. Long shadows down off the top where we were. Down thru grey morning shrubs and low cries of waked up animals. (9)

This is an exceedingly ticklish symbolic scenario of the breakdown of traditional, orthodox values. "The first sun we see each other in" is the old sun, the traditional Western world view, now smudged through the cynical shadows of skepticism, a process which renders the idea of a transcendent, noumenal realm not only unattractive to Baraka, but also starkly elusive and pale. "Down thru grey morning shrubs and low cries of waked up animals" suggests the dawn of the nihilistic era in which the search for absolute truth is abandoned. This in turn leads to the psychological "breakup of my sensibility" (9). The asceticism of the transcendent morality is also summarily called into question:

Even that asceticism you pulled in under your breast that drunks & school friends thought of as "sense of humor". . . gone, erased, some subtle rot disposed in its place. Turning towards everything in your life. Whatever clarity left, a green rot, a mud, a stifling at the base of the skull. No air gets in. (13)

What is left after the devaluation of the transcendent morality is for Baraka an aimless becoming in which all dialectical tensions between good and evil, between the veridical and the delusory, appear to have tailed off. We are set adrift, left apparently with nothing, no support, no inspiration. Conscious of that, the protagonist, Roi, cries out passionately: "I feel sick and lost and have nothing to place my hands on. . . Everything I despise some harsh testimonial of my life. The Buddhism to affront me" (14). "The Buddhism to affront me" suggests the extreme form of nihilism which Nietzsche regards as the European form of Buddhism. Like Nietzsche, Baraka equates Buddhism with Christianity; both are perceived as religions of exhaustion and negation. With its nirvana, Buddhism seeks a pure state of freedom from karma, the extirpation of desire, passion, the empirical self, instinctual drives, those things that validate the here and now.[2]

But by far the most nihilistic scenario in *The System of Dante's Hell* involves the brutalization and flagrant desecration of the deistic, natural, and creative world order. Baraka portrays this desecration in terms of violence "against one's self,/ against / God, Nature and Art" (36). For both novelist and philosopher, God exists in the creative activities of nature and man. It appears that Baraka, like Nietzsche, finds in the dynamic forces of the cosmos and the eternal Viconian cycle of destruction and creation, death and rebirth, the very basis of the unity of immanent God, nature, art, and the creative genius of man. Thus, reality for Baraka does not necessarily lie exclusively in the Christian transcendent realm alone, but instead with nature and the art which mirrors it, of which man is an integral part. We recall Goethe's conception of the universe as a cosmic unity of God, nature, and man (see Pfeffer 167). Baraka's nihilistic spirit is a spirit that places no faith in a transcendent God, but in a God immanent in this world, whose effulgence is fundamentally linked with the productive, regenerative forces in nature, man, and his creative expressions. The destruction of this unity engenders a fundamental loss of purposefulness, a fundamental shattering of a moral world order. Roi no longer possesses ideals and absolute goals toward which to strive:

Nothing to interest me but myself. Disappeared, even the thin moan of ideas that once slipped through the pan of my head. The night is colder than the day. Two seconds lost in that observation. The same amount of time to stroke Nijinski's cheek. One quick soft move of my fingers on his face. That two seconds then that same two if they would if there were some way, would burn my soul to black ash. Scorch my thick veins. (15)

In despair and dread, Roi faces the dilemma of existence without the comfort and security of eternal goals, normative constructs, and categorical imperatives in which he was once schooled. He is now a black man, lost, without a Westernized God, and for now, at least, without the promise of a better, meliorist world.

Baraka's nihilistic spirit reaches its fever pitch in "Seven (The Destruction of America" (35-36), in which nature, mingling with the grisly scenario of dead Indians, provides a kind of apocalyptic vision of the social condition in America, the destruction of which the author finds infinitely desirable for its own sake, independent of any constructive social engineering or willed mobilization.

However, for Nietzsche and Baraka, the crisis of nihilism should not be a pretext for man to will nothingness, to accept the void as his eternal guide or companion. Nihilism, as a historical movement, is for both philosopher and novelist not destructive but tragic, containing within its negative ideology and rhetoric the very basis for regenerative growth. As in Baraka's *Preface to a Twenty Volume Suicide Note* (1961), *The Dead Lecturer* (1964), and *Black Magic* (1969), a nihilistic current is latent in every creative fount of black history in which an affirmative cultural plane is achieved, in which there is a gem of what Clyde Taylor calls "creative orientation" (113). In his *Unpublished Notes 223*, Nietzsche underscores the point succinctly: "The symptoms of decline belong to times of enormous growth; each creative, powerful movement of humanity has at the same time produced a nihilistic movement." The next task beyond the nihilistic stage is to find what Nietzsche calls "the exit and hole through which one arrives at something," to construct a new culture that can lead mankind out of the suffocating hole of nihilism (Pfeffer 79). For Nietzsche, constructing this new culture is metaphorized into an act of philosophizing with a hammer. But the hammer, for Nietzsche, is not only a tool of destruction but also an instrument of deconstruction and reconstruction—both functions are involved in the vital creation of new values. Nietzsche declares: "He who hath to be a creator in good and evil—verily he hath first to be a destroyer, and break values in pieces" (Wright 155).

In Baraka's novel, where belief in the whole system of Western values and meanings Roi had lived by is lost, Roiman is abandoned to himself and faces nothingness. Roi tells us: "Nothing to interest me but myself. Disappeared, even the thin moan of ideas that once slipped through the pan of my head" (15). But the void does not drive Roi into futile resignation, or into weak pessimism and permanent nihilism. Being a higher individual, a Nietzschean hero, he feels the void both as loss and as liberation. It is not mere nonbeing and perpetual darkness. Roi understands Nietzsche's argument that this kind of void is the greatest challenge in human history, including his own black history. Consequently, for now he becomes fully responsible to himself. Roi is convinced that he is a survivor. The narrator tells us that "he had survived the evilest time. A time alone, with all the ugliness set in front of his eyes. His own shallowness paraded like buglers across the dead indians. Some time, some space, to move" (19). It is essential that Roi survive these evilest times in order to be assured a second chance to tap his creative spirit. His expression of the tragic spirit boils down to the personal resolve to move within a distinctly phenomenal space: "All I want is to move. To be able to flex flat muscles" (19).

What Roi wishes for is a space to move; the void left by the collapse of the deistic, natural, and moral world order is for him a Nietzschean space, a space of freedom. It is not the space of Democritus and Dante, which is empty; it is not even a space for the ontological interpretation of evil. Instead it is for Roi a new positive, affirmative space. Paul Tillich, in *The Courage to Be*, states that "no actual negation can be without an implicit affirmation" (176). While Nietzsche manifests this implicit affirm-ation by wielding the hammer, Baraka through Roi will be "frank in armor thrust[ing] out his sword" (21). He will never surrender his will. He must remain defiant: "I am awake in your cold world" (28). The void that he faces is a potential space of freedom, freedom to create new values and alternative systems of meaning. For Baraka and Nietzsche, freedom can be achieved only after the destruction of the old idols and empty traditions. In axiological terms, it is a departure from the Christian and Dantean conception, in which freedom exists only in the transcendent world of the Christian *paradiso* of the Kantian noumenal, and is based on metaphysical and moral beliefs and attitudes that negate or "condemn life."

The new space that Baraka's Roi longs for exists "beyond good and evil," independent of traditional moral categories and their transcendent, metaphysical assumptions, which Roi characterizes as a pack of lies (32). It is not based on a rigidly dualistic world order, but is meaningful for this life only, the life of the senses, of conflict and despair. It is the foundation of a new article of faith and secular piety. Roi's talk of putting on his armor and sword (21) embodies a celebration of the heroic will to destroy and, in destroying, to build and create anew. Like Shaw's Undershaft, Roi finds this creative will in the devil, whom he sees as the spirit that eggs him on to "break out" (36), insistently heeding the call: "Let us create a new world. Of Sex and cataclysm. The rest, let them languish on their Sundays. Let them use shadows to sleep" (51). Baraka calls this heroic will "high tragedy" (52).

Thus, the meaning of the tragic spirit is the courage to face something that can infinitely outweigh all struggle and anguish. It is the affirmative spirit which can aid the black man in America in this age of anxiety to surmount racial injustice, cultural displacement—in short, the whole nihilistic foundation of modern life—without recourse to what Rose Pfeffer describes as the "optimistic illusions and mechanisms of escape" (36). It is an affirmative vision arrived at through the most uncompromising nihilistic position, in full realization of the negative elements of life. For Baraka the basic elements of this tragic spirit are struggle, pain, and opposition; each is metaphysically grounded in and derived from life and a sense of beingness. They cannot be eliminated without destroying life itself. However, as Roi discovers, they can be made to function as cathartic stimulants in the evolution and development of the black personality and culture by a process Nietzsche calls "overcoming."

For Baraka as well as for Nietzsche, the nihilistic and the tragic visions are linked by a certain ineffable complementarity. For Nietzsche, the archetype of this complementarity is the god Dionysus. Dionysus is Prometheus, Faust, Zarathustra; he is skeptic, critic, destroyer, builder, and creator. He is the "Ur-Eine," primal oneness and the ground of being, ever contradictory and ever suffering; he is Schopenhauer's eternally striving will.[3] He is also the will to power, the will to overcome, to affirm, and to create. Dionysus is Nietzsche's symbol of modem man who has lost all traditional values and beliefs and faces nihilism and despair. But he also represents the heroic individual who overcomes nihilism and finds a new meaning of life, one that Nietzsche designates as Dionysian and tragic.

I apply the term Dionysian to Baraka's imagination in *The System of Dante's Hell* in the same way that Nietzsche would employ the term. In *The Twilight of the Idols*, Nietzsche provides this exegesis: "The saying yes to life even in its strangest and hardest problems; the will to life, rejoicing over its inexhaustibility even in the very sacrifice of its highest types, that is what I call Dionysian" (Quoted in Pfeffer 173). I suggest that the last pages of Baraka's novel—that is, the whole of "The Heretics"—dramatize the Dionysian Spirit, which is a spirit of synthesis in which negation and affirmation, suffering and joy, are reconciled. I suggest that Roi's descent into the midnight underworld of the Bottom and the Joint is a descent into the world of Dionysian nuptials. I suggest that Roi is Baraka's black antitype of the Dionysian hero, a hero born out of primal instincts and urges, orgiastic rites and drunken frenzy, all of which Dionysus represents. I suggest that Roi is Baraka's creation of the heroic Dionysian attitude of the higher individual who has the courage to stand alone and self-reliant, neither comforted by Dante's compensatory heaven nor protected by illusory categories of the mind. Roi also recognizes that destruction and annihilation are part of the eternal cycle of life and death, and of the everlasting change that pervades all nature. He knows that contradiction, evil, and suffering belong to the very essence of black life, yet he does not turn away in hatred or, worse still, resignation or negation. In his very failure and despair, Roi the Dionysian man fulfills himself, recognizing that "it is out of the deepest depth that the highest must come to its heights" (see Nietzsche 226). Notice in the following passage how Roi affirms life in spite of, or even because of, tragedy, understanding it in terms of its perils and potentialities, its nothingness and its greatness:

Empty man. Walk thru shadows. All lives the same. They give you wishes. The old people at the window. Dead man. Rised, come gory to their side. Wish to be lovely, to be some other self. Even here, without you. Some other soul, than the filth I feel. Have in me. Guilt, like something of God's. Some separate suffering self.

Locked in a lifeless shaft. Light at the top, pure white sun. And shadows twist my voice. Iron clothes to suffer. To pull down, what had grown so huge. My life wrested away. The old wood. Eyes of the damned uncomprehending. Who it was. Old slack nigger. Drunk punk. Fag. Get up. Where's your home? Your mother. Rich nigger. Porch sitter. It comes down. So cute, huh? Yellow thing. Think you cute. (134)

Earlier on we have heard him affirm life even in the face of benumbing death and deathness:

And
they tell me there is one place/
  for me to be. Where
  it all
  comes down. &
  you take up

  your sorrowful
  life. There/
  with us all. To
whatever death. (121-22)

In other words, Roi is molded out of the Dionysian myth of suffering and death, of being constantly sundered from himself. ("Split open down the center, which is the early legacy of the black man unfocused on blackness" [153], Baraka writes near the end of *The System* .)

Roi's suffering is the Dionysian pathos connected with the age-long concept of *Rausch*, which Nietzsche defines as "the psychology of the orgiastic as an overflowing feeling of life and power where even pain has the effect of a stimulus" (Nietzsche 173). In simpler terms, Rausch is a Dionysian quality which refers to states of alcoholic intoxication and to the orgiastic abandon experienced in impassioned dancing, sexual intercourse, and the like. Let me suggest that the story of the Bottom underworld, like that of the Joint and the Cotton Club, is an exploration of the psychology of the orgiastic. The Bottom is the consummation of the tragic culture achieved through the Dionysian passion which recognizes suffering, pain, and contradiction as essential elements in the productive activity of life and art, which, in order to create, must first destroy; in order to affirm, must first deny and annihilate. The central motif of this Dionysian psychology of the orgiastic is the dance, music. Baraka describes it with remarkable succinctness:

> The dancing like a rite no one knew, or had use for outside their secret lives. The flesh they felt when they moved, or I felt all their flesh and was happy and drunk and looked at the black faces knowing all the world thot they were my own, and lusted at that anonymous America I broke out of, and long for it now, where I am.
>
> We danced, this face and I, close so I had her sweat in my mouth, her flesh the only sound my brain could use. Stinking, and the music over us like a sky, choked any other movement off. I danced. And my history was there, had passed no further. (129)

Let me suggest that, like the Dionysian music, the music of the Bottom brothel, to which its inebriated customers dance, transports them into a state in which the artificial boundaries between people, black and white, and the limits of space and time, are broken down, leaving them to savor a sense of quasi-mystical oneness, a sense of what Levy-Bruhl identifies as *participation mystique* (de Laszlo 77). The music reveals a world that is unknown and seemingly unknowable to reason with its fragmentizing, isolating activity, a world which instead can be grasped intuitively by feelings and instincts. It penetrates to the primal force of life, which is, to Baraka and Nietzsche, the human will in its unadulterated form. Nietzsche has said that in the Dionysian music "the gospel of universal harmony is sounded; each individual not only feels united and reconciled with his fellow man, but at one with him, as if the veil of Maya had been torn apart and there remained only the vision of mystical Oneness" (Nietzsche 121-24).

I submit that what Roi actually experiences in the dithyrambic, syncopated rhythm of the Bottom music is a state of Dionysian frenzy, a state of exultation which includes suffering and pain as part of the primordial definition of the black experience. He feels deeply a sense of joy and realizes that, in spite of terror, pain, racial persecution, and relative deprivation, life is at base indestructibly powerful and creative.

And yet there is another sense in which the brothel rite is linked with the Dionysian unconscious; this is the area of "creative madness." According to Walter Friedrich Otto, the Dionysian nature is one of madness, a madness inherent in a world itself, not the passing or lasting derangement that comes as a disease, or even a sickness or degenerative state, but the companion to one's "most perfect health" (142). Roi's transformation from a nihilistic pervert to a more or less extroverted tragic-Dionysian hero is conceived within the mythos of Dionysian creative psychopathy. The first indication of this comes just before Roi descends into the Bottom. As he trudges his way to the Bottom, the whole vision of his mythopoeic quest becomes somewhat trans-personalized into a suspenseful moment of creative insanity:

But it was dusty. And time sat where it could, covered me dead, like under a stone for years, and my life was already over. A dead man stretched & a rock rolled over. . . till a light struck me straight on & I entered some madness, some hideous elegance. . . (119-20)

Like Saul of Tarsus on the dusty road to Damascus, Roi is profoundly moved by this strange encounter. From his deeply felt response to the tragic living conditions in the Bottom comes the second indication of the kind of infinite madness he is up against. The Bottom is like

some life drained off in silence. Under some grey night of smoke. They roared thru this night screaming. Heritage of hysteria and madness, the old meat smells and silent grey sidewalks of the North. Each father, smiling mother, walked thru these nights frightened of their children. Of the white sun scalding their nights. Of each hollow loud footstep in whatever abstruse hall. (125)

The final indication, and perhaps the most direct and deathly, comes from the inscription on the brothel wall directly above the entrance door: "The neon winked, and the place s eemed mad to be squatted in this actual wilderness: 'For Madmen Only'" (126).

These three indications are conceivably part of Baraka's strategy of of stressing the Dionysian mania symbolized by the brothel, a mania which provides a visionary explanation of a state in which man's vital powers are enhanced to the utmost, in which consciousness and the unconscious merge toward the inner growth of the individual. Baraka associates Dionysian madness with the churning up of the essence of black life, surrounded by the eternal storms of death, deprivation, and destitution. Since the tumult of creative insanity lies waiting in the bottom-most depths and makes itself felt in a noisy kind of way, all of life's ecstasy is stirred up by Dionysian paroxysm and is about to frolic beyond the bounds of controllable rapture into an infinitely dangerous wildness. The elements of creative madness associated with Roi's eternally striving will, as in Euripides's *The Bacchae*, provide the underground storm which splits up the stratified civilization of the West epitomized by Dante, the Christian pilgrim, from which Roi has received the conscionable injunction to "break out" (29), to "break, Roi, break" (134).

Finally, a discussion of the Dionysian in *The System of Dante's Hell* will not be satisfactorily conclusive without mentioning its relation to the primordial concept of the "eternal feminine." Peaches is the main symbol of this eternal feminine. Carl Kerenyi suggests that the myth of Dionysus relates to women in terms of their overflowing vitality, their milk and physical energy, their qualities as nurses and maenads (13). J. J. Bachofen states that the appeal of the Dionysian mythos is primarily to women. It is among women, argues Bachofen, that it finds its most loyal supporters, its most assiduous servants, and their enthusiasm is the foundation of its power (101). On the basis of these enunciations, I submit that Baraka's Peaches is the maenad of Dionysus, the Dionysian heroine of Ikarion, the love-stricken Eros who summons Roi, a young black man, a drifter, who also embodies Dionysian qualities, to the hot game of unrelenting love and dance. She and the other prostitutes are the bearers of the brothel's Dionysian cultus, the strange mistresses of wine and wonder. Like the Dionysian maenad, Peaches welcomes a timid youth, then lures, cajoles, and throws him unrepentantly into the seething cauldron of orgasmic and voyeuristic encounter through the mystery of his transformation into a true Dionysian protégé. Notice how Baraka describes their lovemaking, a description which has all the dark trappings of Dionysian intensity:

She rolled on me and, after my pants were off pulled me on her thick stomach. I dropped between her legs and she felt between my cheeks to touch my balls. Her fingers were warm and she grabbed everything in her palm and wanted them harder. She pulled to get them harder and it hurt me. My head hurt me. My life. And she pulled, breathing spit on my chest. "Comeon, Baby, Comeon. . . Get hard." It was like being slapped. And she did it that way, trying to laugh. "Get hard. . . Get hard." And nothing happened or the light changed and I couldn't see the paper woman. (139)

The paroxysms of intoxication and erotica represent the Dionysian via media to the sublimest gratification of the primordial unity. In the erotic encounter between Roi and Peaches, the artificial distance between "opposites" or strangers is annulled, a process which Jung describes as *conjunctio oppositorium*. Thus the Dionysian vision, within the mythos of anima-animus encounter and cohabitation, provides a profound insight into how a renewal of life may come from seeming evil. Renewal comes about through the assistance of the femme fatale and through the painful acceptance of what had hitherto not been cared for, what had previously been rejected or disowned, hence not really internalized. That regarded as evil may have been so, while it was allowed to remain unexperienced.

Baraka had been raised as LeRoi Jones by orthodox Christianity, according to which sex out of wedlock is regarded as lewd and sinful. But Roi experiences what Edward Whitmont has described as "the orgiastic quality of sex" (226), or what I call the metaphor of redemptive eros, the image of the unrealizable maternal unconscious in each one of us, coming to fruition in a moment of transformational erotic encounter, and he becomes bound by Peaches's viewpoint, which is designed to minimize its perceived evilness. This is the moment when traditional evil becomes rebaptized in a cultural, Nietzschean, and Jungian sense. While Dante would affirm ultimate reality by encountering it in ascetic, repressive, and suppressive virtuousness, Baraka, like Nietzsche, would uphold it in the primal majesty of ecstasy and joy expressible in Dionysian orgiasm. To achieve our individual wholeness, we are compelled to risk the experience of our own evil, an act that would allow us the capacity to express its energy in constructive ways. It seems as if the devil, in the shape of our anima, has applied the sting to make us find new ways out of our dilemma.

So then what is the underlying meaning of the Dionysian vision? Nietzsche, in *The Birth of Tragedy*, offers one plausible answer:

Under the charm of the Dionysian not only is the union between man and man reaffirmed, but nature which has become alienated, hostile, or subjugated, celebrates once more her reconciliation with her lost son, man. . . Now the slave is a free man; now all the rigid, hostile barriers that necessity, caprice, or impudent convention have fixed between men are broken . . . (Nietzsche 37).

This sense of reconciliation, this vision of freedom, Roi experiences all around him through his Dionysian encounter with Peaches. The passionate Dionysian orgy of the Bottom awakens him to a new, significant sense of wholeness and affinity with his previously unappreciated heritage. The sun that had once paled during the dark period of his alienation and egotistical inflation now shines in the moment of his cultural epiphany with a bright lustre: "The sun, thru that one window, full in my face. Hot, dust in it. But the smell was good. A daytime smell. And I heard daytime voices thru the window up and fat with optimism" (146-47). Roi is so ecstatic about this moment that he declares gleefully:

And I felt myself smiling, and it seemed that things had come to an order. Peaches sitting on the edge of the bed, just beginning to perspire around her forehead, eating the melon in both hands, and mine on a plate. . . Things moving naturally for us. At what bliss we took. At our words. And slumped together in anonymous houses I thought of black men sitting on their beds this saturday of my life listening quietly to their wives' soft talk. And felt the world grow together as I hadn't known it. All lies before, I thought. All fraud and sickness. This was the world. It leaned under its own suns, and people moved on it. A real world of flesh, of smells, of soft black harmonies and color. (147-48)

Roi, thus emancipated, might very well be overhearing the distant echoes of Nietzsche's voice:

A spirit thus emancipated stands in the midst of the universe with a joyful and trusting fatalism, in the faith that only what is separate and individual may be rejected, that in the totality everything is redeemed and affirmedhe no longer denies. . . But such a faith is the highest of all possible faiths: I have baptized it with the name Dionysus. (Pfeffer 258)

With this feeling of emancipation and joyful reconciliation, Roi arrives at a new sense of self. His transformation is a veritable *rite de passage* in a somewhat Gennepean sense. Roi is no longer another faceless airman running after strange, incomprehensible values, but a truly rejuvenated Peachesman: "Into that sun. The day was bright and people walked by me smiling. And waved 'Hey' (a greeting) and they all knew I was Peaches' man" (149). Roi, as airman, is Nietzsche's "herdman," the thing to be overcome in each of us. Where the herdman's life is shrouded in ambiguity and anonymity, that of the Peachesman is focused—on blackness. Roi is now without question the black inheritor of the Nietzschean Ubermensch, egged on by what Paul Tillich has described as "the courage of despair." We see this courage of despair borne out in Roi's heartful affirmation:

It was a cloud I think came up. Something touched me. "That color which cowardice brought out in me." Fire burns around the tombs. Closed from the earth. A despair came down. Alien grace. Lost to myself, I'd come back. To that ugliness sat inside me waiting. And the mere sky greying could do it. Sky spread thin out away from this place. Over other heads. Beautiful unknowns. And my marriage a heavy iron to this tomb. "Show us your countenance." Your light. (149)

Like the fate of Nietzsche's Overman, Roi's fate is the victory of the human spirit; its ultimate given is not opposition, but synthesis and reconciliation. The result of the Overman spirit in Roi is to see greatness and beauty even in the face of the horrible and ugly in black experience, to exult over suffering and pain, and to affirm the superior creative vitality of native Dionysian Peachesman. Roi is like Goethe's Faustian man, who has turned away from revealed, sanctioned truths and solipsistic pedantry toward hallowed truths, toward communal, chiastic existence as he wanders with Mephistopheles through life's depths and heights, its infamy and glory.

Roi's experience as Peachesman takes place within the struggles and tensions of the heroic will to overcome. His is an experience leveled in tragic vision, one that culminates in an affirmation of life and a savored glorification of the totality of all being, where the devil himself is present in heaven and the horrible and infamous are accepted as necessary and sacrosanct. The path to the Peachesman is like the path of Childe Roland, a path fraught with dangers and risks, and it leads all those who take it through an abyss, to the dark tower, the Bottom. The essential quality of character which Roi shares with Nietzsche's Overman is his titanically striving will, expressed in Nietzsche's will to power and symbolized by Goethe in the Eternal Feminine.

Like Arthur Schopenhauer, Amiri Baraka in *The System of Dante's Hell* is driven by the voluntaristic and pessimistic metaphysics of his age, a metaphysics which parts with Cartesian rationalism and the trans-cenddentalized dicta of Dante Alighieri. Again like Schopenhauer, Baraka believes that the innermost essence of the world which underlies all things is a blind impulse toward existence, an arational, ceaselessly striving, instinctual, and suffering will. This impulse pits Baraka against the fundamental presuppositions of ready-made angelic harmony readily assumed in the Western philosophical tradition of which Nietzsche is a constant critic, and this accounts for the seeming chaos of the plot of the novel. Unlike Schopenhauer, however, Baraka does not see this ceaselessly striving and suffering will as merely alternating between pain and boredom; instead, he sees it as transforming its basic agony through the mediation of the tragic spirit distilled in Dionysian mythogeny into patterns of life celebration and what he himself has once described as the "higher equations of purpose." This is where Baraka's path crosses Nietzsche's and makes Baraka Nietzsche's seeming disciple.

For Baraka and Nietzsche, the final goal of life is not attained through the abolition of the striving and suffering will, but through its tragic overcoming, the spirit of which is borne in the indefatigable soul of the Overman, or what Baraka cognitypically designates as the Peachesman. Baraka, through the mediation of the Dionysian imagination, proves ultimately to be Nietzsche's initiator of tragic culture. Like Nietzsche he sees with sharp clarity the deepest roots of black suffering and anonymity in racist America. With passionate concern though, he searches for a way out of the moral dilemma that America poses. And he finds his escape neither in the noumenal illogic of a futuristic divine order nor in the presumed supremacy of the intelligence of man, *homo sapiens*, but rather in the phenomenal primacy of what Max Scheler calls *home faber*—a creature of instinctual drives and practical needs—in the depths of man's personality and his creative, self-affirming will to power, symbolized by the Bottom (dynatype) and embodied in the body scheme of Peaches (cognitype), the eternal feminine.[4]

Baraka, America, and the Allegory of Racial Sin

At the surface, the skillful blending of romance (quest narrative), comic myth, and cultural freight into tbe lyrical, dadaist-surrealist structure of Amiri Baraka's (LeRoi Jones's) novel, *The System of Dante's Hell*, invites comparison with the banal schematism of John Gower's *Confessio Amantis* or the comic realism of Boccaccio's *Decameron*. But at bottom, seriously speaking, somewhere between *Decameron* and *Confessio Amantis*, *The System of Dante's Hell* parallels Dante's *Inferno*, providing a multi-layered view of experience growing out of a social, cultural, and ideological situation, and subserving a broad range of opinion within a carefully orchestrated framework of moral sentiment.[1] Despite subtle differences in the imaginative conceptualization of Hell, both Baraka's *System* and Dante's *Inferno* are interfaced in the judicious absorption of moral and philosophical issues into literary narrative, as well as the juxtaposition of erotic and spiritual experience, the sacred and the profane, an interface that will serve as a neccessary point of departure for this discussion.

In fact, to follow Baraka in his *descensus ad inferos* (descent into hell) is to traverse a moral topography charged with unusual intensity. It is a descent very much like Dante's crippling voyage through the gates of Hell which, as noted by Irma Brandeis, is in part "a search for understanding of the order and nature of the universe" (16). In *The System of Dante's Hell*, the search is for a black man's understanding of the order and nature of his world (contemporary America), projecting a deontological geography of his sundered soul with the aim of exploring his soul's wandering away from and return to authentic black heritage. It is, as the author suggests in the novel, a search to mend the damage inflicted by the wayward legacy "of the black man unfocused on blackness" (153), and thus be in a strong, uncompromising position to "deliver us from the salvation of our enemies" (153). Like Dante, Baraka draws upon a source which is his own personal experience, the many touching episodes derived from his own private observations. That means that the world we encounter in Baraka's *The System of Dante's Hell*, as in Dante's *Inferno*, is essentially a world constructed out of historical and social realism, quite the opposite of the substantively allegorical construction of Guillaume de Lorris's *Roman de la Rose*, and in contrast to Bunyan's hell. It is, in other words, a socialized hell. The infernal abyss borrows form and color from America; the scenes among the damned are typical American scenes, with the whole design securely related to the moral degeneracy of contemporary America. Baraka thus removes the myth of the quest for a Black Eden from the realm of other worldly utopia/dystopia and gives it an irreducibly historical and geographical sensibility. But behind the vivid immediacy of realistic topography, there is at work a subtle and discriminating moral judgment, an allegorical intendiment.

The novel opens in an atmosphere smothered in moral breach, made even brusquer by Baraka's dystopian imagination. It would appear as though Baraka insists that we go with him, Dantean wayfarer, to discover and possibly overcome the root of this moral breach, to know, and by knowing, vanquish that which has caused the black man's life in white America to become insecure and miserable. It is part of Baraka's thematica that the errant Black soul is rooted in evil American soil. Just as salvation in Dante requires both recognition of the evil depth, and victory over it through Christ, so for Baraka, the black man's redemption lies in his recognition of the evil that is his externally imposed cultural deracination and role playing, and in his capacity and will to transcend it not necessarily through the white image of God, but rather through a newly woven image of God consistent with the soulful perception of things so characteristic of the black world view.

In "NEUTRALS: The Vestibule" (Dante's Canto 3), Baraka introduces us to his formal doorway to Hell, where the indulgence in unabated sin has led to "the breakup of my sensibility" (9). The sensibility of negation by mortal sin is complete and thus leads to an atrophied moral darkness, a darkness whose uncanny silence is broken only by "low cries of waked up animals, by ill-tempered "dogs wetting on the buildings in absolute content," and by the ceaseless, disconsolate wailings of the damned and the pitied. The entrance to the American Hades is by a gate, bearing a superscription, which for Baraka is partly explanatory and partly terrifying. Just beyond the gate, in that part of Dante's Hell usually referred to as the "Vestibule," Baraka looks searchingly into the "minds

of darkness. . . breaking out in tears along the sidewalks of the season"
(9).

Baraka intentionally upsets the familiar popular encomiums about
America heard incessantly in the national ultra song—"America the
Beautiful." He thus erects his narrative as a countermemory, as a site of
resistance, a domain where challenges to official cultural memory are
posed. Following in the great tradition of the African American slave
narratives, *The System of Dante's Hell* encourages its readers to develop
what Robert Levin calls "a healthy skeptical relationship to glorified
stories. . .[about America], to rethink sanctioned knowledge, and to break
the hold of official "truth" and the metaphysics of memory, replacing
them with the truth of countermemory" (15). The novel as countermemory text signifies on the prevailing picture as painted by such organs
of officialdom as the Voice of America and the like, by taking seriously
the marginalized perspective of an American cultural outsider such as
Baraka. Like Hawthorne in *The House of the Seven Gables* and Melville
in *Pierre*, Baraka shows that beneath the happy façade of a thriving,
prosperous, democratic America lies an ambiguous history of racial
tyranny, ethnic violation [even ethnic cleansing], deceit and oppression.
We are reminded of similar objective in his play, *Dutchman*, where the
complex formation of images and myths, including Biblical myth, and
the legend of the Flying Dutchman, all are linked by Baraka with the idea
of a prior curse brought about by slavery. Slavery ensured the loss of
American innocence quite early in its history, counter to official memory
narrative. *Dutchman* hints that that loss of innocence undermines
America's claim to some kind of functional idealism.

So with brutal realism of contemporary America right in his face, and
having peered into the minds of darkness, Baraka, the fire and brimstone
moralist, now begins to unleash his judicatural power by graduating the
sins and vices of modem day America. In this regard, he becomes like
Dante both the self-styled prosecutor, officer, and executioner of ethical
justice. From this point on, his language is transformed into an
instrument of moral castigation with a tone marked by angst, sarcasm,
and sneering severity.

The first group of sinners at whom he directs his moral outrage is the
'neutrals.' Like Dante's 'neutrals,' these roam aimlessly. In their vain,
empty lives, they lack conviction. They hold no belief of their own, nor
subscribe to other beliefs outside of themselves. Their imperviousness to
other lives, other responses, is fiercely inexorable. They are marked by
their noncommittal passivity. They range from the "Sheridan Square blue
men under thick quivering smoke," to those who "run jewelry shops and
shit in silence under magazines;" from "women who disappear into

Canada," to the tinsel cadre borne on vanity who "wore rings and had stories about them." To these their noncommittal lives have predisposed them to believe that "ideas are ugly," insulated themselves from the positive throb of the world, causing "their histories [to] die in the world" (9-10).

Given this kind of indulgence, it is hardly surprising why Baraka chooses to depict his American hell as a grim place; its grimness is totally unrelieved by any durable hope. Although here and there Baraka fiddles with wry humor, mostly, however, it is a scene of untold suffering, sorrow, and private shame beneath a veneer of material contentment. The following passage bears this scenario out: "The mind fastens past landscapes. Invisible agents. The secret trusts. My own elliptical. The trees' shadows broaden. The sky draws together darkening. Shadows beneath my fingers. Gloom grown under my flesh" (10). Thus in *The System of Dante's Hell*, everything strikes the voyager as impemetrably dark and infinitely terrible; it is evil unmitigated, unvitiated.

From the "Vestibule," Baraka takes us right into the center of the first Circle of Hell—"Heathen: No.1" [and] "Heathen: No.2." Here, on the brink of the great abyss of Hell, Baraka pauses and hears the importunate cries of the poverty-stricken. Like Dante's spirits, they are not necessarily damned, but merely suspended between a dignified social scale and a "lower middleclass poverty. . ." Unlike Dante, however, Baraka does not show admiration for the heathen. In fact, taking aim at America's public policy, he shows instead that the black world is very much like the heathen's, a world of suspended animation, a suburban ghetto of confinement, racial neglect and criminal abandonment.

Excluded from the paradisal "bliss" of the American dream, and segregated from the well-to-do white communities, the "heathens" of the ghetto turn against one another in a seemingly endless cycle of mistrust, betrayal, even murderous rage (black on black crime): "You've done everything you said you wdn't. Everything you said you despised. A fat mind, lying to itself" (13). What comes true here is a numbing sense that these black ghetto residents, like Dante's infernal prisoners, are in limbo. That is why there is a persistent emphasis upon enclosures, upon dark, dreary rooms, devoid of life and light, nestled and wedged in a strangely neutral, aberrant, and lifeless scene. The heathens are living literally in desire without hope. To our moral voyager, this apparent paralysis is more than enough to cause him "to feel sick," to bemoan the fact that "everything I despise some harsh testimonial of my life. . . Left outside I lose it all. So quickly. My youth wasted on the bare period of my desires" (14).

With this overwhelming sense of hopelessness blinded by personal lust, Baraka wanders into the second circle of Hell (Dante's Canto 5). This is the world of the incontinent and the lascivious. Baraka skips the graphic picture of Dante's Minos figure, and moves immediately to the second circle proper. Here he comes hard face to face with the sensualists. The chief sensualist is one Petrus Borel, and Baraka's impression of him is quick and poignant. "Petrus Borel is a lascivious man" (23), the narrator tells us. With this dominant impression, Baraka takes a quick swipe at a street not far off, literally infested with other sensualists. Some of them, with dull, expressionless faces, droop over bottles of liquor on the pavements outside of bars.

The voyager has to strain his eyes, for the canopy under which the sensualists indulge their incontinence has created an eerie cloud of darkness. The scenario gets increasingly scandalous. At a downtown brothel is another bedabbled crowd, this time a random jumble of common folks, factory workers, reverend ministers, law men, etc. They are all bonded in this macabre brotherhood of unbridled concupiscence. As in Dante, these lascivious street sinners appear to Baraka as birds. At the end, though, Baraka is distressed, lumpish, angry, and fearful, distraught about the hour of lustness which "hung in my flesh." The last sentence—"and the lust in the world fashioned into snow" (25)—summarizes the fate of a young man who has lost his ethical innocence, the soul's second encounter with personal and collective sin.

This violated innocence serves as an eye opener to our moral voyager as he makes his way to the third circle (Dante's Canto 6), inhabited by another, much deadlier group of sinners—the gluttons. In Dante's scheme of sins, gluttony follows lust, and this is usually considered more serious and so more punishable. Although in *The System of Dante's Hell*, Baraka makes gluttony follow lust, the order, however, is not significant. What is significant, though, for Baraka is that the moral voyager has moved from a sin that is mutually enjoyed (for instance, that with the street sensualists) to one that is more or less solitary, one indulged privately for its own sake. To Baraka the harshness of northeast winter is a function of the crass greed and and voracity very much a part of northern city life. He pictures city men and women as wolves in sheep's clothings. He too has begun to behave that way, to gloat over the excesses of the city, to set his evil eyes on its blossom, its flower (like Baudelaire flowers of evil), its alluring, seductive magic. The final statement is an affirmation of a moral voyager turned wolf-hound, corrupted by wolfish appetite, and yet somehow manages to maintain some semblance of sanity. The voyager himself says: "If my flesh is sweet, my mind is pure. I am awake in your cold world" (28).

Savoring the sweetness of carnality, the voyager traverses circles four, five, and skipping circle six for the moment, enters the seventh circle titled: "Seven: The Destruction of America" where he encounters one of the brutal consequences of gluttony, and of pitiless greed. One of those consequences is violence which may be directed "against others, against one's self, against God, Nature and Art" (36). The goriest example of this kind of violence is the one unleashed upon the Indians by the white man, under the pretext of creative civilization (*la creatrice civilisation*), in what is clearly a reminiscence on the part of Baraka of the time when the first white settlers set foot in America. But the white man's almost natural penchant for violence is not just a thing of the past; to Baraka the same ineffable instinct survives even today, except that the black man not the Indian is now the whiteman's latest victim. The white man, by enslaving the black man and keeping him enslaved through Jim Crowism, and by robbing him of his essential dignity, has acted violently against him. And the black man, by chasing after things white, has indeed done violence to himself—"My name, like Indians. Dead hard ground" (36). So the moral castigation here is complete and somewhat impartial.[2]

Like Dante Baraka knows that the root of all evil is demonic. The descent into the city of Dis, renamed by Baraka in *The System of Dante's Hell* as "Bottom" and later as "The Joint," is literally an encounter with Satan or Prince of moral darkness. In Circle Six—"The Heretics"—the demon is at work in the prostitutes of the Bottom brothel tempting Baraka to sin and impeding his way toward repentance and spiritual salvation. In some ways, they are like the devil prowling around like a roaring lion, seeking someone to devour. Peaches, the chief prostitute, at first acts as the demon's maenad by luring Roi, Baraka's alter ego, into sexual incontinence. Peaches, before her mythological transfiguration by Baraka into a kind of parody of Dantean Beatrice, serves as a prima facie symbol of the entanglement with earthly, carna things and desires.

And I twisted my ann away, moving faster as I knew I should toward the vague smell Peaches was touching and tugging a little at my sleeve. She came around and robbed my tiny pecker with her fingers. And still I moved away. . . When I got outside she moved in front of me. (131)

The temptation scene here is, as Rosemary Woolf suggests, reminiscent of the common scene in Medieval morality play where vices entice man to the tavern or the brothel.

Other forces have also attempted to get in the way of the moral voyager. These include: the Wrathful (33-34); the Seducers and the Treacherers. . . . Bolgia 1 (37-39); the Flatterers. . . Bolgia 2 (41-45); the

Sirnonists . . . Bolgia 3 (47-48); the Diviners. . . Bolgia 4 (49-54); the Hypocrite (s). . . Bolgia 6 (61-68); the Thieves. . . Bolgia 7 (69-78); the Makers of Discord. . . Bolgia 9 (93-100); the Personators and Falsifiers. . . Bolgia 10 (101-105). All these groups of sinners, each serving as an abrasive foil in its own right to one another, are brought clear to us by the force and virulence of Baraka's comical, satirical, and symbolic imaginative energy. His comic-satiric fancy depicts their foibles with such care, poignancy, and picaresque virtuosity that our laughter is summarily aroused. The stories about these fallen men and women are generally a free mixture of exempla, moral in intentionality, and marked by a high degree of obscenity, jestings, and mild moral abuse. What predominates is a general air of jocularity and mild Dantesque satire, a kind of technique very much reminiscent of the days of Menippus of Gadara (3rd century BC Cynic philosopher) and Varro, and one which has influenced such writers as Petronius, Apuleius, Voltaire, Swift, Rabelais and Sterne. Needless to say that the brief encounters with these sunken forces and lost souls link the story of Baraka's descent into real-life American racial Hell not only with the death and resurrection of Christ and his victory over the Devil, but also with the myths of great classical heroes such as Hercules, Odysseus, Theseus, and Perseus.

The moral topography of *The System of Dante's Hell* thus is an ingenious conflation of quasi spiritual pilgrimage and neo-cultural *miserere*. In it Baraka traces the progress of a black man, Roi, his tortuous passage from moral darkness, coterminous with cultural destitution, to the light of cultural enlightenment, coterminous with spiritual illumination. It is a painful search for understanding of the order of the universe as it relates to a primal, conscientious knowledge of one's own cultural identity and the spirit of *participation mystique* that cements that identity. Thus a discussion of the moral saga of *The System of Dante's Hell* must conclude by experiencing the novel from a double perspective: from the perspective of a concrete moral experience, and from the bastion of a secular judgment which Baraka interweaves with the lives, histories, and actions of characters who embody certain passions and sentiments prone to changing moral states.

This writer would venture to submit that the greatest appeal of *The System of Dante's Hell*, in fact, its power to elicit very much the kind of sympathetic hostility so characteristic of Shavian (George Bernard Shaw's) dramaturgy, lies in the special moral appeal, an appeal not merely that of the cultural intellect, but of the urbane faculty of responding to the reality of intense moral experience. The motive of Baraka's voyage through the hellish terrain of contemporary America is cultural repentance, a rise of new native spirit almost to vertiginous heights which contradicts earlier moral and cultural aberrations, a rise which is very much conceived as a movement of discovery or what Northrop Frye calls "points of expanding apprehension" (326). There is, however, no conscious attempt in the novel to reduce the black experience to any rigid set of simple moral maxims. Nor does Baraka look for that kind of systematized didactic confidence and conviction which invests the Dantean pilgrimage. Rather, the moral gradation here is rendered in terms of an eclectic melange freely constructed upon the notion of casual arbitration by an avid cultural referee. A writer has said that "the logical end of pilgrimage is the meeting of the soul with its Creator" (Ruggiers 40). The end of Baraka's symbolic journey in *The System of Dante's Hell* is the meeting of the prideful black soul with the earthy prime movers of his culture through a perilous moral terrain.

8

Gwendolyn Brooks's *Maud Martha*: Narrative as Allegory of Initiation

In a brilliant essay in *The Journal of Aesthetics and Art Criticism* titled: "What Is an Initiation Story?" Mordecai Marcus defines with remarkable succinctness the quintessence of the initiation story this way:

An initiation story may be said to show its young protagonist experiencing a significant change of knowledge about the world or himself, or a change of character, or of both, and this change must point or lead him toward an adult world. It mayor may not contain some form of ritual, but it should give some evidence that the change is at least likely to have permanent effects. (181)

From this compelling beginning, Marcus then proceeds to calibrate a typology of the initiation story, identifying in the process three main forms. This is what he says:

. . . First, some initiations lead only to the threshold of maturity and understanding but do not definitely cross it. Such stories emphasize the shocking effect of experience, and their protagonists tend to be distinctly young. Second, some initiations take their protagonists across a threshold of maturity and understanding but leave them enmeshed in a struggle for certainty. These initiations sometimes involve self-discovery. Third, the most decisive initiations carry their protagonists firmly into maturity and understanding, or at least show them decisively embarked toward maturity. These initiations usually center on self-discovery. For convenience, I will call these tentative, uncompleted, and decisive initiations. (181)

Marcus's definition not only foregrounds the initiation story's essential paradigm, propelled as it were, by its central defining metaphor—the metaphor of growth, development and temporal kinesia consociated with the creative process—but is itself corroborated and deepened by other authoritative sources.[1] For example, Theodore Ziolkowski describes the process as the "triadic pattern of humanization" which constellates the essential notion of the individual progressing in his or her growth and development through three distinct but inseparable stages.[2] For Martin Swales, the narrative remains, for the most part, "a [veritable] novel form that is animated by a concern for the whole man unfolding organically in all his complexity and richness" (14). Wilhelm Dilthey maintains that it is, by and large,

a regulated development within the life of the individual (which) is observed, each of its stages (having) its own intrinsic value and (being) at the same time the basis for a higher stage. The dissonances and conflicts of life appear as the necessary growth points through which the individual must pass on his way to maturity and harmony. (394)

Susan J. Rosowski is convinced that the initiation story is a narrative, true to type, which recounts the growth of a young man [or woman] attempting to learn the nature of the world, discover its meaning and pattern, and acquire a philosophy of life and 'the art of living' (49).

Gwendolyn Brooks's *Maud Martha* which predates its other African American counterpart, or better still, antitype—Ralph Ellison's *Invisible Man*—belongs unequivocally in the first category of the intiation story identified by Marcus. At the time that Brooks wrote *Maud Martha* (1953), the initiation story as a quest narrative in American literature was, sadly enough, largely male-oriented. Quite often, in most male initiation stories, the true story of the female was left sadly untold. The female was often portrayed as a temptress, or at best, as some unconscious instrument by which the male, not the female is humanized and redeemed. There was no proper definable image that fitted her checkered experience. A demand for answer to the nagging, persistent question—what is my own story?—is quite often ignored or at best treated with some degree of benign levity.[3] At least that was the sad state of affairs until the auspicious turn of the century when the long ignored female initiation narrative (otherwise known as the female bildungs-roman) began to emerge and to assert itself with unmistakable candor and clarity. According to Carol P. Christ, the female bildungsroman is a celebration of the woman's perception of the world, not just as shadows living "in the interstices between their own vaguely understood experience and the shaping given to experience by the stories of men," but as viable authentic subjectivities (5). And because of this fact, argues Christ, "new language must be created to express women's experience and insight, new metaphors discovered, new themes considered" (7).

In *Maud Martha*, Gwendolyn Brooks intends that the black woman question can no longer be dealt with solely through the muffled trajectories of the male quest. It has to be confronted in her own turf, on her own irrevocable terms, both from within and without her unique sense of self and subjectivity. From without, her struggle to gain respect, equality, and genuine freedom in society—in the work place, in the home place, in politics, and in social intercourse involving other women, men and children—is starkly ventillated. From within, her awakening to the depths of her soul and significant selfhood, as well as her unique position in the universal and destinal order is explored (Christ 8). For Christ, as for Brooks, these two aspects of being are not mutually exclusive but rather two dimensions of a single inexorable struggle in which women seek "a wholeness that unites the dualisms of spirit and body, rational and irrational, nature and freedom, spiritual and social, life and death, which have plagued western consciousness" (8).

It is this syncretistic approach to the feminized variety of the initiation story that is at the very core of *Maud Martha*. It is what essentializes its rhetorical domain. Brooks's heroine, Maud Martha Brown's story is explored within and without the world of her sense of self and subjectivity. Her story is a story of growth toward the self as a symbolic site of objective transpersonal reality within which the social phenomena of her life point toward the experience of the ineffable, toward the redefinition of self. Within the fluidity of this redefinition, we become acutely aware of the intrinsic conflicts of the heroine's existence—conflicts of leanings and loves, responsibilities and commitments. Those intrinsic conflicts are recognized by Brooks's heroine in terms of their symbolic meaning as expressions of the drama of life. The heroine's drives and urges now demand to be vocalized for the sake of an integral wholeness of her total being.

In *Maud Martha* Gwendolyn Brooks appears to employ the intiation narrative paradigm identified by Marcus in the chronicling of her heroine's growth from childhood to adulthood, from frail innocence to chastening adult experience. In unraveling that, she insists that we see in Maud's progress some reflection of the traditional male quest plot or initiation story.

The evolution of Maud Martha Brown can be divided into three major stages, very much like the Wordsworthian exemplar of the three ages. Each stage represents a distinct phase in that evolution, displaying itself in a peculiar structure of feeling and emotional responses. The first stage I would designate the nostalgic/eidetic. This is the stage marked by vivid recall of visual images—images of innocence, of naiveté and spontaneity. The second is the dialogic/dialectic which initiates the language of liminal encounter. Here the loss of innocence leads to an encounter with the harsnness of the wider social environment. This is the phase of sensitive regard, of critical awareness, the awareness of the limitations of the nostalgic and the dialogic, and the attempt to break away from their curtailed hopes and ambitions through a self-conscious mode of recovery and the struggle for self-expression. In passing through all these stages, Maud seeks to learn the nature of a race-conscious world, to discover its meaning for herself as well as for all black people, and from her observation and participation, hopefully, to acquire an overall vision of life and the purpose, if any, that undergirds it.

The first stage begins with the description of the personality of Maud Martha, a young girl intensely observant of the natural landscape. There is a sense of withdrawal to a garden, the garden of dandelions, under the overcast western graciously viewed from the backyard veranda" (1).[4] The garden is both a physical and a symbolic landscape. Here, alienated from a cherishing love, Maud is thrown back on herself. Gwendolyn Brooks casts her in the image of a Cinderella-figure nestled within the myth of her childhood. Like Simone de Beauvoir's prototypical heroine, Maud is "locked" in a garden of dandelions, passive, quiescent, innocent and inexperienced. One of the early choices of her childhood is one made between the lush landscape of lotus or China asters and the Japanese Iris, on the one hand, and between meadow lilies and dandelions, on the other.

But Maud's capacity for choice does not necessarily mean that she has attained as yet the kind of critical awareness necessary for sustained self-actualization. As we watch Maud locked in her back porch, peering intently at the garden of dandelions with their modest affectation, their ordinariness and ubiquity, we get a sense that she is a child nurtured in a kind of rural innocence and isolation, uncorrupted for the most part by the priveleges of sex and beauty, with an unsullied if not modest sense of her own consequence (this modesty comes through in her recognition of her sister's—Helen's—beauty in contrast to her own ugliness or plainness). In short in Chapter I (1—3), Brooks portrays her as the true traditional innocent, forcing the reader to regard her with a fairly patronizing or matronizing air.

Gwendolyn Brooks also portrays Maud as a delicate, impresssionable young girl whose life is molded by romantic ideals drawn from childhood reading of fairytales. At this very point, the author employs the testimony that is decidedly known to Freudian/Jungian cultural functionalists and psychological folklorists that fairytales fulfill some very basic psychic needs for the individual and society.[5] One of the ideals/fantasies which fairytales habituate in children is the fantasy of escape or attempted flight coterminous with our heroine's sense of awakening. For example, no sooner had Maud seen the image of an escaped gorilla in a dreamscape, than she began to long for some kind of freedom. When Maud awakens, she awakens not only to the possibility of innocency of escape, but also awakens to the danger of social paralysis which she notices all around her. So the functionality or the practical utility of the gorilla's escape subserves the fundament of Maud's hope, the hope that she too might be able to escape not only the cloistered life of the dandelions, but also the emotional paralysis resulting from a feeling of social, economic, and racial inconsequence.

But Maud's dream of escape is not going to have immediate results. Brooks's heroine's attempts to escape harsh human realities (first, her escape into the cloistered garden of dandelions behind her back porch; second, her escape into the world of dreams and fairy tales), are almost impossible, at best a pipe dream. She does this by counterposing to Maud's dream of escape with the gorilla, characters and situations that tend to oppose, challenge, or perhaps slow down the process of actualization of the self. Either symbolically or quite literally, Maud's attempted dream flights are thwarted by these forces into even stricter confinement. Notice the mental torture of the death-room in which Maud's Grandma lies dying (11−15). It is a grotesque version of the Sleeping Beauty of Snowdrop's coffin scene, or perhaps, like the red room in which Charlotte Bronte's Jane Eyre is confined at Gateshead.

Notice also the inhibitiveness of the brick structure of Maud's school. The description of the landscape is a chromatic medley of beauty and ugliness, freedom and confinement, though images of ugliness and confinement predominate. Maud would very much have wished there were promises embedded beneath the nightmarish cast of predominantly grotesque landscape, but as we will soon discover in the second stage of Maud's growth, as adumbrated in the first stage, they are overpowered by uncanny images of growth inhibition.

Before we part with the first stage, we need to dwell more on the landscape factor because of its thematic and phenomenological significance in the evolution of Maud Martha Brown's sense of selfhood. The landscape vignette—"Description of Maud Martha"—one of several such vignettes which opens the novel in which Maud emotionally empathizes with the garden of dandelions, is not a wholly isolated scene. Unlike the conventionally emblematic lotus, or China asters or Japanese iris, or meadow lilies, these dandelions have an intense concreteness of presence upon which young Maud's abstraction of a love ethic hinges.

Thus at the formative stage of her life as a woman in a man's world, the landscape of dandelions reminds her of a spontaneous life of love which she cherishes, but is denied. There is also an imaginative evocation of natural beauty and a world of innocence, the innocence of a child intent on taking imaginative possession of the world. This evocation of natural beauty enables Maud to compensate her feelings of loss and alienation in an uncherished and uncherishing world. The primal ambience of innocence is intensely animated in a way that suggests a kind of Carlylean projection of Maud's emotion on the dandelions. It is also suggested in the gradual assimilation into the natural landscape. "For in that latter quality she thought she saw a picture of herself, and it was comforting to find that what was common could also be a flower" (2).

The dandelions and the allurement of the flower have the intensity of felt experience. Clearly for Gwendolyn Brooks, the theme of childhood is not far removed from a feeling for nature which is reminiscent of Wordsworth. The memory of the Wordsworthian harmony of man, nature and self evidently constitutes one of Maud's touchstones of anticipated joy and wholeness, but one which unfortunately would soon be shattered by the intrusion of other external forces like sexism and racism. In this latter sense, the seeming edenic lushness and serenity of the dandelion garden, much like the coral garden that delights the imagination, may prove less a fair play of rhythmic consonance with Maud's inner terrain and more a measure of what she lacks fundamentally—a cherishing love. All that Maud has ever wanted is to be loved and cherished, in stark terms of endearment.

For Maud Martha Brown, the infirmities of childhood shadowed by the "allurement of any flower" reflects a quasi-Arnoldian landscape emblematic of a fledgeling consciousness premodern in its spontaneity, premoral in its cool awareness of adolescent passion, and presocial in its sheltered seclusion.[6] Thus Brooks's use of the floral landscape, particularly that of the dandelions, is calculated to unveil a world of frail, innocent, and transcient beauty, a state of naive consciousness, of spontaneous simplicity, intensely characteristic of adolescence itself. In fact, Maud's incipient and fledgeling consciousness of the world outside is an outgrowth of the inner depths of her unconscious conceived in terms of a vegetal meadow mass. For Maud it means taking the ordinary dandelion and lifting it out of its humdrum ambience, and making it almost inorganic by imagining it in a world of seemingly infinite mythologem. There she contemplates it and then associates it with love. For Brooks it is delightfully startling the way that she, much like the cubist painter, Juan Gris, takes seemingly insignificant things and objects and then transmutes them into icons of profound meaning. The meadow is, to an adolescent mind, a kind of timeless order in which Maud, the feminine child archetype, feels sympathetically at home, and looks at the rest of the outside world like the changing images within a crystal. The dandelion, therefore, represents Maud's inner order or trajectory, her golden flower of the psyche, the very nerve center of her fledgeling self, a self for whom feeling, instinctive life, is primary.

If the first phase of Maud's intiation into life and the forces that shape its destinal alterity could be said to be the phase of over-protective innocence, the second phase might well be described as the phase of lost innocence, of paradise lost. Brooks engages it by erecting a dialectic between the apparent peace and loveliness of natural landscape and the endless disquiet of the contemporary city. In this latter setting, Maud, for the first time, becomes conscious of other lives, other responses, other modes of existence. Though still an adolescent, Maud can now hear clearly other sensitive children chattering about fixing curls and about Joe Louis, of Duke Ellington, and of Bette Davis (5). The figuration of the action with which the second chapter opens thus foreshadows the psychological shift from the benign and gentle pastoral terrain of dandelions to a harsher, more menacing landscape of the school yard which is described in images almost Dantesque.

The dilemma posed in juxtaposing a frail innocence in a seemingly prelapsarian garden of dandelions and the present illusion or doubt is evident in the various sets of antithetical images which objectify the dialectial tensions in the novel—childhood/maturity, past/present, solitude/society, seclusion/freedom, hope/despair, black/white, male/female, light/darkness, beauty/ugliness. These opposing, dialectic images convince Maud that the recourse to the dandelions as the abode of pristine serenity is nothing but a vacuous daydream. Maud now realizes that the only alternative that exists for a young black girl growing up is the encounter with the world outside of the self. The first real indication of her initiation into this world begins in Chapter 6 at age sixteen—"At the Regal." Here Maud mingles gleefully with the heavy outflowing crowd assembled in the lobby of the Regal Theatre at Forty-seventh and South Park. The occasion is the live performance by a celebrity singer, Howie Joe Jones, with rugged honey voice.

But to Maud Martha, the society of Howie Joe Jones is nothing but a society in which few choices exist for a colored girl, despite the tokenism of flamboyant airs of a few lucky ones of her kind. Howie Joe Jones stands, for most men and women, as a symbol of those molded in the image of society, for whom the image-making process is everything. Despite the evanescence of this society-induced image, Jones nonetheless revels in it because it serves his opportunistic and materialistic end. A staunchily outer-directed person, Howie's sense of worth and dignity is defined exclusively in social terms, especially among a race of people for whom success was a rarity. On the contrary, Maud's sense of pastoral worth lies in the opposite direction. It is inner directed, defined in terms of her good naturedness and personal virtue. Although the audience had applauded at the end of Howie's live performance, Maud remains largely unimpressed by the whole superfluous buzz about Howie Jones, and had actually stormed out of the lobby, [and] headed home as soon as the whole show was over. Her emotional impulse is primarily a longing for freedom from the intolerable pressure of quick, evanescent, and socially-conditioned fame. Fame is fundamentally a social construction laced with false ego and paradoxically inimical to one's sense of proportion.

Thus the voice that Howie Joe Jones has is the voice of a mob gloating over its short-lived vanity beneath a cancerous veneer which is like a "lightgaze across its little miseries and monotonies" (20). So that the dialectic of voices provides for Maud the basis for a search for a new paradigm for personal joy, social participation, and above all, self-fulfillment. It would be a dialectic of inward movement which has greater potential for self-knowledge, except that in Maud's case, given the nature of her society, that self knowledge leads inexorably to a disclosure of a cleavage between knowledge of self and the painful realities of a racist culture. Maud is soon to realize that for a woman, and a Black woman, for that matter in white America, such self- knowledge is very difficult of practical attainment because it summarily leads to socially conditioned restraints.

Maud's sensitive choice for an inner sense of worth, grounded as it were in good naturedness, ironically betrays a passivity that would prove counter-productive. By electing to donate to the world a goodly chaste Maud Martha, Maud quite ironically accepts the label put on women by society as tender and holy virgins, as toasts of society urged to be chaste, retiring and modest. In a sense, Maud impreceptibly internalizes the same damaging stereotypes about women as ploys, an image which she seems to be trying to cast off. She further succumbs to this perception by entertaining romantic fantasies of love and matrimony based fundamentally upon societally-induced Cinderella image in which passivity, domesticity, and a morbid paternalism are dominant trademarks. First, there is her high school date, Charles. The love relationship here is one between a male benefactor and a humble female recipient of kindly gifts. Second, there is the fantasy in the love relationship between Maud and Russell, whom, we are told, does and says things with a mien, "a dazzling, long, and sleepily swishing flourish" (41). Third, there is the love tangle with the fop, David McKemester, a student whose personality reminds her of a perfect "English country gentleman. . . roaming the rustic hill" [side] (42), possibly with a pipe in hand. And then there is the knot-tying with Paul Phillips, an impercunious young man. It is a marriage beset by one unfulfilled desire after another, and finally is docked in divorce.

In all these relationships, Brooks portrays Maud as a men's pawn. We see her frustration of youthful ambition, the felt discrepancy between the ideal of romantic love which seems to Maud at first to be actually attainable and the exigencies of the real world of men which impose themselves with irritating authority. When she visits New York, she apprehends the meaning of modernity in terms of the hopes and frustrations that attend the search for love. Diva Daims and Janet have said that

the conventional heroine is severely limited in her activity and relations to other people. Her relations to the men in the novel are usually confined to the roles of mother, sister, daughter, nurse, and assistant. . . Her principal functions once she has won the hero's affection are to reform, inspire, serve, and marry him, and to sacrifice all to his home and children. (viii)

In several instances, Maud's utterances and actions suggest a young woman for whom the conventional ideology of marriage is a tantalizing, self-indulgent fantasy. The first is in a conversation with Paul. Earlier on Maud had confessed to an almost infatuation, even adulation.

But as Maud would soon realize, the hard way, the yearning for self-fulfillment in conventional love and marriage is delusory matched only by the vacuity of its dreamscape. It is at best a cluttered happiness. The impulse to surrender to male love sanctioned by society may be genuine, but unfortunately for a young woman all too powerless to actualize her dreams. It leads ultimately to emotional exhaustion, to disillusionment, to despair, and female isolation. Toward the end of the second stage, Maud has begun to interrogate traditional agnate ideology as it relates to gender: female chasteness, goodnaturedness; in fact, the whole gamut of the old paradigm of personal and social fulfillment as promoted by society's socialization process, and for the first time, Maud begins to contemplate the possibility of replacing the that old ideology with a new emerging, radical womanist instinct, womanist order.

Maud enters her third and final phase of growth with a grim realization that life for a woman is not a bed of roses, that "alternatives are severely limited to feminine options: the woman must choose between her inner life of romance and the outer life of reality. Either alternative leaves her passive" (Rosowski 54). The truth, continues Rosowski, is that life requires an awareness much sturdier than passive daydreaming and phantasmagoria could possibly afford. The critical question then for Maud is what to lean on for critical support. The answer to this question would gain for her a measure of freedom from the "ridiculousness of men" (179), as well as a measure of aware-ness of herself as a human being with individualizing interests, talents, and capacities. But the reward of her apprenticeship to life is having children, and more children, a kind of perverse increase-and-multiply male-socialized ethic. This melancholy fact compels some resignation, even as it prompts a rejoicing of a rekindled life. While the end of the novel may usher in a salutary weather, bidding her bon voyage, it, however, leaves only a flickering suspicion that the best in calm or storm may yet to come. It remains a bon voyage that offers no real option for meaningful growth except to expect another baby. But alone in the world with her baby, Maud begins to look at the world with mature eyes. Her determination to have another baby is tempered by a more mature vision of the complexity of life which hitherto has been gabbled up in the naive surrender to romantic and social vainglories.

Gwendolyn Brooks's *Maud Martha* is an African American woman's testament on the position of black women in modern, male-dominated, racist society prior to the concrete asseverations of the feminist discourse. In this sense, Brooks joins her predecessors such as Sojourner Truth, the Brontes—Charlotte, Emily and Anne—George Eliot (Mary Ann Evans), Jane Austen, and Willa Cather, and their latter-day successors—Alice Walker, Gloria Naylor, Toni Morrison—in search of authentic female identity. Some of these women writers have sought to destabilize the old paradigm of gender relations; some have merely interrogated traditional society's long-held views about women to match the deeper understanding they believed they possessed, and yet others have looked for new causes with which to identify themselves or new responsibilities outside the narrow or circumscribed life of the past, responsilities that would call forth new powers to meet new needs.[7]

Brooks weaves her own artistic vision out of these possibilities, because the very fact of being a Black woman in America in the 50's demands a vision much more complex. The complexity of the vision is born out of a wedding of sacrifice and agonality and points toward freedom and wholeness. And, because *Maud Martha* is potentially an autobiographical fictional text, it may be read, as Stephen Shapiro suggests about every autobiography, an assertion of the ego's transcendence of circumstance (qtd in Daims). It is in short Brooks's search for female self-authentication, without the kind of "great awakening" we might confer on Kate Chopin's heroine, Edna Pointelier or Alice Walker's Celie. But even if Brooks's Maud has specifically fallen short of this "great awakening," it is because at the time the novel was written, few real choices existed for women, and even much fewer for black women. In both the woman question and the race problem, suggest Ann Julia Cooper, the colored woman "is yet unknown or an unacknowledged factor or both" (133). Even those limited choices left to her were not as clear as one might think. For Alice Walker, only in music have the black women been permitted a measure of artistic freedom.[8] For Mary Helen Washington, "the knowledge of one's self as a black woman was fragmented by a society that could not imagine her" (272).

For Brooks's heroine, Maud Martha Brown, the search for female subjectivity, even without any great awakening, implies an enactment of what Lorraine Hansberry has referred to as "the comedy of concern,"[9] a just balance between the comic and the tragic elements of life, and between the inner life of imaginative release and phantasma and the opposing tyranny of social restrictions, of arbitrary measurements, the "passive embodiment of a social role" (Rosowski 48). According to Patricia Meyer Spacks, "the search for (female) form involves a struggle for the appropriate—both true and emotionally acceptable—image of transcendence, involving a just balance between fact (embodving circumstance) and interpretation through which the writer triumphs over circumstance" (125).

For Gwendolvn Brooks. it implies an attempt to question the old ways of thinking about women within the not-too-fully realized articulate discourse of feminist tradition, and to transcend them through a conscious release of the power of her quasi womanist sensibilities.

9

Redemptive Fantasy and Allegory of the Endtime

From Joachim of Fiore's Trinitarian *evangelium aeternum* to Michaelangelo's *The Last Judgment*, from Plato to Thomas More and then to the science fiction; from Rudyard Kipling to H. G. Wells; from the origins of social theory to militant feminism; from the American revolution to the Bolshevik uprising; from the Hegelian triadism to Marxian demiurge; from Maoism to Castroism; from African-Uhuru nationalism to Ahiara declaration; from Marcus Garvey to Walter Rodney (Rastafarian movement); from the Stoics' pantheistic cosmology to Seneca's *dies irae*; from Epicurean hedonism to the desacralized eschatology of Lucretius; from Rousseau's radical innocence to Jeremy Bentham's moral arithmetic, from Leibniz's monadian ethos and preestablished harmony to C.G. Jung's *principium individuationis*, from Oswald Spengler's cyclogenic historicism to the Orwellian Big Brotherism, from the moral idealism of Dante to the *mens hebes adverum per materialia surgit* (the dull mind rises to the truth by way of material things) of Suger of Saint-Denis, and from the Christian millennium to Mircea Eliade's myth of eternal return, one of the traditions of the millennial narrative employs elements of heroic fantasy to imagine possible futures. This heroic fantasy is expressed in the millenarian myth which, extrapolating from present milieu and knowledge, objectifies the hopes and fears of its time, creating infinite models of social possibility by which it evaluates the present. These models of social possibility express their visionary rhetoric through an allegorical frame termed the "chiliastic vision" which is, at bottom, a vision of the grand conception of the final human destiny as shared by people bound together by a common yet profound experience.

The chiliastic vision has its narrow beginnings in Christian millenarianism which, according to Norman Cohn, "referred to the belief held by some Christians on the authority of the Book of Revelation (xx, 4-6), that after his Second coming, Christ would establish a messianic kingdom on earth and would reign over it for a thousand years before the Last Judgement" (15).

Conceptually, it belongs to that part of literature, terminal literature, which W. Warren Wagar designates as "a creative act of secular imagination" (5), and which for the most part, maintains Wagar, tends to be upbeat and future-oriented, rather than depressive and retrospective. As a mythical expression, the vision, by and large, is a subjective ingrowth of the primordial mythos of transformation, viewing the end as an opportunity for passage to a radically new world, most often to a better one. It is one of those traditional mythologems, those ancient myths of the glorious paradisiac future, that still actuate modern man not only in his speculations about a remote better end of life days, but also in his reveries or daydreams about worlds that lie in the future in a developmental as well as in a purely temporal sense. These worlds are then placed within our grasp by the creative fantasy of writers. For mythographers like Raphael Patai, the chiliastic image allows us a glimpse of the future, the only kind of future many of us can still believe in in this world of technical and social breakdowns, war and waste, a future in which problems still exist but are always met with determination and tremendous will, "a world that is at once overwhelmingly attractively and ultimately reassuring, a universe in which men have actually become like gods (84–85).

As Patai makes clear, and as revealed in the novels under discussion, the chiliastic image is very much an inextricable part of the substratum of primordial fantasy, particularly, heroic or apocalyptic fantasy.[1] According to Herbert Marcuse, "phantasy links the deepest layers of the unconscious with the highest products of consciousness, the dream with the reality; it protects the archetypes of the genus, the perpetual but repressed ideas of the collective and individual memory, the tabooed images of freedom" (140–41). The critical utility of phantasy and the chiliastic image lies in its refusal to accept as final limitations imposed upon freedom and happiness by the reality principle, in its refusal to forget what can be (149). The concepts of freedom and happiness are themselves the essential ingredients of the chiliastic fantasy, both involved in the millenarian struggle for a redemptive society. David Elton Trueblood identifies one of two motives present in any struggle for a redemptive society: the motive of liberation (89—91). Vittorio Lanternari writes that millenarianism, politically speaking, is the "religion of the oppressed, the striving of subject peoples to become, emancipated" (vi). Its strident phraseology, according to Kenelm Burridge, always envisages a new set of rules, new kinds of moral obligation, in short, a new earth in which heaven is more brightly mirrored (165).

The vision of a new earth, new heaven, provides an expanded sociopolitical context for one of two forms of literature broadly identified by Andre Rousseaux and discussed by Charles Moeller. In *Man and Salvation in Literature*, Moeller explains Rousseaux's dichotomy between the literature of happiness and the literature of salvation. The literature of happiness tries to show man how he can create a happier life for himself. Its intention is to make man more human, supposing that man is already human; and thus intends to embellish and improve his life (3—4). On the other hand, continues Moeller, the literature of salvation, the creative by-product of apocalyptic imagination, takes its starting point from an awareness of a situation that human life has come to a stage that is subhuman. It is a threatening and dangerous situation fraught with dread and wretchedness. Declares Moeller: "The literature of salvation is marked by the anguish of not being able to live a [normal] human life" (6); it is also characterized by "the human condition under the sign of menace and death" (9), with feverish anticipation of what Frank Kermode describes as "a new historical dispensation" (12).

Each of the six novels to be discussed here—Soyinka's *Season of Anomy*, Baraka's *The System of Dante's Hell*, Ekwensi's *Survive the Peace*, Reid's *New Day*, Sembene's *God's Bits of Wood*, and Lamming's *In the Castle of My Skin* is an example of the literature of salvation and redemptive fantasy; each is preoccupied with the objective and subjective aspects of secular salvation identified by Moeller as justice, life, and love. And each projects an optimism and a principle of hope, in the words of Frances Carey, "promising renewal. . . [and a]. . . fulfillment of a redemptive plan for history" (270). We begin with Soyinka's *Season of Anomy*.

In *Season of Anomy*, we discover aspects of fantasy in literary myths woven very neatly into the fiber of a millennial text. Soyinka uses the sub-genre of a lost/civilization of Aiyetomo, to provide special atavistic access to a period of the past through the activities and rituals of contemporary Aiyero. In other words, the fragments of prevenient Aiyetomo cultural civilization provide Soyinka with a variety of artistic possibilities in his attempt to create a distinct millennial world. I am not suggesting that *Season of Anomy* is an archetypal lost civilization novel per se in the same way as, for instance, Alan Quatermain's *King Solomon's Mines*, or John Beynon Harris' *The Secret People*. Rather what I am suggesting is that through a conflation of historical romance and some elemental trappings of lost civilization sub-genre, Soyinka reconstructs a social ambience that pacifies our thirst not only for an atavistic past, but of a millennial proleptic era.

Beyond the trappings of the lost civilization sub-genre, there is a suggestion that in *Season of Anomy* Soyinka heeds Mircea Eliade's injunction to abandon 'the terror of history' "and return to a more or less archaic stratum of belief in supra-temporal 'archetypes,'" which are quasi platonic static models of cultural affirmation represented in ancient myths and religions. Eliade would replace today's world of "future shock with a timeless and mythic world of the future which would be oriented only to the externally regenerative past suffused with paradisal or escha-tological myths of the [pristine] golden age. . ." (*The Myth of the Eternal Return* 88). On a broader conceptual scale, the novel is an ingenious conflation of Yoruba mythopoetic thought and Judeo-Christian eschatology, although the former is clearly dominant with the latter playing a somewhat complementary, borrowed role. Soyinka appears to have no problem conflating the two because like Ernst Cassirer, the two paradigms—cyclical (Yoruba/mythopoeic) and linear (Judeo—Christian)— cohere in finding the world meaningful and the end of the present order of things inevitable.

As a mythopoetic writer, Soyinka creates his millennial text by distending his mythopoeic mind to thoughts of decline, winter, calamity and the end. Aiyero as traditional culture, like all traditional cultures, has its own eschatology. It is an eschatology that is grounded in pantheistic cyclical vision or what Eliade calls the myth of the eternal return. It has a fundamental optimism, and according to Eliade, "this optimism can be reduced to a consciousness of the normality of the cyclical catastrophe, the certainty that it has a meaning and, above all, that it is never final" (*The Future of Eternity* 35). The apocalyptic vision is thus expressed in the mythopoetic formulation of the novel, a function of the movement of history identified by Fung Yu—lan as "progressive degeneration" (159). It is a correlative of the eschatology of the myth of eternal return which in turn expresses not only Soyinka's belief in the wisdom and superior vitality of creative antiquity, but also the fact that the golden age of man lies largely in the past and only peripherally in the future. Whatever redemptive hope there may be for the future of Soyinka's Ilosa rests in the possibility that humanity would have to return to Aiyero-type ancient virtues and traditional rites to have any real chance of surviving. The greatest threat to the Aiyero ideal is the Cartel—Junta hydra conglomerate which in its policies has created such a nihilism and cavernous metaphysical void that has alarmed redemptive futurists like Ofeyi and the head of the Aiyero commune, Pa Ahime.

Soyinkas's Aiyero is the cultural storehouse of man; without it man's great sense of cultural continuum and wholeness remains pathetically hollow. Besides it does contain something infinitely practical and utilitarian for its citizens at a future time and place. The following assertion by Pa Ahime, the custodian of the Aiyero legacy, summarizes succinctly the very quintessence of Aiyero. This is in response to the pointed question by Ofeyi, the novel's monomythical hero.

The vision Soyinka paints of Aiyero is the vision of a pastoral eden, grounded in the ideal of human freedom and the right of political and royal dissent. Like H.G. Wells's Time Traveller, Soyinka presents Aiyero as a kind of prelapsarian world now on the verge of being defiled by the leviathanic forces of the Cocoa Cartel with their babylonian mentality. Aiyero is in many respects a place of wounded innocence where traditional agronomy which fosters a unique sense of sympathetic relatedness is still nurtured, this in spite of the destructive inroads of modern technology and mechanization. Eric S. Rabkin and others have said that "often the utopian world is a pastoral one by virtue of the exclusion of technology" (3). The elegant simplicity of Aiyero is summed up rather neatly and laconically by Pa Ahime as he officially welcomes Ofeyi and his amorous partner, Iriyise: "We are simple people in Aiyero" (19). This simplicity is evident even in their most "complex" traditional ritual ceremonies, some of them rituals of the end of Aiyetomo history and the beginning of Aiyero history. There is a kind of pastoral equanimity associated with the Aiyero commune, a commune which reminds us of Gerrard Wistanley's cooperative Digger's Movement of the mid-17th century, Denis Diderot's glorified Tahiti of the late eighteenth century, and the Brook Farm project of the nineteenth century. The following passage describes Aiyero's pastoral climate and the fit of frenzy which grips it as it witnesses the ravages wrought on the land by the Cocoa Cartel.

Part of the appeal of the Aiyero commune is atavistic "a reversion to a vision of an earlier humankind in closer and happier relation to necessity and nature and self" (4). It is Soyinka's attempt to demonstrate the communal basis of pastoral millennium, to re-establish the harmonious and healthy community of an imagined golden age. This vision is given sublime poignancy in the funeral rites and ceremonies marking the death of the Custodian of the Grain, the founding patriarch of Aiyero (see *Season of Anomy*, especially pp.7-18). Behind the intense solemnity of the ceremonies is the mythogenic role of ritual in recapturing the spirit and power of an arcane, mythic past, in reliving events which occurred *in illo tempore* before the world began its slow process of eco depletion and dissolution under the corrupt and rapacious regime of the Cocoa Cartel, aided and abetted by the military junta. On a more personal level, the ritual celebration allows Ofeyi to escape from *le temps vecu* to the *temps mythique paradisique* of childhood, to merge with, in his own words, "The life of the community. The parallel life of a child from seed. . ." (20).

The cosmogonic myth of Aiyero is rich in psychological meaning as well. It parallels the Greek myth of the golden age, and Plato's original man. The funeral rites alluded to earlier and the euphoria felt by Iriyise in tune with the Aiyero earth dramatize man's original oneness with nature and deity, and for Iriyise especially, a tremendous nostalgia for the original unconscious state. In that state one is freed from all the metaphysical void, the *danse macabre* of nihilism, and the modern sensation of the abyss. Iriyise's desire to stay on in Aiyero, and the unique sense of inner peace she feels about her while there, represents a peculiar kind of eutopic nostalgia and shows how each one of us wishes to return to that primordial wholeness out of which we were born. For her this is healing.

Soyinka is not only interested in utopia but in dystopia as well, here partly embodied by the Cartel and partly by the military junta. Where the Aiyero ideal is distinctly pastoral and edenic, the Cartel's and its cohorts, the military junta, anti-pastoral and hellish. Unlike Aiyero, the Cartel confronts nature only in the form of the rapacious bloodhound that sucks everything in its way. The juxtaposition of utopian Aiyero and dystopian Cartel makes *Season of Anomy* a twin work—a work of hope, the hope of radical pastoral innocence and a work of grim foreboding, the foreboding that sinister forces of systematic destruction have been let loose. In this dialectic, the author's genuine effort to reestablish human contact, which is the Aiyero ideal, is graphically visualized as a reversion to childhood, and the Aiyero commune serves as the first metaphysical step in the renaming of the contents of the phenomenal universe. The novel closes on an optimistic note—"in the forests, life began to stir" (320)— a longing for an atavistic return to Eden or aboriginal home.

In another sense, Soyinka's utopian conception parallels Thomas More's vision in his classic treatise, *Utopia*. Like More, Soyinka is disturbed by a society of heavy-handed tax system where, as More has stated, "rich men buy all to engross and forestall" (*Utopia* 23, 27, 28). In Soyinka's Ilosa, it is money that gives both form and substance to vanity and vice or what More has called "riotous superfluity" (*Utopia* 66). At the beginning of *Season of Anomy*, there is the setting forth of the actual injustices of contemporary revenue laws and the suggestion that the Aiyero commune might provide for a more equitable distribution system

Like an avid practictioner of political allegory, Soyinka's cryptic attack on the lopsidedness and inherent inequities of the capitalist system represented by the Cocoa Cartel parallels not only More's critique of a money economy and acquisitive mercantilism, but also Karl Marx's critique of the formation of capitalism. It may be suggested that Aiyero is Soyinka's utopian panacea to the monstrosity posed by unchecked private property and money economy. In this context lies Soyinka's social humanism, and we are invited early to share in its power and integrity. That is why the novelist places Aiyero on a higher scale of values and invests her with a potency; that out of the coarse and vulgar Cartel's rapacity will arise a new respect for man's dignity. It is a dignity rooted in and deriving its just strength from the primal memories of a hallowed communalism, a vision of the immemorial past when property was held in common and there was concord, simplicity and pastoral serenity. And Soyinka invokes these time-hallowed memories to counteract the schism, the corruption and deathliness of his day, and thus is able to construe his pastoral eden as a real existent.

Finally, a significant part of the millennial and terminal vision of *Season of Anomy* lies in its depiction of the scenario of death and decay. In this sense, the novel can be regarded as a veritable danse macabre. Wagar maintains that nothing is more universal in terminal fictions than death. "Since the certainty," writes Wagar, "of an ultimate personal endtime is also the most overwhelming datum of the human condition, it is safe to guess that every public endtime in fiction serves its readers to some degree as a metaphor and reminder of their own mortality" (70). For Soyinka, the vision of the endtime is the vision of distinctions of sorts, the sharp distinctions between edenic pastoralism represented by Aiyero, and infernal cosmopolitanism and the dystopian world of the Cartel and the military junta, between life-affirming principles as represented by the former and the death-dealing forces embodied in the latter. The following passage shows not only a ghoulish image of unrelenting deathness, but also a deepening crisis of man's fall from the pastoral grace of eden (not a *felix culpa*, however) which corresponds roughly to an endtime in Soyinkan sense:

... Twenty miles from Irelu a woman was dragged from her bed, sliced open at the belly. She was not even dead when they left her guts spilling in a messy afterbirth between her thighs. A tax assessor, she had beggared many ruthlessly in slavish obedience to the Cartel.

. . . .

The assailants stuffed her mouth with a roll of the; court orders she had served on them and set the grotesque cigar alight.

. . . .

A family of twenty, three generations in all wiped out in a noon of vengeance. An agent on the run from mob rage had fired wildly into his pursuers felling two, fled and barricaded himself in his own house. He was still scrabbling for more cartridges when they came upon him, a huge wave borne solely on pain and rage. (109-110)

This is a gory picture of political and ethnic violence directed against the Aiyero people, presented first as a kind of pharmakoid act of savagery, and seen as a perverse act of motiveless malignity. As in Thomas Hood's poem, "The Last Man," or better still as in Jewish holocaust fiction, men, under the inciteful banner, first of religious zealotry, and second of political tribal instigation by the Cartel and the Junta, have become a grisly pack of psychopaths and murderers. Like Edward Bryant in "Among the Dead," Soyinka carries his terminal vision to its ultimate grotesquerie. For example, Soyinka's description of the ghoulish scene near the Labbe bridge has all the eerie reverberations of an actively willed evil and motiveless malignity. [see p. 193]

Apart from human exhaustion, nature too is exhausted. The Cartel's operation also bears witness to the exhaustion of nature's energy. Aside from the Cartel's destruction of the virgin forests of Aiyero, there is also the wasted emanation that is the Cross River topography. With dwindling trees, scrawny leaves, scorched sky, 'gorges whose precarious sides sheered into the netherworld,' what remains is nothing but a "maisma which hung over [and seemed] to seep from a source of hidden putrefaction" (174).

But seen from an intensely eschatological perspective, the destructive energy of the Cartel as well as the seemingly interminable process of unrelenting natural degeneration stands as the mythic killing frost that comes in winter, providing a double band metaphor for a morally and physically exhausted earth as well as a gateway to a new life. As in Samuel Beckett's *Endgame*, what predominates in *Season of Anomy* is a crippling feeling that everything is dead; nature no longer exists or is in abeyance, seeds will probably never sprout again; the sky has turned gray; the environment stinks of makeshift morgues. How-ever, unlike the eschatological vision in Eugene Ionesco's absurdist play, *Le pieton de L'air*, where, beyond the fiery curtain which consumes saints as well as sinners, there is no heaven, no survival, in Soyinka's *Season of Anomy*, on the other hand, the terminal paradigm of the myth of eternal return means that the wasted emanation in nature and the wanton destruction of human life represent the burning away of the accummulated debris of the ages, one that may be necessary for the world to undergo rebirth. According to Wagar, "in short, the end in traditional cultures is the gateway to new life" (35). Any wonder then why Soyinka ends his millennial tale with intimations of rekindled life: "Temoko was sealed against the world till dawn. The street emptied at last as the walls and borders shed their last hidden fruit. In the forests, life began to stir" (320).

In Baraka's *The System of Dante's Hell*, the terminal metaphor is presented against the skewed background of contemporary decadence and cultural despair (i.e. disenchantment) brought about by antiblack racism and other American ills. In fact, the pervasive sense of this decadence and disenchantment forms a serious and meaningful part of the novel's eschatological and apocalyptic rhetoric. Wagar has said that "of all the symptoms of disenchantment in our culture, visions of the end are the bluntest and the most. powerful" (7). The black man, Roi, is disenchanted about the present state of affairs, an unsettling state of affairs in which traditional values appear to have tumbled down, and in their place has emerged a kind of existentialist reductionist world, which is at best a surreal metaphor for quick movement and death. The first thirty-four pages of the novel are rife with images of agonizing despair and age-long lament. In "Seven: The Destruction of America" (35-36), these images cluster into a frightening penumbra of altered conscious-ness, the consciousness of a world gone desolate and mad. The section, which parallels Circle Seven in Dante's *Inferno*, contains a high dose of apocalypticism. It contains a insistent suggestion of the final destruction of the unrighteous and violent men in a purging conflagration engulfing America, and the rise of the lowly just (dispossessed Indians and enslaved Black people) to a purified world of social justice, cultural illumination, knowledge-synthesis and relative social bliss, a kind of Black eden.

The protagonist, Roi, is our sole witness of this endtime, a quasi heroic and salvational role given expression in a trenchantly cynical response to a world that may not endure its present form. He becomes a nay-sayer: "My substance dark and talked of now odd times when everybody's. . . dressed up. Forgive me"! (34). . . "Tell your lies some other time" (32).—and his nay-saying helps prepare the way of the black prodigal in apparent quest for a better world in a melioristic and cultural sense. The terminal vision is finely blended into the millenial vision, the latter beginning with a bland sense of radical innocence exacerbated by a kind of erotic intemperance. Baraka weaves this vision into the broad theory of *felix culpa*, the happy fortunate fall of man. Roi, like the old Adam, commits the act of primal disobedience by tasting the forbidden fruit of sex, thus signing an unwritten pact with Mephistopheles (the Devil himself):

Big Apple (myth says) knocked down a horse, split open a basketball player's skull.

For him, let us create a new world. Of sex and cataclysm.

The rest, let them languish on their Sundays. Let them use shadows to sleep. (50-51)

The straddling of biblical allegory with secular defiance in the preceding passage skillfully dramatizes Roi's sexual awakening and the generational strife it betrays. As a writer of utopian apologue, Baraka knows pretty well that sexuality of a perverse kind can be a destabilizing phenomenon. In pointing up a future for a black prodigal, Roi, fallen from the unfulfilled promises of the Judeo-Christian eden, looking for that distinctly black eden, Baraka knows that he must deal with the power of sex; and he uses the first half of the novel to remind us of the Christian paradise that perverted sex once cost us, and then the second half to anticipate the Black paradise that creative sex promises us. Roi as new Adam is like the original Adam, guilty of the sin of defiance. Roi's Peaches, however, is neither the temperate Eve nor the holy Beatrice of Dante, but rather the eternal feminine of Goethe beckoning him to her bossom so that she can regenerate his darkened world with the seed of her generous flesh.

What is being suggested here is that the terminal-millenial vision in *The System of Dante's Hell* is depicted in Freudian and Jungian terms. The millennial story can be read as the conquest of thanatos (embodied in Roi, the new Adam) by Eros (embodied in Peaches, the eternal feminine), and of father-hatred (embodied in Western paternal literary figures like Eliot, Dante, later to be abandoned by Roi) by mother-love (black heritage embodied in Peaches), with Roi finding peace by descent into the deepest caverns of the maternal unconscious. Roi graphically describes the whole millennial and redemptive process of illumination in starkly voyeuristic terms:

She loved me, she said. Or liked me a lot. She wanted me to stay, with her. We could live together and she would show me how to fuck. How to do it good. And we could start as soon as she took a pee.

. . . .

Oh, we can have some good times baby. . . She put the book down and scratched the inside of her thighs, then under one arm. Her hair was standing up and she went to a round mirror over the sink and brushed it. And turned around and shook her big hips at me, then pumped the air to suggest our mission. She came back and we talked about our lives: then she pushed back the sheets, helped me undress again, got me hard and pulled me into her. I came too quick and she had to twist her hips a few minutes longer to come herself. "Uhauh, good even on a sof; But I still got to teach you." (146)

All the central impulses of Eros, Roi's hedonistic wish for life and love, come into vital play in the typical eschatological scenario such as this, propelling him and Peaches and the other nocturnal visitors to the Bottom and the Cotton Club through the endtime struggle for a Black eden. Even though initially thanatos (death by perverted sex), with its demonic lust for conquest and self-destruction, gets the better part of Roi, Baraka generally takes pains to show that his own sympathies as well as Roi's nonetheless lie with Eros.

The very scene of carnal encounters between Roi and Peaches is a psychological and allegorical accompaniment of the millennial imperative in the novel. It is an articulation or replication of those first man's sexual beginnings when there was minimal awareness of ethical constraints. The implication is that before the new Roi can be realized, a period of being rather less than human has to be endured. The wishful prelude to entering upon a new eden, the black eden, is a millenial condition of beingness in which all artificial taboos and moral proscriptions are cast off, unconscious primal desires sanctified. Roi and Peaches are black free-movers, free spirits, in that golden age when no rules were necessary. For Baraka such a millennial state must be realized by giving free reign to man's creative sexual impulse. Once thanatos is transformed alchemically by Eros, a black form of millennium is consummated, one in which there is a profound expression of earthy joy, boundless optimism and ethnic contentment. The following passage neatly exemplifies Roi's personal actualization of that millennium: "Into that sun. The day was bright and people walked by me smiling. And waved "hey" (a greeting) and they all knew I was Peaches' man" (149).

In Cyprian Ekwensi's *Survive the Peace*, we have a conflation of eschatological and millennial paradigms. The novel, without question, is an example of the literature of secular eschatology. As in traditional Jewish and Christian apocalyptics, the end in *Survive the Peace* is also the beginning. When I say that the novel is eschatological, I mean that it belongs partly to the science of last things. According to Wagar, "eschatology seeks and analyzes the question of what will happen at the end—the end of time, the end of man, the end of civilization" (6). For the author Ekwensi, the end of the Biafran nationalist gamble is something supremely crucial for those who survive the throes of its failed revolutionary secessionist dynamics. The seething end of the conflict becomes paradoxically the center, the axis, the focal point of the novel's central action.

The novel opens with a frenzied group of reporters in a newsroom who, between clatters of war-bedevilled typewriters and light-hearted jokes, nick answers to what might possibly happen when the Nigeria—Biafra war does finally come to an end. Let's look at the following bantering exchange:

'When this war will end, it will be like the abomination of desolation which was spoken of by Daniel the prophet standing in the Holy Places, he that heareth let him understand. . .'

That remark had made them break out into a nervous laugh, easing the tension.

'And he that is on the rooftops,' laughed another, 'let him not come down to take anything out of his house—'

'And woe to them that are with child, and give suck in those days—'

'And pray that your flight be not in winter—'

'There's always winter in Biafra'—and the laughter redoubled. Back and forth, to the rhythm of clattering typewriters went to nervous quotes, until James Odugo mentally withdrew into the private world of chain—cigarette smoke. That had been one of those days that stuck in his memory. $(3)^2$

Beyond the uneasy jocularity of the exchange, beyond its parodic nature, the reference to Prophet Daniel of the Old Testament has very serious apocalyptic implications for those trapped in the throes of that war. The Book of Daniel, one of several Biblical origins of the apocalyptic tradition, and also one of only two apocalypses in Christianity admitted into the canon (the other being the Book of Revelation by St. John, the Divine) foretold of a great tribulation that the Jews would endure in the hands of their oppressors and of how at the end the God of the Jews would avenge the injustices of His people and would eventually free them from the tyranny of Babylonian rule. For characters like James Odugo, Senior Reporter, *News*, Daniel's prophecy, however much they try to steel themselves with a jocular parody of its apocalyptic message, seriously hope that the endtime of this war would usher in a period of exceptional celebration. But for them also the expected end of the civil war raises serious fundamental questions of survival, foremost of which is economic and biological survival. He finds to his chagrin that the cost of living, which soared in the thick of the war, is now seemingly unsurvivable. As the narrator relates this grim statistic, he vividly paints one of the most eschatological scenes in the novel:

Nothing could be further from Odugo's mind than the end of the war that January afternoon in 1970 as he crossed the market square at Umunevo, on his way to the newsroom. He suddenly found himself standing under a tree surrounded by chattering women waving chickens at him and he thought, 'let me price one of these. . . see if Odugo can still afford to buy one chicken. (5)

The preceding passage appears to suggest that, as an eschatological novel, *Survive the Peace* not only helps the readers cope with fear of good times lost, of death and separation, brought on by the war, but also grants individuals like James Odugo a unique opportunity to face the stiff problems of personal and collective survival brought on by a certain sense of powerlessness in the face of a war-shattered economy. Odugo is like the representative last man or one of a handful of last men of eschatological fiction, one driven on by an indefatigable spirit and an unconquerable will.

In *Survive the Peace*, Ekwensi draws an acute relationship between the Biafran melee and the foreknown millennium of postdisaster peace. Michael Barkun has contended that "those who regard the millennium as imminent expect disasters to pave the way" (1). A vivid scenario is Umunevo, where Odugo, pondering seriously the grave consequences of the Biafran forlorn adventure, runs into a cross-section of the Biafran population, among them runaway soldiers gaunt with popped-out eyes (9). Among the general population there is a nervous, perhaps prayerful anticipation that good times are ahead and would replace the evil times of mass destruction; that in fact, these destructive times may indeed have acted as a cleansing rite so that life can be regenerated, both morally and physically. In this apparent cleansing act, there seem to be two polarities and extremes; on one extreme is disaster, on the other millennium; on one is upheaval and perdition, on the other promise. Between these dizzying extremes is a kind of what Barkun describes as "nervous anticipation." The belief in the inevitability of the collapse of Biafra and in the imminence of a post-war peace has a psychodynamic potency that most members of the public simply could not resist.

In a significant sense, therefore, *Survive the Peace* is a millennial and apocalyptic text because the events after the anticipated end—the scuttling into hiding until the disaster syndrome abates, the reuniting of long, separated families, the raw courage to pick up the pieces and resume normal life speculates what would happen at the end of the war. It speculates about extreme alternatives—death and chaos, renewal and salvational order, the latter seeming more probable than the former. In this connection, Odugo's surmise as to how he might cope with the end of the war is a surmise that blends elements of nostalgia, romantic agony and: proleptic frolic.

Odugo's musings about the end of the war are significant in another sense. They assert the eschatology of what Martha Wolfenstein has called the "post-disaster utopia" (189), a period of exceptional social harmony immediately subsequent to any kind of catastrophic happening, remembered with nostalgia by the participants in later years. For Odugo, the attractiveness of the post-disaster utopian scenario finds its trenchant expression in the confrontation with the grim statistics of death. It enables him to imagine himself heroically evading death, like the very close call when Umunevo comes under a vicious barrage of enemy mortar and aerial offensive. It does also, almost quite literally, offer Odugo the unique opportunity to relive anxieties of separation from loved ones, and the therapeutic healing that accompanies the formation of new ties and friendships and the restoration of old bonds and acquaintances. In fact, the formation of new ties and the restoration of old ones represent the main pivot of postdisaster utopia as presented in the novel.

The readers' attention is soon markedly drawn to Odugo's anxiety as he tries relentlessly to relocate his family trapped behind the battle lines in the remote village of Ifitenu; his avidity to forge new ties, as, for instance, between him and Vic, on the one hand, and between him and Gladys Nwibe, on the other; and finally his sense of elation at reuniting with Pa Ukoha's family at Obodonta. In each critical instance, *Survive the Peace* proves a veritable terminal novel, par excellence, in its start depiction of "scenes of food-getting and feasting, erotic gratification, the formation of warm and loving relationship among survivors, new simplicities and rough comforts that compare favorably indeed with the humdrum, or the decadence of pre-disaster society" (Wagar 1). For Odugo, surviving the peace is, in an eschatological and apocalyptic sense, analogous to a fondly remembered childhood or to the ideal home, family and social circles that he and others, beyond the identity crisis, dream of either forming or restoring.

Each of the preceding novels is a mini-drama of the myth of eternal return. Each is concerned with conscious and unconscious mental processes aimed at returning to an earlier time when man was happy and at peace with himself, with his milieu, with God and nature. Except, perhaps, for *Survive the Peace* in some respects, there is a virtual absence of sustained revolutionary imperative as seen in such novels as V. S. Reid's *New Day*, Ousmane Sembene's *God's Bits of Wood*, and George Lamming's *In the Castle of My Skin*, where there is an intimation of a new ideal social order that would emerge out of the ruins of the old colonial suzerainty primarily through the revolutionary mythos of the Marxian demiurge (Wagar 71). In these three latter novels, apocalypse and eschatology unite in the seething cauldron of dialectical materialism,

for Marx reveals what was to happen in the end of days: the unification of the workers of the world, the global conflict between the bourgeois and working classes (echoes of the pre-messianic war of Gog and Magog), and the ultimate taking over of the means of production, including, in the first place, the ownership and control of the industrial plant, by the working class. (Patai 96–97)

As apocalyptic texts, the three novels are bound together by a supreme sense of history, played out in terms of three aspects of millennialism discussed by Theodore Olson in *Millennialism, Utopianism, and Progress*: the interpretation of history as one story consisting of significant events, the interpretation of history as drama, and the drama as propelled by conflict among contending forces in a dialectical fashion

(15).[3] In the specific context of the three novels, the drama is the conflict between the imposition of western colonial power and the determined struggles of the oppressed natives of Jamaica, Senegal and Barbados to be free. The struggles are presented as millenarian and apocalyptic processses, where hope is seen as what Henri Desroche identifies variously as "waking dream. . . collective ideation. . . exuberant expectation."[4] In order words, in *New Day*, *God's Bits of Wood*, and in *In the Castle of My Skin*, the consciousness of history as millennial and materially dialectical process is manifested in the idealized futuristic imagery of collective violence in a brave people willing to defy the present, to sacrifice everything in pursuit of the "always elusive, but eternally attractive, enticing, and inspiring mythos of the future" (Patai 93).

The parallels between and among these novels suggest a manifestation of the redemptive phantasy. For instance, the rebellion of the indigenous peoples of Jamaica, Senegal, and Barbados against the colonial establishment represents a contemporary acting out of the depths of resentment mankind has always felt against what they feel are the iniquities of the social order in which they live. The young radicals and putative New Leftists like Deacon Bogle in *New Day*, Mr. Slime and Mr. Trumper in *In the Castle of My Skin*, and Diaw Falla, Oumar Faye and Tiemoko in *God's Bits of Woods* are the latter-day heirs of a long line of dreamers about a utopian future whose main features are fashioned after that old myth of the paradise.

Although *New Day*, *In the Castle of My Skin* and *God's Bits of Wood* are linked by a common catalysis of revolutionary mythos; although in all three novels, in their discussion of the radical evolution of an ideal, free and egalitarian society, use terms and concepts which are vague and generalized, a use which, of course, adds to the attractiveness of the revolutionary idealism in the eyes of those who are dissatisfied with the present state of affairs in colonial society, some distinction still exists between *New Day* on the one hand, and *In the Castle of My Skin* and *God's Bits of Wood* on the other. It is the kind of distinction that would normally be made between the biblical/animistic myth of the future and the mythos of the science fiction. *New Day* belongs to the former; while *In the Castle of My Skin* and *God's Bits of Wood* belong to the latter. Although in all three novels, we have revolutionary prophetae imbued with varying prophetic and soteriological roles, prophetae who must employ their revolutionary rhetoric to reassure their followers about their future, but who must do so by depicting the dangers and horrors that lie ahead as a way of projecting and concretizing the phobia of the present lodged in every citizen's heart, in *New Day*, however, the revolutionary mythos takes on an added spiritual dimension.

The revolutionary mythos in *New Day* draws its basic inspiration in a large measure from the Judeo-Christian eschatology. Specifically, the pattern of revolutionary myth in the novel is resonant with solemn echoes of the pre-messianic war of Gog and Magog, and subserves the whole Judeo-Christian messianic ideology: the very final battle between Good and Evil which is easily comparable to the apocalyptic battle between Christ and Antichrist, followed by the total victory of the former. In short *New Day* differs from the other two novels in its addition of a religious, or more precisely, Christological component. The use of Deacon Bogle's pulpit at Stoney Gut as a rallying point for the political struggle shows a peculiar kind of eschatological myth, one in which there is a parallel between suffering Jesus and the redeeming role of the just of Morant Bay whose suffering is destined to alter the social condition of the Jamaican masses.

The prophetic role attributed to Deacon Paul Bogle echoes the messianic mission of Christ. In carrying out this role, in preaching "Secession! Total freedom!,"[5] from the perspective of a Christian man, Bogle expresses a recognition of the phenomenology of the God-image in the national Jamaican Self and its ineradicable link with the Judeo Christian eschatological mythos. The implication is that a society that yearns for a change must be transformed not only materially but also spiritually. Thus at the base of the millenarian struggle in *New Day* is a crystallization of the religious function of the self and the question of its rapport with the God-image. This crystallization is enkindled and then re-enkindled in Pastor Humphrey's Church, solemnly honed in the recitals of Bro' Ira D. Sankey's pilgrim hymns:

There are shadows in the valley where our
Tired feet must go
But we hear the peaceful waters as they
Murmur soft and low (35)

. . . .

Sunshine on the hill, there is sunshine
on the hill
There are shadows in the valley, but 'tis
Sunshine on the hill (36)

This crystallization is also echoed in the narrator's prayer between what amounts to as the dark night of the soul and the consummate but paradoxical song of victory of the oppressed people:

And Lord O—how our people are a—sing! They ha' seen the young light o' new day, and like deep-running water is the song that pours from their throats to greet this new day. With steadiness they sing, just like how I know they will go steady with one another when we march on the new road England has shown us. (369)

The pilgrim hymns of Brother Sankey, the consummate doxology of the narrator, the solemnity of Deacon Bogle's politicized homilies, and the importunate entreaties of Pastor Humphrey for divine reparation—all clearly evidence that the millennial struggle for a redeemed, new Jamaican society free from the colonial stranglehold of imperial England holds out not only the hope of secular salvation but also divine benevolence. All suggest a leap of faith beyond the mortal faith in man's own ability, intelligence and ingenuity. They also suggest that in the final analysis, just as the Israelites realized, man's last and ultimate defense must be God's, without whose blessings the Jamaican people could not do it all by themselves alone. Of particular note is the fact that revolutionary participants such as the narrator, Deacon Bogle, Pastor Humphrey, and everyone else at the Stoney Gut congregation, who believe in the metaphysics of divine intervention conduct themselves in accordance with the demands of the Biblical myth of the future, a myth of the future conceived and presented in an age in which man knows himself to be a weak and powerless creature who could survive emotionally only by relying on great transcendent cosmic powers.

To men of God such as Bogle and Humphrey, the humbling lessons of the story of the Tower of Babel are all too clear. Pretty much in the tradition of the black struggles in America, they are convinced of the pivotal role of the church and liberation theology. They realize that to secure the future of a just, free and egalitarian Jamaica without God's help or even against His will is an exercise in futility and defeatism. They seem to understand well the metaphysical implications of Patai's statement that "those who relied on God, or those whom the gods favored for reasons of their own, although the ship was tossed by inimical tempest, were destined to reach safely the coveted shores of their islands of the future" (87). Thus the connection between the Christ element and the millenarian struggle for liberation must be assumed as an inalienable imperative. Within the psychology of the unconscious, political independence is an outward manifestation of inner collective wholeness. Christ is the cognitype of this wholeness, the psychological phenomenology of the collective Jamaican self.

Before we part with the unconscious dimensions of the revolutionary myth in *New Day*, we need to explain the water symbolism as used in the narrator's glorious song and its meaning within the entire revolutionary struggle. The Jamaican struggle for independence is not only a search for a concrete objective, but also a quest for a collective image which would permit an understanding of the vicissitudes and displacements shared by all Jamaicans. The objective of those who participate in the struggle is, in part at least, to find an expression for their psychical bond, which is both an archaic image of God as well as the rebirth of the national self. The conflict is not merely the conflict between oppressor and oppressed; it is also one between the will created by colonial imperative and the counter will created by the desire for liberation, mediated by the Christological image.

At the center of the Christological image is the arcane symbolism of water, which is equivalent to the symbolic archetype of rebirth. The deep running water in the narrator's soulful lyric is the symbolic font which frees the song of the oppressed people from the ensnaring channels of material darkness, offers it a new gradient, and canalizes its dreams into a spiritual lyricism of liberation. The Jamaican people, by participating in and winning the struggle for independence, are like those who set out for the water and plunge into the dark depths of the unconscious where they find the pearl on the bottom, which in turn becomes the symbol of the savior, the harbinger of national healing. The descent into the watery depths of the psyche always seems to precede the ascent, which for Jamaicans, means the ascent into political autonomy, social emancipation, and spiritual renaissance with God of Moses right in front of them.

Unlike in *New Day*, in *God's Bits of Wood* and in *In the Castle of My Skin*, the struggle for a redeemed nation is stringently secular and Marxian. It is a revolutionary struggle somewhat demythologized. Instead of a reliance on divine intervention, we see the omnipotence of the soteriological will of the proletarian man insistently emphasized, a will which is anchored in the fountainhead of human history, or as Karl Marx describes it, in dialectical materialism. In dealing with the unconscious, nonrational dimensions of the revolutionary struggles in *God's Bits of Wood* and in *In the Castle of My Skin*, Sembene and Lamming have used two very vital mythic patterns. The first pattern is what has been boldly identified as the Marxian-Hegelian demiurge, or what

Edmund Wilson has described as the "myth of the dialectic" (179–98). The second is the Sorelian myth of the General Strike. The first pattern refers to the Hegelian concept of the dialectic as Karl Marx understands it—the dialectic of the thesis, antithesis, and synthesis. The demiurge haunted Marx for whom, according to Wilson, it took the form of a triad which "was simply the old Trinity, taken over from the Christian theology, as the Christians had taken it over from Plato" (190). In applying the Hegelian triad to his futuristic vision of society, Marx equates thesis with the traditional bourgeois society, the antithesis with the proletariat, the down-trodden working class, those living on the margins of society, and the synthesis with the millennium—the overthrow of the bourgeoisie and the rise of the dictatorship of the proletariat.

In *God's Bits of Wood*, the thesis is the French colonial economic monopoly, the draconian monopoly of the port—railway —construction industry. In *In the Castle of My Skin*, the thesis is represented by Mr. Creighton and his land ownership, his estate form of feudalism. The antithesis in Sembene's novel is represented by all the impoverished masses of Bamako, Thiès and Dakar—wage-earners, port and railway workers, construction workers, tradesmen and junior civil servants. In Lamming's the antithesis is represented by the displaced and dispossessed villagers and peasants of the Creighton Village as well as the urban workers. The synthesis in both novels begins in the people's awareness of their common plight, the plight of being condemned to a seemingly endless cycle of poverty, social injustice, pain and misery, but above all indignity in their own God-given land under the oppressor's reign of terror. This is the phase of the intellectual ferment, a phase during which the down-trodden become infused with the passionate and conscientious call to rise up and overthrow the oppressor and somehow inherit dominion over the whole earth under their feet.

In *God's Bits of Wood*, the valiant spokesman for the intellectual ferment is Tièmoko:

"We're the ones who do the work," he roared, "the same work the white men do. Why then should they be paid more? Because they are white?. . . It does no good just to look at our pay slips and say that our wages are too small. If we want to live decently we must fight!"[6]

In *In the Castle of My Skin*, the distraught narrator, in his account of the disparity between the lifestyles of the colonial masters and the hapless natives, captures that extreme sense of frustration the people feel about their lives.[7] Note, for instance, the living conditions between the poor inhabitants of Creighton's village [those who live in the valley] and the opulence of those who live in Belleville. Beyond the intellectual phase is the call for concrete action which would hasten the process of dismantling the colonial apparatus and thus elevate those down-trodden—the last shall be first. In both novels the strategy for taking, head on, the oppressive gauntlet is the general strike. In *God's Bits of Wood* we have the general strike organized by Tièmoko and Bakayoko in the three provinces of Bamako, Thiès and Dakar. The general strike in *In the Castle of My Skin* is led by the urban workers like Mr. Slime. The result of the two general strikes is remarkable. In *God's Bits of Wood* it leads to a new egalitarian order in which the workers' demands are met. In *In the Castle of My Skin*, the strikes and the riots end Creighton's reign of terror, even though his departure ushers in a new order which turns the poor masses' dreams into a partial nightmare.

The use of the general strike in the two novels to effect the kind of radical change envisioned by the masterminds and thus realize the millennial aims of those who participate in the struggle is of significant note. It is significant because it incorporates the vital myth which is at the core of Marxian dialectic. This is the myth that is generally referred to as the Sorelian Myth of the General Strike. The term "Sorelian" derives from Georges Sorel, the French social philosopher, who in his *Reflexions sur la violence*, argues that socialism or similar revolutionary movements need an image of the future, a revolutionary myth, to reassure the people regarding the final outcome of the struggle they are embarking upon. According to Sorel, this revolutionary myth, of which socialism such as we have witnessed in *God's Bits of Wood* and *In the Castle of My Skin*, is a part, is a product of the apocalyptic imagination, and manifests its psychological energy in persuading people of the rightness of the movement and by imbuing them with a belief in its ultimate victory, in motivating them to action in its service, often in spite of all sober individual judgement (Quoted in Patai 90). Sorel insists that it is futile to try to speculate whether or not the utopia envisioned will ever materialize. What is truly essential, contends Sorel, is the sense of expectation, the unconscious nonrational potential of the myth of the general strike as a "neoclassic example of the myth of the future acting on the present, the unattainable [gem] brought within reach, the mythical belief that collective violence can bring about Utopia (Quoted in Patai 91).

What is clear, from the preceding discussion is that the apocalyptic imagination, or what might very well be referred to as the myth of eternal return and revolutionary mythos, shares in one essential element. The vision is a shared one, evocative of the sentiment shared by an individual or group of individuals in an organized struggle for an alternate social order, a struggle which is, allegorically speaking, an objective manifestation of a deep, unconscious urge for peace, pros-perity, and happiness.[8] As Mircea Eliade once stated, it is an imagination that is essentially something of the borderline of transition, but on the threshold of the new world, light is born which gives meaning to the world which is passing away.

The Black millennial text, of which the six novels just discussed are eponymous, is, forged from the seething crucible of black man's fate as perceived by each of the writers concerned. Often times, it is a crustacean fate of pain, wretchedness, destruction and deprivation. The dynamics always is toward a sanctified moment, a way out of the vicious circle. The language of a typical black millenial text conceals a unique metaphysic which conceives the world, as each writer intends it, in terms of the conflict between two very different human impulses: the one, a dissolvent force, urging blacks towards hostilities, toward depressive wretchedness and infamy, the other, a centripetal force, urging them toward a telluric communalism, toward pastoral in-nocence and human relatedness, toward regenerative love and authentic selfhood, and toward political redemption and cultural pride as an intrinsic good. The plot of a typical black millennial text, be it novel, poetry or drama, is an allegorical expression of a profound teleological search for a meaningful order, a search for some sense of purpose in life, beyond the clangor of crotchets which surrounds our lives. It subserves an ideal, utilitarian-Benthamite raison d'être, the doctrine that the basic aim of moral, social, economic and political actions should be at all times the largest possible balancing of pleasure over pain, loyalty over mistrust, peace over war, eros over thanatos, and freedom over tyranny.[8]

10

A Cosmic Postulate of Eros: Reading Harris's *Palace of the Peacock*

Critics of Guyanese novelist Wilson Harris have often noted with acute interest the remarkable way in which his fiction is driven, quite literally, by a single dynamo—the symbol-forming imagination which constructs phenomenal space as a protean theater for dramatizing in stark relief and reflective processes its underlying metaphysical reality. Harris's fiction reads like an intricate network of symbolic vignettes pregnant with evocative power and propelled by incredible moral eloquence. If proverbs are for Chinua Achebe the palm oil with which words are eaten, symbols and symbolic inscriptions are for Wilson Harris the cerate by which logos, character, locus and circumstance are invested with profound meaning.[1] Quite often in his fiction, the phenomenal prefigures the spiritual and immaterial essences (the noumenal realm). Harris himself has admitted the fact that his fiction foregrounds "a symbolic landscape-in-depth—the shock of great rapids, vast forests and savannahs—playing through memory to involve perspectives of imperilled community and creativity reaching back in the pre-Columbian mists of time" (292). Although critics have pointed out some of the patterns in these symbolic inscriptions, what has not been fully discussed is how Harris's fiction transforms the symbolic object into a spiritual truth, extrapolating from fictional language some deep spiritual significance, leading to a fundamental transformation of mind and persona, a kind of *metanoia*. And yet that is exactly what is happening in his first *tour de force* novel—*Palace of the Peacock*.

In the novel, Harris exploits creative symbolism toward the search for individual and collective wholeness. I will designate this process as the voyage from thanatos (death instinct/aggressive faustianism) to eros (life-love instinct), a voyage understood as a microcosmic inflection of the spiritual quest for the center of the universe, a quest which shows the complexities of the creative function of the active, dynamic aspect of the psyche, of its symbol-forming power, which manifests itself in the creation of symbolic rites and fantasy images. Harris taps this symbol-forming energy of the human psyche, using it to constellate primordial images which dramatize this voyage in terms of the process of individuation, of the realization of the spiritual self, the real or wholesome personality in all of us. Thus at a fundamental level, the voyage from thanatos to eros is constructed by Harris as a tenacious process of creating a timeless order in which man, fallen or sunk in matter, rises to encounter the divine within himself. Both eros and timeless order as employed in *Palace of the Peacock* will be able to help Donne (the novel's monomaniacal protagonist) reconcile his nature with spirit, and thus prepare him in the end for a new birth of self.

Although Sandra E. Drake contends that "despite the arduous journey and the final vision at the end, this is not really a tale of either salvation or redemption" (68), evidence abounds in the novel that Donne is on a voyage of spiritual rebirth, a drama of inwardness resulting in the inner transformation of being. And this rebirth is consummated within the creation of a timeless order, the magical realm of experience, an act which would not only compensate for the "threatening tension between the opposites"[2] (the faustian man as opposed to the man of eros), but would also transform the peculiar agonies of this experience into a moment of joyful equilibration. The significance of this timeless order lies in Donne and crew renouncing their faustian drive and recognizing the ultimate futility of aggressive, seemingly unbridled masculinist territoriality. The narrator is our sole witness here. He says of Jennings, the engine driver:

"Ah got an idea," he announced. He spoke with hopeless obstinacy. His face was no longer the same as before: it had changed into a dream, the dream of an unnatural unshaven dead man's beard and growth. The cheeks were hollow as the caves in the wall and the blackness of this skin had grown lighter and greyer into an older drier mask and presence lying within. The lust and soul of rebellion had been killed abruptly in a manner that left him suddenly empty. He felt now only the loss of an opposition and true adversary within himself. His eyes had lost all rude fire and in their blindness and loneliness they spun deeper than nature's darkness and light. (118—19)

For Donne and crew, the veil of the faustian ego and pomposity is torn, and in its place,

> a longing [which] swept him [Donne] like the wind of the muse to understand and transform his beginnings: to see the indestructible nucleus and redemption of creation, the remote and the abstract image and correspondence in which all things and events gained their substance and universal meaning (130).

The "indestructible nucleus and redemption of creation" for which Donne now longs is the magical center of the timeless order and of the ultimate unity of all existence, which Jung, using the terminology of medieval natural philosophy, identifies as the *unus mundus*. The objective domain of this timeless order is the cliff, at the foot of which Donne and crew are marooned. The cliff is Harris's chief allegorical symbol, his mandala in the depths of his unconscious maternal psyche. It is the eikistic equivalent of the *philosopher's stone*, the alchemist principle which is capable of achieving the spiritual regeneration of man; for Harris, purifying Donne from the corrupting influences of the faustian ego.

Standing tall, imposing and rugged above the roaring sea, the cliff stands as a maternal symbol of order and meaning in a world torn asunder by the absurd masculinist faustian ego. As a mandala of cosmic nature, Harris's cliff is the feminine model of the godhead and the cosmic order. It is conceived out of a deep primordial vision which wells up from the novelist's unconscious. The curiosity with which Donne gazes at the windows on the cliff shows that man has finally confronted something unknown of fundamental import. Thus the cliff, as an archetypal symbol, is both an image constellated in the objective psyche as well as in the subjective domain, as a trope of a final trans-personal order.

In fact, it can be said that *Palace of the Peacock*, particularly from Day One of the journey beyond Mariella (Book 3—"The Second Death," Chapter 8) to Day Seven (Book 4—"Paling of Ancestors," Chapters 11 and 12), is an allegoric re-enactment of the mystery of existence, the unknown in the qualitative kinetics of creation. Jung assumes that in the deepest level of the collective unconscious, we encounter a bit of unknown "Nature which contains everything, also, therefore, what is unknown, including matter" (von Franz 246). Harris's narrator echoes this Jungian vision as he and others prepare to embark on the ill-fated voyage beyond Mariella: "We stood on the frontiers of the known world, and on the self-same threshold of the unknown" (92). The concurrence of known and unknown thresholds of existence is a paradox of concrete

continuum which underscores the unity of all existence. To play out this
concurrence, Harris uses the magical number—7—which corresponds to
the seven days of Christian divine creation and respite. In fact, the
change that is going to occur in Donne and his crew as they journey
beyond Mariella takes place in phases, and these phases are indicated by
the number seven, which reflects a distinctly Harrisian groundplan of the
whole cosmos which is, in the end, mathematical.

The journey beyond Mariella is the search for the ultimate unity of all
existence which, as we have indicated earlier, Jung calls the *unus
mundus*. In *Mysterium Coniunctionis*, Jung defines the concept of the
unus mundus as follows:

Undoubtedly the idea of the *unus mundus* is founded on the assumption that the
multiplicity of the empirical world rests on an underlying unity, and that not two
or more fundamentally different worlds exist side by side or are mingled with
one another. Rather, everything divided and different belongs to one and the
same world, which is not the world of sense but a postulate whose probability is
vouched for by the fact that until now no one has been able to discover a world
in which the known laws of nature are invalid.[3]

In *Palace of the Peacock*, Harris describes the experience of the *unus
mundus* as the opening of the window on eternity into the eternal world.
The insistent and persistent references to "window," through which
Donne perceives the larger significance in the scheme of things, suggests
that it serves as the gateway through which the man of matter can feel his
way into the unknown side of the psyche. At every step of the way in his
ascent up the treacherous walls of the cosmic cliff, Donne is greeted by
all manner of windows. Harris describes them with the energy of vivid
detail. On page 131 alone, there are three references to "window"—"A
swallow flew and dashed through the veil and window.". . ."He
hammered against the wall and shook the window loud." . . . "His eyes
were darker than the image of the sky and the swallow that had flown
towards him was reflected in them as in window-panes of glass." On
page 132, there is a direct reference as well as an implied
reference—"Donne felt himself sliced with this skeleton-saw by the
craftsman of God in the window-pane of his eye. . . . "Finger-nail and
bone were secret panes of glass in the stone of blood through which
spiritual eyes were being opened." Other references include, "the
window panes reflecting the brightness of star and sun" (133), the
"windowsill with the dying light of the sun" (134), the "window-pane
clouded a little with the mist of falling evening and water" (135), the

misty window-pane of the carpenter's room (136), the window behind which the new moon vanished (137), the second window in the wall (137), the windows associated with the consummated job of universal creation and natural life (146-47), and the windows of the soul which looked in and out of the palace of the universe (146-51).

All these descriptions of and references to the window are deeply rooted in the experience of the Self and how this experience can help men like Donne and crew extricate themselves from the stifling prison of a conscious image of the world that is too narrow, so that they can be open to the noumenal, and so that, at the same time, the noumenal can touch and move them on the path of regeneration. The narrator tells us that for Donne,

> it was the unflinching clarity with which he looked into himself and saw that all his life he had loved no one but himself. He focused his blind eye with all penitent might on this pinpoint star and reflection as one looking into the void of oneself upon the far grater love and self-protection that have made the universe. (140)

At this point in his ascent, Donne's experience on the cliff can be compared to the sartori experience of Zen Buddhism or with the samadi of Eastern teachings or with the awakening to the Tao in China. He now realizes that his finite, material life, which he had previously sacrificed on the altar of Faustian deviltry, now has meaning only when it is related to the infinite through the "window on eternity." Of this linkage, Jung offers some general thoughts:

> Only if we know that the thing which truly matters is the infinite can we avoid fixing our interest upon futilities, and upon all kinds of goals which are not of real importance . . . If we understand and feel that here in this life we already have a link with the infinite, desires and attitudes change. In the final analysis, we count for something only because of the essential we embody, and if we do not embody that, life is wasted. In our relationships to other men, too, the crucial question is whether an element of boundlessness is expressed in the relationship.
> The feeling for the infinite, however, can be attained only if we are bounded to the utmost. The greatest limitation for man is the "self"; it is manifested in the experience: "I am only that!" Only consciousness of our narrow confinement in the self forms the link to the limitlessness of the unconscious. In such awareness we experience ourselves concurrently as limited and eternal, as both the one and the others.[4]

That is why the experience of the Self, for Donne and crew, is an exceedingly excruciating glimpse through the window upon eternity, a growing away from the limited bounds of the faustian ego to the boundless energy of the timeless and the eternal embodied in all of us. Through the windows on the cliff, Donne perceives not only the underlying unity of all human beings, but also the unity of all cosmic existence visualized in the arcane symbolism of the cliff

Harris's depiction of Donne's *unus mundus* experience has trappings of Chinese Taoism and of the ancient Egyptian liturgies for the dead. In both instances, a genuine experience of the *unus mundus* is always hoped for as an event which happens only during or after death. In certain ancient Egyptian liturgies for the dead, for instance, writes von Franz, there is a depiction in moving language of the way in which the dead become one with all the gods and all the matter of the World-All and are thus finally united with the primordial father Nun, the primordial ocean itself, from which the world was created. The deceased can then pass effortlessly through all crude material objects and "go into and out of all forms."[5] In *Palace of the Peacock*, Donne and crew realize that within the inner chamber of timeless order death is, on the one hand, alienation from the God-within, and on the other, a gateway to the eternal and the noumenal. Donne comes to this self-realization as he yearns importunately to gain entry into the carpenter's room. The narrator tells us:

All sound had been barred and removed for ever, all communication, all persuasion, all intercourse. It was Death with capitals, and when he saw this he felt too that it was he who stood within the room and it was the carpenter who stood reflected without. This was a fantasy, this change of places, and he hammered again loud. The image of Death in the carpenter stared through him, the eyelids flickered with lightning at last in the midst of the waterfall (133).

The cosmic consciousness appears intensified as he nears the end of his gruelling ascent. It is a consciousness that enacts the eternalist journey beyond the dualistic categories of material intelligence. Again the narrator is our sole witness:

It is better to be a doorkeeper in the house of the Lord ... he mumbled foolishly. He stepped over the eloquent arms that reached to him in a fixation of greeting. DaSilva was dead he knew. He entered the corridor over the dead body and stood himself at strict attention by the lion door. He had stopped a little to wonder whether he was wrong in his knowlege and belief and the force that had divided them from each other and mangled them beyond all earthly hope and recognition was the wind of rumour and superstition, and the truth was they had all come home at last to the compassion of the nameless unflinching folk. (143).[6]

In Chinese Taoism the same affinity with the *unus mundus* is at work. Of this, Chuang Dsi writes in *Das Wahre Buch von sudlichen Blutenland*: "He [i.e., the man who has encountered the *unus mundus*] walks on air and clouds; he rides on sun and moon and travels beyond the world. Life and death cannot change his self." The *unus mundus* self also understands how "to make the innermost essence of nature his own, and to let himself be moved by the changing primordial powers, to wander there, where there are no boundaries."[7] This concept of the unity of all cosmic existence as an irrepresentable and irreducible back-drop to the material world is captured vivdly in the narrator's final sense of elation at Carroll's song:

I was suddenly aware of other faces at other windows in the Palace of the Peacock. And it seemed to me that Carroll's music changed in the same instant. I nudged the oracle of my dreaming shoulder. The change and variation I thought I detected in the harmony were outward and unreal and illusory: they were induced by the limits and apprehensions in the listening mind of men, and by their wish and need in the world to provide a material nexus to bind the spirit of the universe.

It was this tragic bond I perceived now—as I had felt and heard the earlier distress of love (148-49).

Very much in the esoteric traditions of the Oriental, Harris employs the mythologem which foregrounds the dialectic symbiosis of the sun and the moon in order to capture the very state of Donne's mind.[8] For instance, Donne begins his ascent of the cliff during the day. It is also during the day that he encounters the first window that leads into the carpenter's room, during which time the rays of the sun greet the chastened wanderer/pilgrim. But with the approach of darkness, daylight is soon followed by the flickering moonlight. The shifting states of Donne's mind are reflected in the narrator's words:

The carpenter looked blind to the stumbling human darkness that still trailed and followed across the world. He closed his window softly upon Donne and Jennings and daSilva.

Jennings cried slipping suddenly in the dark upon a step in the cliff. His wrist gave way too with the shaft of his dreaming engine snapping at last as a branch in the flight of the stream. They both answered him but their voices were drowned in the waterfall and they saw nothing save the ancient winding horn of the moon falling from the sky like the bone of his metal and wood.

Darkness still fell upon the cliff and the horn of the new moon vanished in the
end behind the window of the wall as into a longfeared shelter in the earth rich
with the frames of humility of God's memory and reflection. (136-37)

The depiction of the diurnal cycle of day and night, coextensive with
the dynamics of Donne's and the narrator's minds, shows Harris's
alchemical strategy at work. It is an alchemical strategy rooted in a network of coded images for self-realization in which Donne and crew
could pass on to the threshold of enlightenment. It is Harris's quasi-yogic
strategy of harmoni-zing and blending the nerve currents of matter and
mind, a strategy infinitely essential toward the reinvention of the
wholesome man in Donne, a material ego dismantled into cosmic self.
The psychological basis of high moral states in the process of
individuation represents an interchange of energies between the solar and
lunar chambers of Donne's mind. This fundamental dualism in Donne's
mind, in response to the diurnal tide of day and night, is equivalent to the
dualism of contrarious impulses represented by thanatos (the faustian
instinct of animus) and eros (the life-love instinct of anima). That aspect
of Donne's mind in ordinary waking consciousness—which uses rational
yearning as the chief means of making sense of the seemingly inscrutable
reality of the cliff's denizens, as well as that used by the narrator to
manipulate verbal symbols—represents masculine daytime consciousness.
Complementing and contrasting with it is the night time, lunar
consciousness. In the novel, the lunar consciousness is the feminine
consciousness, the realm of dreams, intuition, and non-verbal communication. The narrator tells us:

Darkness still fell upon the cliff and the horn of the new moon vanished in the
end behind the window of the wall as into a longfeared shelter in the earth rich
with the frames of humility of God's memory and reflection. The stars in the sky
shivered as they crawled once more up the fantastic ladder and into the void of
themselves.
As they climbed upward Donne felt the light shine on him reflected from
within. He had come upon another window in the wall.. . . The room was an
enormous picture. It breathed all burning tranquility and passion together—so
alive—so warm and true—. . .
The room was as simple as the carpenter's room. . . . Yet it all looked so
remarkable—every thread and straw on the ground, the merest touch in the
woman's smile and dress—that the light of the room turned into the wealth of
dreams. (137-38)

The description of the carpenter's and the woman's rooms points up
the existence of two distinct aspects of material intelligence that stand in

dialectical relation to each other as the sun and moon in the sky. We can even regard the carpenter, because of the various associations with which his room is vivified, as the representative of daytime, solar consciousness. His complement, the woman dressed in a long sweeping white garment—like the virgin moon gooddess who appears in the celestial hierarchies of so many cultures—symbolizes the night-time, lunar consciousness. These two symbols, in their dyadic complementarity, represent affective depictions of the nature and potential of the two phases of the human material consciousness. They can also be seen as Harris's primeval representations of the basic dualism of astrological reality—the sun and the moon, as correlative designations of the masculine and feminine aspects of human consciousness.

Harris's relentless, almost heavy-handed association of the carpenter's and woman's rooms with the firmament of the stars, the starry vault of heaven (*Palace* 136-41), shows a peculiar way of conceiving what Paracelsus has called *lumen naturae* (light of nature), which is a metaphor of inward voyage. It also reminds us of "the characteristic alchemical vision of sparks scintillating in the blackness of the arcane substance."[9] Or perhaps Harris, like Paracelsus, sees the darksome psyche (here Donne's false ego) as a star-strewn night sky, whose planets and fixed constellations represent the archetypes in all their luminosity and numinosity.[10] And when Harris describes the carpenter's room as the room which "became a dancing hieroglyph in the illumination of endless pursuit, in the subtle running depths of the sea, the depths of the green sky and the depths of the forest (135-36), we are reminded of the Hieroglyphica of Horapollo, where the starry sky signifIes God as ultimate Fate.[11] Thus either room has the potential meaning of eternity or the cosmos in miniature form. Donne is greatly comforted by the beauty and luminous visions perceived in either room, which on the one hand are introspective intuitions that mirror the state of the unconscious, and on the other are Harris's intussusception of the fundamental Christian concept of eternity. The anagogic implication may very well be that the palace of the peacock is the miniaturist version of the *vaicuntha* of God ("It is better to be a doorkeeper in the house of the Lord. . . ," Donne whispers to daSilva [*Palace of the Peacock* 143]), the God that fills the entire universe in his coextensive transcendent-immanentistic effulgence, and rules over it by means of the powers of vision that proceed from His face, and to which man's own visionary powers are contemporaneously subjugated, interfaced and interconnected.[12]

But of particular awed fascination to Donne is the woman's room. As Donne and crew stare at the woman-figure, Donne, in particular, experiences a sudden infusion of Spirit, the spirit of the anima. According to Paul Tillich,

Spirit is first of all power, the power that drives the human spirit above itself towards what it cannot attain by itself, the love that is greater than all other gifts, the truth in which the depth of being opens itself to us, the holy that is the manifestation of the presence of the ultimate" (84).

The narrator conveys this ascendant sense of power as is felt by Donne in the following long passage:

Nothing could match this spirit of warmth and existence. Staring into the room-willing to be blinded-he suddenly saw what he had missed before. The light in the room came from a solitary candle with a star upon it, steady and unflinching, and the candle stood tall and rooted in the floor as the woman was. She moved at last and her garment brushed against it like hair that neither sparked nor flew. He stared and saw her astonishing face. Not a grain of her dress but shone with her hair, clothing her threadbare limbs in the melting plaits of herself. Her ancient dress was her hair after all. Falling to the ground and glistening and waving until it grew so frail and loose and endless, the straw in the cradle entered and joined it and the whole room was enveloped in it as a melting essence yields itself and spreads itself from the topmost pinnacle and star into the roots of self and space. (139)

Thus the woman in the long, sweeping white garment can be regarded as Donne's "Astronomia," his anima of light. She is coextensive with the starry firmament, and as such, she drives Donne toward the wisdom of the infinite. Her light is an inborn spirit given to the inner man, the hidden treasure in the inner chamber of eternally transfigured and true life-love man. In short, the woman appears to Donne as what Paracelsus calls *primum ac optimum thesaurum, quem naturae Monarchia in se claudit* (the first and best treasure which the monarchy of nature hides within itself).[13]

The power that Donne feels is the power of Eros; and once he feels that, the Faustian demon in him appears exorcised. As he stares at the wonder woman, there is a kind of subliminal message that filters through him. That message is that his ultra-masculinist life has been one empty and meaningless void, but that given the power of Eros embodied in the virginal anima, there is a distinct possibility of a new life waiting before the eternal door of his inner self to fill the void and to conquer his morbid fear and damnation. As he and the surviving crew contemplate the meaning of the consuming image of the woman, her spirit awakens them to a contrary or complementary desire to strive not toward death and damnation, but toward the sublime of eternity wherein lies the feminized God-within. For the first time Donne, in the true Nietzschean spirit, overcomes his ennui and begins to say yes to life, in spite of the destructiveness that has hitherto marked his life of territorial conquest and despoliation. The spirit of the anima begins to reveal to him subliminally that he has hurt everyone: his crew for leading most of them to a senseless and needless death on the perilous seas; Mariella, the old Arawak woman and the Amerindian folk, for forcing them to flee from his rage and terror—but all that has changed now; in the paraphrase of Yeats, a terrible beauty appears to have been born. It would seem as though his anima has given him the right image that reunites these people even in death with him, in love and equanimity.

At the end of the dream, there appears the peacock, which, in the alchemist doctrine, means the completion of the work—creation and recreation. The appearance of the divine Self at the end, symbolized by the peacock, is the birth of a feminine Eros because it is the dream of a woman. The last two paragraphs of the novel are quite revealing:

One was what I am in the music—buoyed and supported above dreams by the undivided soul and anima in the universe from whom the word of dance and creation first came, the command to the starred peacock who was instantly transported to know and to hug to himself his true invisible otherness and opposition, his true alien spiritual love without cruelty and confusion in the blindness and frustration of desire. It was the dance of all fulfillment I now held and knew deeply, cancelling my forgotten fear of strangeness and catastophe in a destitute world. (152)

The music referrred to in the passage is Carroll's music, which is a primordial metaphor that distills and inosculates the diffuse inner being into a cosmic unity so that it can come into affective and cognitive life in the figure of the One. The circle of man's consciousness of the divine is thus widened, and the manichean tension between thanatos and eros appears to have been eased. The palace of the peacock represents that eternalist and indestructible monad inherent in the majesty of the divine Self. The cliff is the theater of initiation and wisdom. It is an arena of sufferance through which the Faustian ego becomes conscious of the Self, where thanatos is redeemed in the virginal melodies of an anima.

Jung says that whoever finds himself on the path of individuation cannot evade that suspension between the opposites. For our tragic protagonist, Donne, the suspension between the last vestige of thanatic drive in him and the promise of divine eros is a source of frustration and despair. But as Jung maintains, just at the deepest point of suffering, the content of the next stage appears, "the birth of the inner man," that is, the Self, or the stone of the wise.[14] Since the transformation of the thanatic or thanatized man takes place on the cliff, the cliff can be said to symbolize the lapis, the philosopher's stone, in which the entire sacrificial drama takes place. Donne's ascent up the cliff demonstrates allegorically how the divine/anagogical process of change manifests itself to our human understanding and how man experiences it, first as punishment, torment, and death, and then ultimately as transfiguration and triumph. Drawn into the cycle of death and rebirth of the universal, destinal order, Donne experiences an allegorical transformation which is a function of a sacrifice mystery entified by the cliff. In the solemn act of Donne's sacrifice, the Faustian ego, once dethroned, decides against itself, subordinating itself to an authority defined by divine Eros. Central to Donne's and everyone else's transformation is Carroll's music. The narrator says:

"The music Carroll sang and played and whistled suddenly filled the corridors and the chosen ornaments of the palace; I knew it came from a far source within—deeper than every singer knew. And Carroll himself was but a small mouthpiece and echo standing at the window and reflecting upon the world" (151).

In fact, Carroll's music is not the aesthete's "mere architecture in sound" (Holbrook 233), but the kind of soulful music described by Deryck Cooke in *The Language of Music*. Cooke writes: "Music is, in fact, 'extra-verbal,' since notes, like words, have emotional connotations: it is, let us repeat, the supreme expression of universal emotions, in an entirely personal way, by the great composers" (quoted in Holbrook 233). He concludes by saying:

We need not feel ashamed that music should have a moral effect only by placing emotional moods in a significant order: psychology has shown that our whole life is propelled by these instinctive urges, and that it is by balancing and ordering them that we achieve a valuable creative attitude to life (Holbrook 233).

In fact, judging from the spontaneous response and the narrator's elation over Carroll's song, it is reasonable to conclude that through Car-

roll's music, Donne and crew can achieve a creative attitude toward life.
The music acts as the via media through which the perilous quest to
discover the truth about themselves is crystallized and consummated. It
is, as Cooke suggests, the language of the emotions by which inward
truth is explored and ordered. All of them now are

free from the chains of illusion we had made without—the sound that filled us
was unlike the link of memory itself. It was the inseparable moment within
ourselves of all fulfillment and understanding. Idle now to dwell upon and recall
anything one had ever responded to with a sense and sensibility that were our
outward manner and vanity and conceit. (151)

The illusion referred to here is the false ego in man which sometimes
conditions him to think that he is separate from the divine. Thus
Carroll's music functions as a conduit for leading man back to the
God-within. It activates Donne's and the crew's higher consciousness
and canalizes their thoughts into a state of what R. M. Bucke describes as
"cosmic consciousness" (Quoted in Holbrook 233), an awareness of the
life and order of the universe, a state of moral exultation, an
indescribable feeling of elevation, elation, joyousness, and a quickening
of man's moral and spiritual sensibility. The peak of this anagogic
experience, as a form of changing one's outlook on life, is attained when
the narrator tells us that

this was the inner music and voice of the peacock I suddenly encountered and
echoed and sang as I had never heard myself sing before. I felt the faces before
me begin to fade and part company from me and from themselves as if our need
of one another was now fulfilled, and our distance from each other was the
distance of a sacrament, the sacrament and embrace we knew in one muse and
one undying soul. (152)

Carroll's music, therefore, is the kind of inner ambience of knowing,
which a writer identifies as that which "goes beyond the body, [where
nothing will] . . . ever hurt you or bother you, not even death." (Quoted
in Harman 208-09).
     The growth of the Faustian man from thanatos to eros is a fundamental
transfiguration, a voyage from death to life, a rebirth, an emergence of
the inner archetypal mediators of divine power, a creation of a new kind
of ego-functioning where the ego is the servant of the divine, not its
betrayer. The emergence of Self expressed in Carroll's music is bound up

with the muse essence, what R. D. Laing calls "cosmic foetalization" (106) It is a voyage from masculine death impulse to the eternal body of the feminine, the anima figure of the universe. Of the significance of this female body for the growth of man, Harry Guntrip writes:

In the mother's body man knows the universe, in birth he forgets it at bottom. It remains the secret foundation of the stillness, security and peace . . . a foundation which must be preserved and developed in postnatal growth through identification to object relationship . . . In the deepest unconscious it is never lost, and human beings struggle to return to it when their "ego" is most desperately menaced. (269)

For Donne and crew the ultimate realization is that "Being" is discovered not in the Faustian will to power or territorial possession, but in the will to transcendent meaning, which is a function of relinquishing and going beyond the masculinist ego and penetrating the silent core of oneself wherein dwells divine eros. This is higher consciousness, the eternal part of man. This higher form of reality is mystic reality, an "experience of detachment from the world of objective reality as the centre of existence,"[15] a private dream which hovers in the fringe of communal myth, in which, according to Kristian Smidt, "the visible world is no longer a reality, and the unseen world no longer a dream."[16]   .

The lesson of *Palace of the Peacock* is that, at the end, one no longer sees himself as an isolated point on the periphery of existence, but as part of the One in the center. It is the center that consummates the enantiodromic union of opposites[17] through the middle passage—that most fundamental element of inward experience, the most legitimate fulfillment of the meaning of the individual's life.[18] Only the subjective consciousness of the Faustian man is isolated. When, however,. in Carroll's song and in the tested experience of the cliff ascent, subjective consciousness relates to its center (the anima, divine eros), it becomes integrated into wholeness and finds in the midst of suffering and nothingness a meaning beyond all futile pursuits. As the narrator states in his moving peroration: "Each of us now held at last in his arms what he had been for ever seeking and what he had eternally possessed" (152).

11

A Woman Transfigured: Reading Derek Walcott and Wilson Harris

The nature of the colonial and imperial experience in the Caribbean/West Indies (the murderous adventures of Christopher Columbus, the self-serving conquests of the invaders: the Spaniards, the Dutch, the French, and the English, and of course, the brutality of the Atlantic slave trade) has left one intransigent problem in its wake—the absence of authentic self-knowledge. Edward Brathwaite, one of the critically acclaimed writers of the Caribbean, frames the problem this way:

The problem of and for West Indian artists and intellectuals is that having been born and educated within this (the Caribbean) fragmented culture, they start out in the world without a sense of "wholeness". . . Disillusion with the fragmentation leads to a sense of rootlessness. The ideal does not and cannot correspond to perceived and inherited reality. The result: dissociation of the sensibility. . . The second phase of West Indian and Caribbean artistic and intellectual life, on which we are now entering. . . is seeking to transcend and heal it. (30–31)

Thus one of the dominant themes in modern Caribbean/ West Indian literature, the search for identity, in a historical and personal sense, has meant overcoming what Amon Saba Saakana describes as "the schizophrenic attitudes, neurosis, mental trauma and double consciousness of the Caribbean writer" (102). And this search for identity has crystallized around two familiar motifs—landscape and woman. The landscape (the sense of place) has come to represent the determined efforts of the West Indian people to repossess their own land after a century of what Derek Walcott has called "historylessness," while the West Indian/ Caribbean woman has become the allegoric conduit through which the symbolic power of the landscape is amplified and thus realized. Evidently, Caribbean writers' artistic representation of the West Indian woman takes the form of a soulful odyssey which the West Indian writers feel religiously bound to undertake in order to discover a mean-

meaning and a pattern as an alternative to their seemingly desolate lives. The attendant feeling is one that seeks both an encounter with the inner self, as well as the release from a sense of personal and historical emptiness. The fragment that Brathwaite speaks of is the sense of fragmentation which pervades West Indian consciousness, an acknowledgement of the universal Caribbean condition of interruption. The Caribbean life comprises a concatenation of discontinuous pieces. As people who put fragments together, Brathwaite and other Caribbean writers such as Walcott, Harris, and others become what Lévi-Strauss designates as a *bricoleur*, one who is "a marginal figure who transforms the materials the world has rejected" (Elsley 168), to engage in a kind of dialogue with his native land. To the West Indian writer, this kind of engagement is healing.

For Walcott especially, exploring the West Indian woman, particularly as a sublimation of the unconscious desire for identification with the land (i.e. rootedness—a sense of place), sometimes means a close encounter with authentic love, which in turn underlines his unflinching devotion to his artistic vision. For him the West Indian woman provides an indispensable articulate image for the downward journey into the inward region of his psyche. For Wilson Harris, she is the spirit of place and love of place (topophilia), the kernel of native spirituality pitted against the faustian soullessness of a ruthless invader and conquistador. To encounter the West Indian woman, the way Walcott and Harris have in their respective works, is to encounter an anima that exposes the West Indian person's sense of emptiness, loneliness, deprivation and rootlessness, as well as affirm his dire need for psychic emancipation and what Arthur Drayton has called "cultural synthesis" (129).

It is the unique quality of Walcott's *Another Life* that the mythical images and the questing artist intermingle in the passionate intensity of heroic allegory. The long poem is basically an autobiographical quest narrative. Lloyd Brown has correctly pointed out that *Another Life* falls into the pattern of Walcott's three earlier poetry collections in which "the poetic experience as a private odyssey is clearly implied throughout the themes of personal self-exploration, self-discovery, and self-expression" (133). But it is a quest narrative with a somewhat different meaning and thematic construct. Different, that is, from what we had in his earlier twelve-cantoed *Epitaph for the Young* (*Another Life* was published in 1973, *Epitaph for the Young*, 1949). In *Epitaph for the Young*, which Maria Cristina Fumagalli in her book *The Flight of the Vernacular: Seamus Heaney, Derek Walcott and the Impress of Dante*, regards as the first instance of a consistent Dantean echo in Walcott's poetry" (41), the poet-hero is cast in the image of Telemachus, of Stephen Dedalus, in search of a father, of a source of patriarchal authority and tradition, from which he has been severed.[1] That means that the poet, like Joyce's Stephen Dedalus, has to leave his native St. Lucia island in order to forge in the smithies of his soul the uncreated conscience of his race.

In *Another Life*, on the other hand, the poet, a wounded exile is on a homecoming, back to his native land where he finally forges the uncreated conscience of his psyche in a symbolic West Indian woman nurtured in native pride. It is a prodigal's home-bound odyssey that culminates in his passionate self-discovery in maternal beginnings. The transition from *Epitaph* to *Another Life* represents an unfoldment of a poet's destiny through a kind of noble wretchedness and a nomadic and precarious life to a noble endowment with, maternal privileges. It is no wonder then that the note of unrelieved despair, the pathos which characterizes   *Epitaph*   is   somewhat   relatively   restrained.   Its compassionate tone, its blend of idealism and sordid realism, appropriate to the plight of a returning wounded artist-exile, offers the best gateway to the kind of Baudelairean *ecstase* insistently suggested in the poem.

Divided   into   four   movements   or   books,   *Another   Life*   is   an autobiographical   narrative   poem.   As   such,   it   is   self-focused   in   a relational kind of way akin to what we find in African American autobio-graphies where   authors   as   individual   selves   are   defined   relationally, viewed within the context of their relationship with other lives. It is, as Laurence A. Breiner has pointed [black autobiography "moves beyond mere self-assertion to produce representtative texts, witnessed to a shared experience. Writers who might elsewhere be inclined to define their own individuality against their surroundings here tend to link their personal development with that of the society" (3). But the self is not totally effaced. Instead Walcott, the homecoming self, is still the center but a different kind of center. It is the center, as Miller suggests, "of an ever-widening circle that expands to embrace the world and the universe" (148). Walcott still remains the arranger and apprehender of this world, this universe, through the use of his active imagination. What Walcott does in *Another Life* is akin to what Walt Whitman does in his poem "There Was a Child Went Forth." In this long poem, Whitman cata-logues a variety of contents of the world of a child, from "early lilacs" to the old drunkard staggering home. For Walcott, readers get a clear sense of his personality through his relationships with such persons and things as his old mother, Anna, Harry Simmons, Gregorias, and the West Indian/St. Lucian dialect. Just as Whitman speaks in metaphors, so does Walcott, collecting and reinventing the world of St. Lucia in memories, impressions, storing them away inside him there to mingle with his inner being, to form an inextricable part of his consciousness. All of that reads like a narrative allegory of his life and like that narrative as marking a circle with him at the center.

Henry James once admonished young budding writers assembled in front of him to utilize the impression of life colored by each of their individual conditions to make a picture, to transmute that into a vivid picture, a picture framed by their own personal wisdom (29). Derek Walcott, on this all-important homecoming, heeds James' admonition by capturing and retrieving those elemental aspects of his past into this gigantic picture of life in St. Lucia. And with that life is enmeshed his own life of pain and fun, joy and sobriety, into a field-harvest of great illumination. If Walcott recreates himself, he does so through the memory of those individuals he had associated with in the past; in other words, with the help provided by a sympathetic environment.

Thus *Another Life* charts the tortuous course of the homecomer-artist humbled by guilt against the background of a quintessential mother and a brooding symbolic landscape. But two movements/books, "The Divided Child" and "A Simple Flame," stand out in particular as the most eloquent and sustained expression of the instinctual self-portrait of the artist. Earlier, we have seen the guilt that has enveloped him. It is the kind of guilt that manifests the critical oscillations of conscience yet unmolded, a guilt which usually greets the hopeful traveler, who in his present lucidity is appalled by the reality of his exile and earlier wasted engagement. The elusiveness of a maternal instinct in exile, and the agony of the poet's life while there, are weighed against his present odyssean courage. In exile, the poet's creative impotence is seen as the sad consequence of his venality, his pathetic failure to probe the depths of his own participation in the collective maternal unconscious. So as the poet sails across the Caribbean sea bound for native St. Lucia, he feels an overwhelming sense of insufficiency. The sea serves as a steno symbol both of depth, the hoary depth of the collective St. Lucian psyche, from which he has been estranged, and of bitterness that recalls in the poet's own personal unconscious the unsavory fruits of his errant past.

When "The Divided Child" opens, the poet has landed on shore, left the port of entry, waddled across the St. Lucia marshland, and come right in front of his mother's old compound. There, standing before his mother's old house the poet espies the moon, a typical matriarchal symbol. Edward Baugh in *Derek Walcott, Memory as Vision: Another Life* suggests that the moon is a matriarchal symbol, and as such, effect a transition from chapter one to chapter two (25). The remarkable thing here is the way in which a simple, concrete-walled house, with its modest contents, is suddenly beautifully transformed through the very power of poeticized language into a living archetypal feminine image.

The description of the poet's mother's house[2] is significant on two levels. On the literal level, it describes the gothic architecture of St. Lucian buildings, with all their imposing grotesqueness and intricate carvings. On an allegoric level, it creates a psychically altered experience for the returning poet, almost dwarfing him. The city's high rises, behind which the poet's mother's house is nestled, now appear grossly out of proportion with him, suggesting his own diminutiveness in the face of a larger and greater force. They shock the poet out of his normal perception of reality and render him ultimately at the mercy of the maternal unconscious within and beyond his limited self. The poet, however, appears to savor the moment since it contains for him the badly needed altered perspective of his own reality, a change from an anguished ego lost and confused in the abysmal condition of exilic consciousness to a "prodigal" self encouraged into a keener perception of the self and his native soil and the altered link between the two.

The moon that shines around the poet's mother's house illuminates this changed perception, lending it a somewhat extraordinary mysterious power. While the moon lends her lace to a barefooted town, it sets aglow the matriarchal spirit needed for the transformation of the poet from a divided child to mature artist. The power of memory to effect this kind of transformative power is exhilarating. It grounds the poet in the here-now. As David Farrel Krell suggests on the process of remembering, memory or

remembering instigates a peculiar kind of presence. It 'has' an object of perception or knowledge without activating perception or knowledge as such and without confusing past and present. For while remembering, a man tells himself that he is now present to something that was earlier. (15)

The moon is more than an ordinary luminous body. It is a way for Walcott to tap into the universal reserve of primordial images. Selden Rodman in *Tongues of Fallen Angels* writes that Walcott has been consistently hostile to any force which seeks to limit his creativity or restrict his access to anything which might feed it (252). Rodman paraphrases Walcott's assertion that most black writers cripple themselves by a certain separatism. "you can't be a poet," argues Walcott, "and believe in the division of man." According to Rodman, Walcott believes that "the truly tough aesthetic of the New World neither explains nor gives history. It refuses to recognize it as a creative or culpable force." He finds in poets such as Neruda, Césaire, and Perse an "awe of the numinous," the "elemental privilege of naming the new world which annihilates history. . . They reject ethnic ancestry for faith in the elemental man" (Walcott, "The Muse of History" qtd. Rodman, 252).

As indicated earlier, the moon has become for the poet an anagogic symbol of the matriarchal sphere, with his mother as its immediate objective manifestation. It is curious how the moon, as the luminous aspect of this one night in Virgie (the poet's hometown), merges with the pervasive presence of the poet's mother and the expression of her essential spirit, humanity, and wholeness which constitutes one of the objects of his quest. And because the poet so loves his native St. Lucia, he sees the moon as forming a primary maternal totality in the background against which his evolving artistic-cum-cultural consciousness takes place. The moon is made identical with the figure of the "way" which his mother, as the "Great Mother," now symbolizes for him. For the path to ultimate consciousness is the lunar way, whose matriarchal essence the poet now links to his mother. By shining upon and around the house, the moon becomes the symbolic companion of his mother and a symbol of that keener perception for which he longs.

Against this background, the poet's mother enters, and the depth psychology of the matriarchal moon-night begins to take on a marked personal note. At this point both mother and house merge in a convivial starburst of infinite celebration. The merging of mother and house is one of the oldest arcane symbols in the repertoire of mythic symbolism. This is the symbolism of the mother archetype as the protective and containing vessel. The poet's mother speaks of her tireless domestic chores. This is the picture of the feminine as the provider of shelter and sustenance, while encompassing the life of the poet's family in the symbolism of the house. This sheltering and nourishing personality of the poet's mother, that sense of being sheltered, protected and warmed in the maternal house, has always reflected, for the poet, the original containment of the womb. It is not surprising, therefore, that the poet chooses the house as a backdrop for exploring the primordial strength of character of his mother. For within the primordial mysteries of preservation, the house is the prerogative of woman, and is thus a symbol of the great mother. As we watch the poet's mother perform feverishly her daily chores— rising early at six in the morning to prepare coffee and fry scrambled eggs for her children, we get a clear picture of woman as the primordial nourishing principle and the ruler over food. This control over food and nourishment marks the poet's mother out as the sendentary archetypal female functioning as the center of the dwelling, the symbolic home to which the normadic male poet returns. Returning to this house is like returning to the womb. The poet insists that her mother's house sings of balance, of permanence and orderedness.

The poet's ideal, according to Baugh, is to attain the conditions of the old house (27). This is because the age-long house is a critical part of the poet's memorial psyche, giving off the impression that it is a primordial symbol of memory. The old house, against the immanent presence of the moon, therefore, is for the poet at least, the luminous feminine spirit which, in spite of the ravages of catastrophic change, is enduring, even attaining immortality. And by conssociating his mother's house with the forest and the ocean, the poet enlarges its fundamental significance. The poet now realizes that to get to his goal implies first of all a journey through the maternal forest. But in this primordial world of vegetation, the poet encounters "the thorns of the bougainvillea/ [moulting] like old fingernails,/ and the flowers keep falling/ and the flowers keep opening/ the allamandas fallen bugles, but nobody charges." The poet experiences a sense of decay and decline. The maternal forest has become linked with the cycle of pain, "shrinking every room, [and] shining in every womb. . ;" and with the morbid images of physiological dysfunctions "with their constellation of cancer,' et cetera, and finally with the imagery of natural aging, in the words of Baugh, "to embody a sense of mortality and the inevitability of time" (26). Here defecation is experienced as loss and castration, and the consequent pain of mortality appears to weaken and overwhelm the artist's vision rather than provide him with the necessary path to self-actualization. The consequence of all of this is terrible for the poet as he breaks down mentally. Chastened by his own mortality, he is immediately confronted with imminent dissolution both in terms of his subjectivity as well as his artistic consciousness; in fact his whole creative enterprise appears to be in jeopardy, given these overwhelmingly negative and frightening contents of the maternal unconscious.

But all is not lost. For this poet whoever turns to the mother-figure also invariably relies on her ineluctable power and regenerative life-principle. That is why this poet must take recourse to his mother, symbolized by the old house. At a time when everything is in a state of flux, at a time when values have tottered and vision cantled, at a time when consciousness is faced with immediate peril, one falls back upon the aboriginal world of the Mother to derive the faith and strength necessary to promote and sustain social and artistic conscience. This is the paradox that is at the heart of the symbolism of the maternal unconscious which the poet finds, however, infinitely ennobling. Thus while some flowers are falling, others are opening up. The psyche as flower, the mother-figure as flower, all that symbolizes the flower-like maturation of the highest psychic and spiritual conscience that the artist is seeking. It is the epitomizing flower of artistic sustenance which his mother represents.

The poet's mother is also associated with the mythic Mother of Songs. We are told that she is a vivacious woman "singing your iron Hynm." She has the inspiring power of a Muse and can lead the poet through dissolution and death to vision and the word. And because the old house as mother also bears the depth of an ocean, the poet's mother has become the wisdom-bringing waters. The humming of her waters in those depths is for the poet the "outside" utterance of her very own unconsciousness which rises up in her like the water that not only contains, but also nourishes and emancipates. So if, therefore, the old house bears the depths of an ocean, and if the mother is the original preserver of the old house, then it seems reasonably clear that the poet should anticipate a new birth from the depths of the earth-mother vessel and expect that in his artistic drift and aimlessness, his mother, as the Great Mother, the feminine principle identical with the primeval waters, will hold him fast, providing him the much needed direction to avert the tragedy that otherwise might overtake him and his fledgling art. And If the poet has entrusted his life, his commitment to his art, in his mother's hands, it is because he sees her as the great sustainer of his unique destiny as an artist. Her mother, as sustainer, is a primordial embodiment of her role as shelterer and preserver.

As we observe the poet's mother sing through her sewing, stitching and weaving, we are comforted with another primordial mystery, that of weaving and sewing. She becomes like the Great Mother who weaves the web of her children's lives and then spins the thread of their destiny. For the poet, striving for artistic prominence and clarity implies a basic recognition of his mother as weaver of fate, busily engaged in marking off the field of his future artistic enterprise as he enters into mature life. In mythic iconography, the woman must not only provide the clothing of man in the literal sense, but also must clothe him with the body of fate she spins and weaves. Thus existing simultaneously with the negative images of maternal chthonic depths are the images that promise not only a new birth, the regeneration of the individual, but also the formation, broadening and transformation of the poet's conscious-ness.

If in "The Divided Child" the poet has discovered the redemptive feminine principle constellated in the primordial depths of the forest and ocean, in "A Simple Flame" Walcott, like Jean Toomer, finds her in the aboriginal ideals of feminine beauty and in the symbolic flame of seemingly requited love. Away from his mother's house, the poet happily encounters Anna, short for Andreuille Alcée, supposedly his one-time sixteen year old flame, when the poet was still on the island of St. Lucia, and as a boy coming into manhood. The poet, as young voyager, passionately regards his young love as the very center of the universe. He idealizes Anna and himself as Adam and Eve in their original state of innocence, as the poet admits, the first guests of the earth, with the prerogative to create and to name.

For the poet, Audreuille has become transfigured into all Annas, from Okigbo's Anna of the panel oblong to Tolstoi's Anna Karenina. Very much like Joyce's Molly Bloom in *Ulysses* or the protean ALP in *Finnegans Wake*, Andreuille has become, in the words of Robert Hamner, the female of all Nature. "You are all Annas, enduring all goodbyes,/ within the cynical station of your body,/ Christie, Karenina, big-boned and passive." As the center of the revolving disc of the world and the cosmos, Anna is the lubricating wheel of life, the unity of all life amid the eternal flux of the seasons, amid the apocalyptic blaze that nearly destroyed Virgie. In fact, as already mentioned, she is like Okigbo's "Anna of the panel oblong." As the cosmic center, she not only bears and directs life and the poet's psyche in particular, but also the light with which the poet can faithfully prod his way through the labyrinth of life, to ford the direst depths of the sea and savor the nourishment he needs to sustain that journey. Earlier on, in the second movement—"Homage to Gregorias"—the poet had told us that Anna's "body downed with the seasons,/ gold and white, Anna/ of the peach furred body, light/ of another epoch, /and stone-grey eyes."

We are reminded here of Soyinka's Simi with the skin of light pastel earth and of Jean Toomer's Karintha with a skin like dusk in the eastern horizon. Walcott highlights this beautiful anatomy against the backdrop of exotic Gregorian landscape. And later, she walks like Judith with Holofernes' lantern in her hand. Indeed for the poet, Anna is the light of the world. The Holofernes' lantern which Anna presumably carries with her symbolizes the ascending structure of the poet's world whose base and center is relativized in herself. This is transformed into the incandescent vegetal light sprewn across the wheatfield which is her abode. The poet addresses her in a gleefully gnomic tone. As Anna of the wheatfield, she is for the poet the greatest nourisher. Her association with winter rain suggests that she is a fertility figure whose fructifying rain makes the earth fertile. To her belongs the water and the rain. She is the nourisher of life with its life-bringing seasons. In this connection, the poet may be casting her in the image of the Lady of Transformation who as the goddess of water commands the fertility of the soil. In these two capacities, she symbolizes for Walcott the ineluctable element of *participation mystique* within which to define his own artistic dedication. And the fact that Anna's voice could be heard as the poet journeys back into the unknown recesses of his history, with rain and dew drops pattering allover suggests that the potential for the poet to launch into a new integrative world might yet very well be realized.

Walcott's altered vision of the female is that of a great comforter and nourisher, something resembling the Madonna. He perceives the male as essentially nomadic, always thirsting for wholeness and self-upliftment, always set in motion by a primordial urge deep down in the depths of his own psyche for a healing transformation. Beyond all masculine intellect, beyond all faustian solipsism, beyond all will to power, beyond the devastation of nature, beyond the rape of culture, is a constellation of an opposing archetype, the archetype of the feminine, which is a primordial function of the process of cross-fertilization through the maternal unconscious endowed with a receptive and fruitful womb which can reshape what is strange and hostile and give it a familiar, sympathetic expressivity. And always invariably, the feminine provides the intercessioary channel. To Walcott, the feminine is the incarnation of what he, in his poem, "Laventille," identifies as the widening memory, the symbolic unconscious, the point of primordial kinship with all the inheritors of the middle passage. To forge a distinct human love that endures, to create an art that imparts a characteristic quality of transcendent meaning, to effectively join art and artifice, one that transcends the theme of the broken individual, clearly means that the poet seek a point of relative stability, a point of keener perception, of altered realism. To Walcott that point is the female, cast in all her symbolic grandeur and magnificence.

In Wilson Harris's novel, *Palace of the Peacock*, the quest for the West Indian past is distilled into the search for the unconscious, with woman, Mariella, the anima as the dominant symbol. In *Tradition the Writer and Society*, Harris speaks first about the novel's subterranean emphasis, and the deepening cycle of exploration, and second about its inward dialogue and space (3). To Harris, the woman is the personification of one's unconscious, that compassionate counterpart to the self which, forever fugitive and rejected, nevertheless has to be faced and accepted by the individual (Gilkes 16). She appears in the novel first as the Amerindian mistress, Mariella, then second as decrepit Arawak woman in the whore Magdar in *The Whole Armour*, and the brutalized, illiterate Catalena Perez in *The Secret Ladder*, and Petra, the muse-figure in *Heartland*. She is also the focal center of the short story "Tomorrow," Harris's first published work, and in one of Harris's early novel extants, *Banim Creek*, where we find the attractive Portuguese huckster whose husband mistreats her. Her frequent visits to the Banim Creek help create tides of emotion analogous to the river tides which the men after her must reach. There is something particularly unique about the symbolic female in *Palace of the Peacock*, something that we have not encountered before in the other female and/or matriarchal figures.

Aside from sharing in the fundamental protean quality which characterizes every primordial female, there is a highly orchestrated sense of communal mystique in which Mariella's symbolic personality becomes part of the transpersonalized totality of the West Indian psyche. In fact the law of *para pro toto* is a significant principle in the understanding of her essential nature. It is as, Erich Neumann explains, a principle which seeks to establish an identity between persons and objects and their constituent parts and elements. It posits that every part contains the totality to which it belongs, since the whole acts or is acted upon in the part (447). For instance, at one time she is Mariella, an Amerindian woman left behind by her people, who later is to lead the journey to the Mission outpost. At another time, she is Mariella, the land itself. And yet at other times, she is the old Arawak woman. And yet again she is simply the Mission itself, the Guyanese interior jungle, the collective unconscious of the West Indian psyche, the maternal symbol of its cultural roots, that Donne and his crew must rediscover. The lines separating these various shades of her personality are so thin that. it is not easy to decipher at what point one crosses the other or the other diverges from the one. The end result is a complex, convoluted and multilayered novel.

Harris's awareness of the numerous layers of experience of race and culture, of what he himself refers to in *Tradition the Writer and Society* as the paradoxes of this world (14), forces him to reject any one-sided, deterministic interpretation. It is the author's awareness of the very nature of the psyche, the central qualities of which are a seemingly chaotic multiplicity and order, what Jung would describe as *coincidentia oppositorum* (the union of opposites). The narrator tells us that "Mariella was the [main] obsession we must encounter at all costs, and we needed gifted souls in our crew" (24). Identified with the Amerindian folk, on the one hand, and with the Mission for which Donne's crew is bound, on the other, Mariella becomes the symbolic vase of initiation. Jean-Pierre Durix says that "Mariella guides the men, serves as an interpreter in a land where they do not speak the language" (130).

This complexity in Mariella's personality is part of her primordial mystery in the novel. To the narrator, "she too had become an enigma" (24), and "had existed like a shaft of fantastical shapely dust in the sun, a fleshly shadow in his consciousness" (25). Again as with Soyinka's Simi, we encounter the unconscious image of the phantom Lady. The enigma vitae that Mariella represents is the enigma vitae of the fluid, unstable nature of existence. It is a conundrum that has created for Harris an impelling need to discover an interior validity, to probe in his words in *Tradition the Writer and Society*, "the living drama of conception, the conception of the human person rather than the ideology of the broken individual" (27). Thus the conception of the character Mariella, is essentially both Blakean and Jungian, blending disparate characteristic elements superbly together to effect a complex vision of reality, one in which the woman is the vestigial entrance into the assortment of images, which is the real nature of the unconscious psyche.

The novel opens with a horseman racing down a road at breakneck speed. Then suddenly he comes tumbling down from his saddle, having been wounded by a snipper's lone shot. The horseman, it turns out, is Donne, the European invader, and the gunman, or shall we say, gun-woman is none other than Mariella herself. And the image instant-aneously created is that of a Terrible Mother antitype. As the person who pulls the trigger that kills Donne, Mariella is viewed, at   least momentarily, as the archetypal mistress of death and destruction, the gross mother of the underworld. Mariella is that

someone (who) was watching us from the trees and bushes that clustered the side of the road. Watching me as I bent down and looked at the man whose open eyes stared at the sky through his long hanging hair. The sun blinded and ruled my living sight but the dead man's eye remained open and obstinate and clear. (13)

Erich Neumann reveals that death and destruction, danger and distress, constitute one-half of the language and character of the Great Mother. Mariella at this point partakes of that destructive temper, and the narrator tells us candidly that "the fury of her voice was in the wind" (16). This woman, Mariella, who leads the way; to symbolic renewal is the same one who pursues her victims and guns them down in a rage. Like the Greek Artemis—Hecate, she is the mistress of the road, of fate, and of the world of the dead. The neat constellation of the images of death and rebirth, physical descent and spiritual ascent, reflects the phenomenon of the natural cycle, the apparent paradox of regeneration through chaos and death. And the attempts by Harris to conjoin Mariella with the prison-gate, or what the narrator calls "the curious high swinging gate" (16), where Mariella is held hostage by Donne, is a subtle way of underscoring the fact that she is the mythic mistress of the gate of death, the engulfing entrance to Donne's underworld of solipsistic power and pathos. Donne initially experiences himself only in the eternal tragedy of masculinity, of the faustian will to power. Like the sadistic oppressor that he is, Donne perceives Mariella as an archetypal castrator, a murderer of the phallus.

We are told by the narrator that "though he (Donne) was the last to admit it, he was glad for a chance to return to that first muse and journey when Mariella had existed like a shaft of fantasical shapely dust in the sun, a fleshy shadow in his consciousness" (25), and that "I stood on my curious stone upon the reality of an unchanging presence Donne had apprehended in a wild and cruel devouring way which had turned Mariella into a vulgar musing executioner" (25).

In other words, Donne's projection of his diabolic intellect/ego, his *divide et impera* passion, his bull-headed, racist imperialism, provokes and sustains a double irony, one that summarily intensifies, in fact, accounts for the terrible image of Mariella's deceptively coy femininity; the other egging her on in order to engage Donne's seductive guiles that in some sense would lead predictably to his final destruction. Donne is, without a doubt, meant to represent the early European Colonizer, very much in the style of Conrad's Kurtz. His crew is made up of a mixture of races (African, Amerindian, European, Portuguese) which, in their complex, genetic relationships constitute a truly Guyanese society. In psychological terms, it is Jung's collective unconscious and Levy Bruhl's *participation mystique* given concrete, objective reality.

On a literal level, Donne's quest with his crew is related to the European's first voyage and expedition into the interior Guyanese country. But on an allegorical and visionary level, the quest represents the modern Guyanese dream of repossessing the interior, a phrase that in and by its ultimate meaning stands for the establishment of a genuine sense of cultural, spiritual, and psychological identity. Like Donne, the crew recognizes that only the Amerindians have any real title rights to the land, and in seeking the Mission (called Mariella), they are in fact yearning for a sense of belonging to the land. This is where the woman, Mariella, manifests her essential significance. Because she is that Mission, she symbolizes that inner wholeness sought for by the Guyanese, if not the whole West Indian, community.

The veiled desire of the crew is for a monistic order, a certain oneness or permanence and direction beyond the flux of divided consciousness, divided space and time. Mariella is that permanence, that direction, in short, the entire Amerindian folk living in the hinterland. Cameron knows that, for him, the search for the Folk is truly symbolic. For "he wanted space and freedom to use his own hands in order to make his own primitive home and kingdom on earth" (p. 41). Making one's primitive home and kingdom on earth, and making it above all endure for eternity, implies discovering and rediscovering the maternal essence wherein may lie the secret and power of a forgotten milieu. It also implies a manifest movement toward a reclamation of the inner unconscious life and an extension of the space inhabited by man, both symbolized by woman.

Thus Harris's vision of the symbolic female is one that sets up woman as a metaphor for man's undeveloped inner being. To achieve clarity of vision, man must lose himself in the quintessence of the female both in her objective manifestation as well as in her subjectivity. In that lies man's capacity to lose himself in order to find himself; in that lies the possibility of death, renewal, rebirth and the dignity of self-discovery.

Notes

Introduction: Allegory and the Literary Imagination

1. "Interview with Chinua Achebe," by Anthony Appiah, John Ryle and D.A.N. Jones. *Times Literary Supplement*. February 26, 1982.

2. In *Homage to Catalonia*, Orwell castigates the media for literally causing the verbal corruption he decries. See Angus Fletcher, *Allegory: The Theory of a Symbolic Mode*, p. 3.

3. Fletcher recounts that although Coleridge in the *Stateman's Manual* tries strenuously to differentiate allegory from symbolism, his position he says, however well-intentioned, has been vehemently assailed by modem theorists of allegory such as Walter Benjamin and Paul de Man who, instead, see both allegory and symbolism as sharing in similar, even if not identicaL characteristic element. Paul de Man renders the sentiment of the group best. In his *Allegories of Reading* (1979), he contends that while [the] symbol postulates the possibility of an identity or identification, allegory designates primarily a distance. In other words, allegory and symbol are two sides of the same coin.

4. Both Cicero and Quintilian hold the view that allegory is metaphor. Quintilian in particular, goes further to assert that "continued metaphor develops into allegory. . . presents one thing in words, and another in meaning." See *The Institutes of Oratory*. Tr. H.E. Butler (London & Cambridge, Mass), Loeb Classics Edition, 1953.

5. "On Fiction as an Oblique Process—A Talk with Ralph Ellison." *Ralph Ellison: A Collection of Essays*. Quoted in Michael Meyer, *The Bedford Introduction to Literature*. Boston: Bedford Books/St. Martin's Press, 1993. 198.

Chapter 1: Bessie Head's *Maru*: Existentialist Allegory, Pathology
        of Difference, and the Quest for Conscience

1. The summary of Hegel's, Heidegger's and Sartre's enunciations is culled from Chaptec 5: "Feminism and Existentialism." Josephine Donovan's *Feminist Theory: The Intellectual Traditions of American Feminism*. New York: Frederick Ungar Publishing, 1985.

Chapter 2: Masada as Symbol in *Season of Anomy*

1. Izevbaye's neat summary of the Orphic myth is inspirational. I aJso consulted the following texts for additional maximum insight: Walter A. Strauss, *Descent and Return: The Orphic Theme in Modern Literature*. Cambridge:

Harvard University Press, 1971 and Philip Mayerson, *Classical Mythology in Literature, Art and Music*. Lexington: Xerox College Publishing, 1971.

2. One of the best poems by Wole Soyinka dealing with the ironies of human existence, in particular human invention. For a reading, see the Menthuen edition of *Idanre and Other Poems*.

3. The names of four of the six men immortalized in the bronze sculpture include: Eustache de Saint-Pierre—the leader of the heroic pack, Jean d'Aire, Jacques de Vissant, and his brother, Pierre de Vissant. All six men were said to have stripped to their undershirts in the city of Calais and to have put the yoke around their necks.

4. Numbers 1, 2, 5, 6, and 7 are quoted from Yadin's "The Excavation at Masada" except numbers 3 and 4 which are from his "Masada." *Horizon*. vol. 8 (Winter 1966).

5. In connection with the dead naked woman. it is necessary to point up another irony being played upon here. On p. 272 of *Season of Anomy*, Soyinka mentions the graphics of the sculptor Henry Moore. The irony here is that while Henry Moore's mother-figure statues are, for the most part, an essence of creativity am life, that. of the discovered remains of the woman in the crypt is associated with death and destruction. Notwithstanding, both, however, are ultimately linked to eternal promise and renewal.

6. Flavius Josephus is an 18th century Jewish Roman historian who, at the height of the Masada event, defected to the Romans and later wrote an eye witness account of the tragedy.

7. Another writer in the same mode is N. Avigad, "Moral of Masada." *Jewish Observer*. vol. 12. December 27, 1963.

Chapter 3: Soyinka: From the Failed Narcissus to Heroic Orphism

1. Dan Izevbaye has an excellent summary of the novel's plot from which my own synopsis is culled. See his "Soyinka's Black Orpheus." *Neo-African Literature and Culture*. Ed. Bemth Lindfors and Ulla Schild. Wiesbaden: B. Heyman Verlag Gmbtl, 1976.

Chapter 4: Awoonor, Okigbo, and Soyinka: Nostos, Symbolism, and Prima Donnas

1. In "The Madonna/Whore: Womb of Possibilities, chapter 2 in the book, *The Literate Imagination: Essays on the Novels of Wilson Harris*, edited by Michael Gilkes, Mark McWatt provides a long exposé on the sources of the symbolic female, particularly the dichotomous representation of the whore/madonna figure. The first source is the Bible, which McWatt calls "one of the major

sources of symbolism for western art, including literature." Another source is the Homeric poetry where we find Penelope, on the one hand and Circe, the sirens and a number of threatening female figures, on the other. Other sources cited by McWatt include Spenser's female characters in *Faerie Queen*—Una and Duessa, and the narratives of the romantics.

2. Kofi Awoonor, *This Earth, My Brother*. New York: Doubleday, 1972. All future citations from the book refer to this edition and will occur parenthetically in the text.

3. I am indebted to John Vickery's *Robert Graves and the White Goddess* for the inspiration for this thought.

4. Christopher Okigbo, *Labyrinths*. New York: Africana Publishing, 1971. All future citations from the book refer to this edition unless otherwise indicated and will occur parenthetically in the text

5. Wole Soyinka, *The Interpreters*. London: Heinemann, 1970. All future citations from the book refer to this edition and will occur parenthetically in the text.

6. For a full analysis of the multidimensional, protean aspects of the entire Aphroditic tradition. see Paul Friedrich's *The Meaning of Aphrodite*. Chicago: University of Chicago Press, 1978.

7. It is the kind of love that belongs squarely in the popular folklore tradition. One thinks, perhaps, of Charles Nodier's Trilby in *Trilby* as Simi's male counterpart. Or we can regard Egbo as Trilby. And just as Trilby dwells in Jeannie's hearth and watches over house and farmyard while she sleeps, so Egbo dreams of living under the same protective roof with Simi.

8. The general nature of this pattern is fully discussed in Marie—Louise von Franz, *C.G. Jung: His Myth in Our Time*. Trans. William H. Kenedy. New York: Putnam's Sons, 1975. See especially p. 71.

9. Izevbaye also notes that Soyinka "shows through word play that a myth can be made indigenous by the right manipulation of language, form and social experience. Ofeyi and Iriyise are meaningful names in Yoruba. They may be unusual, but they are not improbable names. And yet they sound like Yoruba descendants of Greek Orpheus and Eurydice" (153).

10. Wole Soyinka, *Season of Anomy*. New York: Third Press, 1973. All future citations from the book refer to this edition and will occur parenthetically in the text.

Chapter 5: Baraka, Marquis de Sade, and the Individual Will

1. New York: Grove Press, 1965. All future citations from the book refer to this

edition and will occur parenthetically in the text.

2. See Donald Thomas's comments in *The Marquis de Sade*. New York: New York Graphic Society. 1976.

3. Hassan insists that, against the background of the omnipotence of the Sadean tyrant-villain and the abjectness of his victim-heroine, the consumation of the Sadean will manifests in death (48).

4. The literature of homosexuality begins with the Book of Genesis. which portrays the Sodomites as evil men who want to rape visitors, violating the tradition of hospitality. When the Lord sends two angels to Sodom to find ten righteous men who might save the wicked city from destruction, they are invited into Lot's house and feast with him. Before they lie down to sleep, the house is surrounded by the men of the city (Genesis 19:5-8). See also Deuteronomy 23: 17, 1 Kings. and Jude 7 for a condemnation of the abominations of the Sodomites and their going after strange flesh.

5. See Michel Foucault, *The History of Sexuality*, trans. Robert Hurley. New York: Pantheon Books. 1978.1:34. See also Walter Perrie, "Homosexuality and Literature." *The Sexual Dimension in Literature*. Ed. Alan Bold. Totowa, NJ: Vision. 1978

6. Freud thought homosexuality was a sign of arrested development and succinctly categorized it as a pathological condition. See his *Civilization and Its Discontents*. In this regard *The System of Dante's Hell* should be of tremendous interest to those concerned with contemporary psychoanalysis.

7. See a paraphrase of Stekel's description in Reinhardt, *Sex Perversions and Sex Crimes*, 142.

8. We recall these lines from Baraka's poem "Red Eye": "The corrupt madness of the individual. You cannot/ live alone. You are in the world. Women, fuck them." In both this poem and in his novel, erotica is rife and the call to hetero-sexuality becomes an urgent call for active and close involvement with reality and the essence or symbolism that lies behind it.

9. For an insightful discussion of the way in which this metaphor has served in the sacred realm, particularly with reference to Indian literature and art, see Walter Spink's *The Axis of Eros*. New York: Schocken Books, 1973.

10. Like the moral observer in the tradition of Balzac, Baraka plumbs the depths of the nonrational impulses of human psychosexuality as a way of exposing the trivial, the demonic urge, and the intensity of passion, and subsequently tran-scending them. This is where his path crosses with the other American writer Joyce Carol Oates. In the Introduction to *The Edge of Impossibility*, Oates writes: ". . . what are we except passion, and how are we to survive when this passion breaks its dikes and flows out into nature?" Art, she feels, is built around

violence, around death; "at its base is fear" ([1972; rpt. Greenwich. CT: Fawcett Books, 1973]). 8.

11. Dolmancé, a character in Sade's *Philosophy in the Bedroom* (1795), is Sade's prototype of erotic cruelty. Like Sade he insists that sexual cruelty is itself a virtue. To Baraka sexual cruelty is not virtuous; it is, on the contrary, a kind of moral deformity or depravity.

Chapter 6: Baraka and the Allegoric Meaning of the Tragic Spirit

1. Pfeffer's book is the sole inspiration for this essay; and I hereby express my total, unqualified indebtedness.

2. For a fuller discussion of the affinity between Buddhism and Nietzsche's thought, see Stambaugh 17-19.

3. We are reminded of Nietzsche's early praise of Immanuel Kant's victory over the optimistic foundations of logic. Nietzsche paid the highest tribute to Kant when he called him "the initiator of a tragic culture." For more on this, read *The Birth of Tragedy* (1872).

4. Dynatypes and cognitypes are two essential manifestations of the élan vital within the human psyche as identified by Ira Progoff. According to Progoff, dynatypes are the roots of the lifestyles to which we are attracted, in which we excel, and with which we find ourselves most easily content. Dynatypes program our vital energies. Cognitypes, on the other hand, release our vital energies. Cognitypes are the eternal verities through which the higher self in man is actualized. For fuller details, see Lonergan.

Chapter 7: Baraka, America, and the Allegory of Racial Sin

1. The moral importunacy of art has long been recognized by writers and critics alike. For instance, F.R Leavis in *The Great Tradition* says that the uniqueness of the great English novelists such as George Eliott (Mary Ann Evans) lies in their vital capacity for experience with a high moral tone. David J. Dooley in *Moral Vision in the Canadian Novel* paraphrases the contention of the Canadian novelist, Huqh MacLennan, that the only way in which mankind can be redeemed from the wasteland of the modem world is through religious and moral commitment Wayne C. Booth maintains that the degree of reliability or integrity of a particular work of art may lie in its capacity for moral clarity. Graham Green in *The Lost Childhood and Other Essays* praises the strong moral vision in Henry James's novels, suggesting that the moral background of a given work of art is a significant part of the "willed appliqués of [artistic] sensibility."

2. To Baraka the alienation of the black man from his cultural roots and sense of identity through a process of alien renaming is the white man's first. savage act of violence. But the black man also comes under the author's moral sting, for he

(the black man) too has given credence to that violence by unwittingly participating and reveling in what amounts to as the grand-style nomenclatural coup de grace of the West. Baraka's prototypical faceless black man either with no name or an appreciation of the ontology of name is the character—46 [See *The System of Dante's Hell*—"The Eight Ditch (Is Drama"— 79—91].

3. Prior to this understanding, Baraka suggests that the disorder and the chaos in the black man's world is due in part to his reckless prostitution of his free will and rational faculty. Beneath the newly found order is a clear vision and a unity which is its very soul.

Chapter 8: Gwendolyn Brooks's *Maud Martha*: Narrative as Allegory of
           Initiation

1. This concept is discussed fully in Chapter 7 of Edward F. Edinger's *Ego and Archetype* (New York: G.P. Putnam's Sons, 1972). Edinger provides an impressive array of thoughts by leading authorities on the subject of what he calls "Trinity archetype." Notable among them are: Jung who gives the trinity a dynamic developmental interpretation in his description of the three phases of psychological development in terms of three stages: oral, anal and genital; Esther Harding's threefold pattern: auto, ego and self; Alfred North Whitehead's three stages in the natural learning process: the stages of romance, precision and generalization; W. R. Inge's *scala perfectionis*, the mystic's ladder: the purgative life, the illuminative, and the unitive or the stage of perfect contemplation; Hegel's historical triad: thesis, antithesis, and synthesis; and Gerhard Adler's use of triadism in charting the instinctual events in feminine natural development and growth.

2. For a fuller discussion of the process, see his *The Novels of Herman Hesse*. See also H.G. Baynes's *Mythology of the Soul*.

3. I am indebted to Edward C. Whitmont in *The Symbolic Quest*. Princeton: Princeton University Press, 1969 for this idea.

4. Gwendolyn Brooks, *Maud Martha*. New York: Harper, 1953. All future citations from the book refer to this edition and will occur parenthetically in the text.

5. For a fuller discussion of this phenomenon, see Bruno Bettelheim's *The Uses of Enchantment*. New York: Knopf, 1976.

6. This Arnoldian landscape is thoroughly explained by William Anthony Madden in *Matthew Arnold*. Bloomington: Indiana University Press, 1967.

7. I am indebted to Diva Daims and Janet Grimes, *Toward a Feminist Tradition* for these ideas.

8. See her illuminating essay, "In Search of Our Mother's Garden: The Creativity of the Black Woman in the South." *Ms Magazine*. May 1974.

9. See her *To Be Young, Gifted and Black*, adapted by Robert Nemiroff. Englewood Cliffs, N.J.: Prentice-Hall, 1969. 17 (IV, 2); 217 (V, 3). Quoted in James E. Miller, *Word, Self, Reality: The Rhetoric of Imagination*. New York: Dodd, Mead & Company, 1974. 120.

Chapter 9: Redemptive Fantasy and Allegory of the Endtime

1. For a discussion of the essential features of heroic fantasy, see Jules Zanger, "Heroic Fantasy and Social Reality: *ex nihilo nihil fit*." *The Aesthetics of Fantasy Literature and Art*. Ed. Roger C. Schlobin. Notre Dame: University of Notre Dame Press, 1982. 226-36.

2. Cyprian Ekwensi, *Survive the Peace*. London: Heineman, 1972. All future citations from the book refer to this edition and will occur parenthetically in the text.

3. Olson calls this dramatic process "the doctrine of historical progress." (3)

4. Desroche argues that the hope of transforming society is carried within the millenarian-dialectical mythos of collective ideation.

5. V.S. Reid, *New Day*. New York: Alfred A. Knopf, 1949. All future citations from the book refer to this edition and will occur parenthetically in the text.

6. Ousmane Sembene, *God's Bits of Wood*. Garden City: Doubleday, 1970. All future citations to the book refer to this edition and will occur parenthetically in the text.

7. George Lamming, *In the Castle of My Skin*. New York: McGraw—Hill, 1954. All future ciations from the book refer to this edition and will occur parenthetically in the text.

8. The struggle is also a search for what Anthony Wallace has conceptually described as "revitalization"—"a deliberate, organized, conscious effort of members of a society to construct a more satisfying culture." Wallace is of the opinion that the revitalization process presuppqses "that the participants in such movements felt that major aspects of the existing culture were no longer viable" (xvii-xviii). See his article, "Revitalization Movements." *American Anthropologist*. 58 (1956): 264—66.

Chapter 10: A Cosmic Postulate of Eros: Reading Harris's *Palace of the Peacock*

1. For further discussion of symbolic inscriptions in Harris, see Sandra E. Drake, *Wilson Harris and the Modern Tradition*; Michael Gilkes, *Wilson Harris and the Caribbean Novel*; and Hena Maes-Helinek, *Wilson Harris*.

2. C.G. Jung, "Answer to Job," 754. Quoted by Marie—Louise von Franz, *C.G. Jung: His Myth in Our Time.*

3. Quoted by von Franz, 249—50.

4. Quoted by von Franz, 250.

5. von Franz, 251.

6. Like the alchemist that he is, Harris selects the cliff as an organic steno-symbol for the God-within image. The choice of Antillean cliff is not only to show the principles of matter, but also to demonstrate that the process of self-realization lies within the reach of every living soul. It is also heaven made accessible to contrite material man. As the material theater in which the drama of the eternalist self is enacted, the cliff appears to emerge as the natural symbol of craved wholeness. It would seem to contain within itself dark, towering vitality constructed at the triple axis of divine encounter, femininity and the human stirrings of the spirit-soul. In the cliff, the cosmic spirit appears to be indwelling; the cliff also serving as the symbol of the inner God lodged in every human heart, arising "from those border regions of the psyche that open out into the mystery of cosmic matter" (see Jung, "Zosimos," par. 127). Additionally, Donne's ascent up the cliff appears to dramatize in its conceptual energy the post-Kantian idealism that asserts the qualitative primacy of the spiritual and the intuitive over the material and the empirical.

7. Quoted by von Franz, 251.

8. The inspiration for this reading of the novel comes Andrew Weil, *The Marriage of the Sun and the Moon: A Quest for Unity in Consciousness.*

9. C.G. Jung, quoted by Violet Staub de Laszlo, ed. *The Basic Writings of C.G. Jung.*

10. Quoted by de Laszlo, 65.

11. See Horapollo, *Hieroglyphica.* Trans. George Boas. New York: Bollingen Series XXIII, 1950. 66. Quoted in de Laszlo, 65.

12. For more on this concept, see Ananda K. Coomaraswamy, *Journal of American Oriental Society* 46 (1946): 145—61.

13. Quoted by von Franz, 64.

14. Quoted by von Franz, 227.

15. Elizabeth Drew. Quoted in Gertrude Patterson, *T.S. Eliot: Poems in the Making,* 174.

16. Quoted in Patterson, 175.

17. Jung calls this union of opposites equilibration. In fact, Jung borrows this concept of opposites from Heraclitus, who had earlier described it as *enantiodromia*. Jung explains the concept of enantiodromia this way:

In the philosophy of Heraclitus this concept is used to designate the play of opposites in the course of events, namely, the view which maintains that everything that exists goes into its opposite. From the living comes death, and from the old, youth; from waking, sleep; and from sleep, waking; the stream of creation and decay never stands still. Construction and destruction, destruction and construction—this is the norm which rules in every circle of natural life from the smallest to the greatest. Just as the cosmos itself emerged from the primal fire, so must it return once more to the same—a double process. See de Laszlo, ed. *The Basic Writings of C.G. Jung*, 77–80.

18. de Laszlo, 77–80.

Chapter 11: A Woman Transfigured: Reading Derek Walcott and Wilson Harris

1. For a brilliant discussion of the perspective on *Epitaph for the Young*, see Robert Hamner, *Derek Walcott*. Boston: G.K. Hull–Twayne Publishers, 1981.

2. Walcott, Derek, *Another Life*. Washington, D.C.: Three Continents Press, 1982. All future citations from the book refer to this edition and will occur parenthetically in the text.

Selected Bibliography

Abel, Elizabeth, Marianne Hirsch, and Elizabeth Langland, eds. *The Voyage In: Fictions of Female Development*. Hanover: University Press of New England, 1983.

Abrahams, Cecil. ed. *The Tragic Life: Bessie Head and Literature in Southern Africa*. Trenton, NJ: Africa World Press, 1990.

Adas, Michael. *Prophets of Rebellion*. Chapel Hill: University of North Carolina Press, 1979.

Anozie, Sunday O. *Christopher Okigbo: Creative Rhetoric*. New York: Holmes & Meier, 1972.

Awoonor, Kofi. *This Earth, My Brother*. New York: Doubleday, 1972.

Bachofen, Johann Jakob. *Das Mutterrecht*. Basel: Gesammelte Werke, 1948.

Baraka, Imamu Amiri. *The System of Dante's Hell*. New York: Grove Press, 1965.

Baugh, Edward. *Derek Walcott, Memory as Vision: Another Life*. London: Longman, 1978.

Baynes, H.G. *Mythology of the Soul*. London: Ryder and Company, 1969.

Benston, Kimberly. *Baraka: The Renegade and the Mask*. New Haven: Yale University Press, 1976.

Berdyaev, Nicholas. *The Meaning of the Creative Act*. New York: Collier, 1962.

Bettelheim, Bruno. *The Uses of Enchantment*. New York: Knopf, 1976.

Bishop, Anne. *Becoming an Ally: Breaking the Cycle of Oppression in People*. Halifax, Nova Scotia: Fernwood Publishing, 2002.

Bloch, Ivan. *The Sexual Life of Our Time in Its Relation to Modern Civilization*. New York: Allied Books, 1912.

Brandeis, Irma. *The Ladder of Vision*. Garden City: Doubleday, 1962.

Brathwaite, Edward Kamau. "Timeri." *Is Massa Day Dead?* Ed. Orde Coombs. New York: Doubleday/Anchor, 1974.

Breiner, Laurence A. "Lyric and Autobiography in West Indian Literature." *Journal of West Indian Literature*. 3 (1989): 3—15.

Brooks, Gwendolyn. *Maud Martha*. New York: Harper, 1953.

Brown, Lloyd W. *West Indian Poetry*. Boston: G.K. Hull—Twayne Publishers, 1981.

_____. *Women Writers in Black Africa*. Westport, CT: Greenwood Press, 1981.

Buchen, Irving. ed. *The Perverse Imagination: Sexuality and Literary Culture*. New York: New York University Press, 1970.

Burridge, Kenelm. *New Heaven, New Earth*. New York: Schoken Books, 1969.

Campbell, Joseph. *The Hero with a Thousand Faces*. New York: Pantheon Books, 1949.

Carey, Frances. ed. *The Apocalypse and the Shape of Things to Come*. Toronto: University of Toronto Press, 1999.

Carter, Angela. *The Sadian Woman and the Ideology of Pornography*. New York: Pantheon Books, 1978.

Christ, Carol P. *Diving Deep and Surfacing*. Boston: Beacon, 1980.

Cicero. *Cicero's Letters to Atticus*. Ed. and Trans. D.R. Shackleton Bailey. Cambridge: Cambridge University Press, 1965. I: 252. Letter 40.

Cohn, Norman. *The Pursuit of the Millennium*. New York: Oxford University Press, 1970.

Cooper, Anna Julia. *A Voice from the South by a Black Woman of the South*. Exenia: Aldine Printing House, 1982.

Daims, Diva and Janet Grimes. *Toward a Feminist Tradition*. New York: Garland Publishing, 1982.

De Laszlo, Violet Staub. ed. *The Basic Writings of C.G. Jung*. New York: MLA, 1959.

Desroche, Henri. *The Sociology of Hope*. Trans. Carol Martin-Sperry. London: Routledge and Kegan Paul, 1979.

Diggs, Marylynne. "Surveying the Intersection: Pathology, Secrecy, and the Discourses of Racial and Sexual Identity." *Critical Essays: Gay and Lesbian Writers of Color*. Binghamton, NY: Harrington Park Press, 1993.

Dilthey, Wilhelm. *Das Erlebnis und Dichtung*. Leipzig & Bern, 1913.

Dooley, D.J. *Moral Vision in the Canadian Novel*. Toronto: Clarke, 1979.

Drake, Sandra E. *Wilson Harris and the Modern Tradition: A New Architecture of the World*. New York: Greenwood, 1986.

Drayton, Arthur. "West Indian Fiction and West Indian Society." *Kenyon Review*. 25 (Winter 1963).

Durix, Jean—Pierre. "Along Jigsaw Trail: An Interpretation of *Heartland*. *Commonwealth Novel in English*. 1.2 (July 1982).

Ebert, Teresa L. "The "Difference" of Post-Modern Feminism." *College English*. 53.8. (December 1991): 886—904.

Eilersen, Gillian Stead. *Bessie Head, Thunder Behind Her Ears: Her Life and Writing*. Portsmouth, NH: Heinemann, 1996.

Eliade, Mircea. *Myths, Dreams, and Mysteries*. London: Harvill Press, 1957.

_____. *The Myth of Eternal Return*. Trans. Willard R. Trask. New York: Pantheon Books, 1954.

Elsley, Judy. "Nothing can be sole or whole that has not been rent: Fragmentation in the Quilt and *The Color Purple*." *Critical Essays on Alice Walker*. Ed. Ikenna Dieke. Westport, CT: Greenwood Press, 1999.

Empson, William. *The Structure of Complex Words*. New York: New Directions, 1951.

Finkelstein, Louis. "Masada and Its Heroes." *Masada: Struggle for Freedom*. New York: The Jewish Museum, 1967/1968.

Fletcher, Angus. *Allegory: The Theory of a Symbolic Mode*. Ithaca: Cornell University Press, 1964.

Foucault, Michel. *The History of Sexuality (Histoire de la Sexualite)*. New York: Pantheon Books, 1978.

Freud, Sigmund. *Civilization and Its Discontents*. London: Hogarth Press, 1930.

Frye, Northrop. *Anatomy of Criticism*. Princeton: Princeton University Press, 1957.

Gilkes, Michael. *Wilson Harris and the Caribbean Novel*. London: Longman, 1975.

Gilman, Sander L. *Difference and Pathology: Stereotypes of Sexuality, Race, and Madness*. Ithaca: Cornell University Press, 1985.

Greenblatt, Stephen J. ed. *Allegory and Representation*. Baltimore: The Johns Hopkins University Press, 1981.

Guntrip, Harry. *Schizoid Phenomena, Object-Relations, the Self*. London: Hogarth Press, 1968.

Hansberry, Lorraine. *To Be Young, Gifted and Black*. Englewood Cliffs, N.J.: Prentice-Hall, 1969.

Harman, Willis W. "The Psychedelic Experience." *Ways of Growth*. Ed. Herbert A. Otto, Sidney M. Jourard, and John H. Mann. New York: Grossman, 1968.

Harmon, William. *A Handbook to Literature*. Upper Saddle River, N.J.: Prentice-Hall, 1996.

Harris, Wilson. *Palace of the Peacock*. London: Faber and Faber, 1960.

_____. *Tradition the Writer and Society*. New York: New Beacon, 1967.

Hassan, Ihab. "Sade: Prisoner of Consciousness." *The Perverse Imagination: Sexuality and Literary Culture*. Ed. Irving Buchen. New York: New York University Press, 1970.

Head, Bessie. *A Woman Alone*. Oxford: Heinemann International, 1990.

_____. *Maru*. London : Heinemann, 1971.

_____. "Social and Political Pressures that Shape Literature in Southern Africa." *The Tragic Life: Bessie Head and Literature in Southern Africa*. Ed. Cecil Abrahams. Trenton, N.J.: Africa World Press, 1990.

Hegel, G.W.F. *Phenomenology of Spirit*. Oxford: Clarendon Press, 1977.

Heidegger, Martin. *Being and Time*. New York: Harper, 1962.

Holbrook, David. *Human Hope and the Death Instinct*. Oxford: Pergamon Press, 1971.

Horapollo. *Hieroglyphica*. Trans. George Boas. New York: Pantheon Books (Bollingen Series 23), 1950.

Hudson, Theodore. *From LeRoi Jones to Amiri Baraka: The Literary Works.* Durham, NC: Duke University Press, 1973.

Hughes, Richard. *The Lively Image.* Cambridge: Winthrop Publishers, 1975.

Ibrahim, Huma. *Bessie Head: Subversive Identities in Exile.* Charlottesville: University Press of Virginia, 1996.

Izevbaye, Dan. "Soyinka's Black Orpheus." *Neo-African Literature and Culture.* Ed. Bernth Lindfors and Ulla Schild. Wiesbaden: B. Heyman Verlag Gmbtl, 1976.

James, Henry. "A Letter to the Deerfield Summer School." *The Future of the Novel.* Ed. Leon Edel. New York: Vintage—Random House, 1956.

Jones, Eldred Durosimi. *The Writing of Wole Soyinka.* London: Heinemann, 1973.

Kerenyi, Carl. *Dionysos.* Trans. Ralph Manheim. Princeton: Princeton University Press, 1976.

Kermode, Frank. "Millennium and Apocalypse." *The Apocalyse and the Shape of Things to Come.* Toronto: University of Toronto Press, 1999.11—27.

_____. *The Sense of an Ending: Studies in the Theory of Fiction.* New York: Oxford University Press, 1967.

Kiell, Norman. *Varieties of Sexual Experience.* New York: International Universities Press, 1976.

Krell, David Farrel. *Of Memory, Reminiscence and Writing: On the Verge.* Bloomington: Indiana University Press, 1990.

Laing, R.D. *The Politics of Experience.* London: Penguin, 1967.

Lanternari, Vittorio. *The Religions of the Oppressed: A Study of Modern Messianic Cults.* New York: Mentor, 1965.

Larsen, Stephen. *The Shaman's Doorway.* New York: Harper & Row, 1970.

Legman, Gershon. *Love and Death: A Study in Censorship.* New York: Hacker Art Books, 1963.

Levine, Robert S. Introduction. William Wells Brown, *Clotel or The President's Daughter.* Boston: Bedford/St. Martin's Press, 2000.

Lonergan, Bernard J.F. "Reality, Myth, and Symbol." *Myth, Symbol, and Reality.* Ed. Alan M. Olson. Notre Dame: University of Notre Dame Press, 1980. 31—37.

MacCabe, Colin. *James Joyce and the Revolution of the Word.* London: Macmillan, 1978.

MacKenzie, Craig. Introduction. *Bessie Head, A Woman Alone: Autobiographical Writings.* Oxford: Heinemann International, 1990.

MacQuarrie, John. *Martin Heidegger.* London: Lutterworth, 1968.

Maduakor, Obi. *Wole Soyinka: An Introduction to His Writing.* New York: Garland Publishing, 1986.

Maes—Helinek, Hena. *Wilson Harris.* Boston: Twayne, 1982.

Marcus, Mordecai. "What Is an Initiation Story?" *The Journal of Aesthetics and Art Criticism*. Rpr. Michael Meyer. *The Bedford Introduction to Literature*. Boston: Bedford Books of St. Martin's Press, 1993. 574.

Marcuse, Herbert. *Eros and Civilization*. New York: Knopf, 1962.

McWatt, Mark. "The Madonna/Whore: Womb of Possibilities." *The Literate Imagination: Essays on the Novels of Wilson Harris*. London: Macmillan, 1989.

Meyers, Jeffrey. *Homosexuality and Literature, 1890—1930*. Montreal: McGill—Queen's University Press, 1977.

Miller, James E. *Word, Self, Reality: The Rhetoric of Imagination*. New York: Dodd, Mead and Company, 1972.

Moeller, Charles. *Man and Salvation in Literature*. Trans. Charles Underhill Quinn. Notre Dame: University of Notre Dame Press, 1970.

Neumann, Erich. *The Origins and History of Consciousness*. Princeton: Princeton University Press, 1970.

_____. *The Great Mother*. New York: Pantheon Books, 1955.

Nietzsche, Friedrich. *The Complete Works of Friedrich Nietzsche*. Ed. Oscar Levy. 18 vols. New York: Macmillan, 1909—1911. Vol. 1.

Oates, Joyce Carol. *The Edge of Impossibility*. Greenwich, CT: Fawcett Books, 1973.

Okigbo, Christopher. *Labyrinths*. New York: Holmes & Meier, 1971.

Okonkwo, Juliet. "The Essential Unity of Soyinka's *The Interpreters* and *Season of Anomy*." *African Literature Today*. 11. Ed. Eldred Durosimi Jones. 110—121.

Olson, Theodore. *Millennialism, Utopianism, and Progress*. Toronto: University of Toronto Press, 1982.

Otto, Walter Friedrich. *Dionysos: Mythos und Kultur*. Frankfurt: Klostermann, 1933.

Patai, Raphael. *Myth and Modern Man*. Englewood: Prentice—Hall, 1972.

Patterson, Gertrude. *T.S. Eliot: Poems in the Making*. New York: Barnes and Noble, 1971.

Perrie, Walter. "Homosexuality and Literature." *The Sexual Dimension of Literature*. Ed. Alan Bold. Totowa, NJ: Vision, 1978.

Pfeffer, Rose. *Nietzsche: Disciple of Dionysus*. Lewisburg, PA: Bucknell University Press, 1972.

Rabkin, Eric S., Martin H. Greenberg, and Joseph D. Olander. Eds. *No Place Else: Explorations in Utopian and Dystopian Fiction*. Carbondale: Southern Illinois University Press, 1983.

Reinhardt, James Melvin. *Sex Perversions and Sex Crimes*. Springfield: Charles C. Thomas, 1956.

Rodman, Selden. *Tongues of Fallen Angels: Conversations with Jorge Luis Borges and Others*. New York: New Directions Publishing, 1972.

Rosowski, Susan J. "The Novel of Awakening." *The Voyage In: Fictions of Female Development*. Eds. Elizabeth Abel, Marianne Hirsch, and Elizabeth Langland. Hanover: University Press of New England, 1983.

Ruggiers, P.G. *The Art of the Canterbury Tales*. Madison: University of Wisconsin Press, 1965.

Ruy, Jules Chaix. *The Superman: From Nietzsche to Teilhard de Chardin*. Trans. Marina Smyth-Kok. Notre Dame: University of Notre Dame Press, 1968.

Saakana, Amon Saba. *The Colonial Legacy in Caribbean Literature*. London: Karnak House, 1987.

Sanders, Roland. "The View from Masada." *Midstream*. vol. 10.2 (1964).

Sartre, Jean-Paul. *Being and Nothingness: An Essay in Phenomenological Ontology*. New York: Citadel Press, 1966.

_____. *Saint Genet: Actor and Martyr*. New York: G. Braziller, 1963.

Savater, Fernando. *Childhood Regained*. New York: Columbia University Press, 1982.

Scheler, Max. *Die Wissenschaft und die Gesellschaft*. Leipzig: Neuegeist, 1926.

Schlobin, Roger C. ed. The Aesthetics of Fantasy Literature and Art. Notre Dame: University of Notre Dame Press, 1982.

Sedgwick, Eve Kosofsky. *Epistemology of the Closet*. Berkeley: University of California Press, 1990.

Shmueli, Adi. *Kierkegaard and Consciousness*. Princeton: Princeton University Press, 1971.

Soyinka, Wole. *Season of Anomy*. The Third Press, 1973.

_____. *The Man Died (Prison Notes of Wole Soyinka)*. London: Rex Collins, 1973.

_____. *The Interpreters*. London: Heinemann, 1965.

Spacks, Patricia Meyer. *Imagining a Self*. Cambridge: Harvard University Press, 1976.

Spink, Walter. *The Axis of Eros*. New York: Schocken Books, 1973.

Stambaugh, Joan. *Nietzsche's Thought of Eternal Return*. Baltimore: Johns Hopkins University Press, 1972.

Swales, Martin. *The German Bildungsroman from Wieland to Hesse*. Princeton: Princeton University Press, 1978.

Szasz, Thomas S. *The Manufacture of Madness*. Syracuse: Syracuse University Press, 1970.

Taiwo, Oladele. *Female Novelists of Modern Africa*. New York: St. Martin's Press, 1984.

Taylor, Clyde. "Baraka as Poet." *Imamu Amiri Baraka (LeRoi Jones)*. Ed. Kimberly W. Benston. Englewood Cliffs: Prentice, 1978. 112–18.

Teskey, Gordon. *Allegory and Violence*. Ithaca: Cornell University Press, 1996.

Thomas, Donald. *The Marquis de Sade*. New York: New York Graphic Society, 1976.

Tillich, Paul. *The Courage To Be*. New Haven: Yale University Press, 1952.

Trueblood, David Elton. *The Predicament of Modern Man*. New York: Harper & Row, 1944.

Wagar, W. Warren. *Terminal Visions*. Bloomington: Indiana University Press, 1982.

Walcott, Derek. *Another Life*. Washington, D.C. : Three Continents Press, 1982.

_____. "The Muse of History." *Is Massa Day Dead?* Ed. Orde Coombs. New York: Doubleday/Anchor, 1974. 1—27.

Walker, Alice. "In Search of Our Mothers' Garden: The Creativity of the Black Woman in the South." *Ms Magazine*. May 1974.

Wallace, Anthony. "Revitalization Movements." *American Anthropologist*. 58 (1956): 264—66.

Warren, Barbara. *The Feminine Image in Literature*. Rochelle Park: Hayden Book Company, 1973.

Washington, Mary Helen. "Plain, Blain, and Decently Wild: The Heroic Possibilities of Maud Martha." *The Voyage In: Fictions of Female Development*. Eds. Elizabeth Abel, Marianna Hirsch, and Elizabeth Langland. Hanover: University Press of New England, 1983.

Weil, Andrew. *The Marriage of the Sun and Moon: A Quest for Unity in Consciousness*. Boston: Houghton Mifflin, 1980.

Whitmont, Edward C. *The Symbolic Quest*. Princeton: Princeton University Press, 1969.

Wilson, Edmund. *To the Finland Station*. New York: Doubleday, 1953.

Woolf, R. "Later Poetry: The Popular Tradition." *History of Literature in the English Language*. Ed. W.F. Bolton. London: Barrie and Jenkins, 1970. 263—311.

Wright, Willard H. *What Nietzsche Taught*. New York: Huebsch, 1915.

Yadin, Yigael. "The Excavations at Masada." *Masada: Struggle for Freedom*. New York: The Jewish Museum, 1967/1968.

Yu—lan, Fung. *A Short History of Chinese Philosophy*. Ed. & Trans. Derk Bodde. New York: Free Press, 1966.

Zanger, Jules. "Heroic Fantasy and Social Reality: *ex nihilo nihil fit*." *The Aesthetics of Fantasy Literature and Art*. Ed. Roger C. Schlobin. Notre Dame: University of Notre Dame Press, 1982. 226—36.

Ziolkowski, Theodore. *The Novels of Herman Hesse*. Princeton: Princeton University Press, 1965.

Index

www.ingramcontent.com/pod-product-compliance
Lightning Source LLC
Chambersburg PA
CBHW030649110726
47901CB00002B/633